THE REFORMATION EXPERIENCE

LIVING THROUGH THE TURBULENT 16TH CENTURY

ERIC IVES

LION

Copyright © 2012 Eric Ives
This edition copyright © 2012 Lion Hudson

The author asserts the moral right
to be identified as the author of this work

A Lion Book
an imprint of
Lion Hudson plc
Wilkinson House, Jordan Hill Road,
Oxford OX2 8DR, England
www.lionhudson.com
ISBN 978 0 7459 5277 2 (print)
ISBN 978 0 7459 5889 7 (epub)
ISBN 978 0 7459 5888 0 (Kindle)
ISBN 978 0 7459 5890 3 (pdf)

Distributed by:
UK: Marston Book Services, PO Box 269, Abingdon, Oxon, OX14 4YN
USA: Trafalgar Square Publishing, 814 N. Franklin Street, Chicago, IL 60610
USA Christian Market: Kregel Publications, PO Box 2607, Grand Rapids, Michigan 49501

First edition 2012
10 9 8 7 6 5 4 3 2 1 0

Cover image
The Blue Cloak (*De Blauwe Huik*), 1559 by Bruegel, Pieter the Elder;
Staatliche Gemaldegalerie, Berlin, Germany / The Bridgeman Art Library

Acknowledgments
pp. 49, 60, 64, 215, 219, 226, 275: From *The Stripping of the Altars* by Eamon Duffy, 1992.
Printed with permission of Yale University Press.
pp. 91, 105, 169, 180, 229, 279: From *The Reformation* by Diarmaid MacCulloch, 2003.
Printed with permission of Penguin Books Ltd.

This book has been printed on paper and board independently certified
as having been produced from sustainable forests.

A catalogue record for this book is available
from the British Library

Typeset in 10/13 Italian Garamond BT
Printed in Great Britain by Clays Ltd, St Ives plc

For Susan

CONTENTS

THE REFORMATION IN ENGLAND

Ask a person in the street about the Reformation and the likely response will be, "What Reformation?" Ask churchgoers and the answer will almost certainly compound misunderstanding and tradition with myth and anachronism. But among historians, Reformation Studies flourish. Indeed, over the last forty years there has been a revolution in scholarship. The old explanations have been consigned to the graveyard of historical invention. The Protestant story of a failing church split apart by the recovery of the original Christian message is no longer credible. Neither is the Roman Catholic story of a church which triumphantly resisted the assault of evil-motivated heretics. And the dismissive view that the whole thing was, in the words of the historian A.L. Rowse, "an idiot controversy" is equally untenable.

Most contributions to this new thinking have been aimed at readers who want or need to study the Reformation in depth, although something has begun to filter down into schools and examination boards. Even so, if given half a chance, students are likely to skirt over the central issue – the massive challenge the Reformation posed to established Western thinking. Instead of ideas they will concentrate on related political, economic, and social issues which are much easier to understand. What is more, such is the postmodern sidelining of belief, that when a student is invited to choose an area of interest for the next essay, the reply is likely to be, "Anything but religion." Yet sixteenth-century men and women were taught – and most accepted – that religion was central to human experience, so to ignore it is to approach the period half blind.

For a person seeking to understand why the world thinks as it does today, or why religion today is configured as it is, the Reformation is – or should be – of direct and immediate relevance. Key social and political fault-lines too can be traced back to it, and not only in Northern Ireland. For those with Christian beliefs the relevance of the Reformation goes, or should go, without saying. Individual denominations, churches, and religious movements have in significant ways been moulded by the sixteenth century, both positively and negatively. They still are. The shape of Christianity worldwide today is substantially a product of the Reformation. Even where this inheritance has been forgotten, the influence is still there in ideas, attitudes, and assumptions which are taken as normal. This is particularly true of the way the Reformation still shapes vocabulary and language.

Because of this conditioning, new ideas and interpretations are not automatically welcomed. They modify and can even threaten self-identity. A myth is a story which enshrines a meaning, and few people, including those who value religious belief, are happy to have their myths destroyed and their heroes shown to have had feet of clay. Similarly with those who are reluctant to accept that religious rather than secular issues are the core to understanding the event. As for the current inter-church scene, the repeated mantra of the ecumenical movement – "our unhappy divisions" – is effectively a wish that the Reformation would go away.

Challenging any or all of this may seem foolhardy in the extreme. Nevertheless, this book sets out to tell something of the overall story of the Reformation in the light of recent scholarship. It recognizes that it will not please everybody, especially as it attempts to be as irenic as possible and to be, as far as is feasible, fair to all sides of the story. Not that this account is neutral; it couldn't be. No writer ever is, and certainly not where the Reformation is concerned. Expecting prejudice from a Roman Catholic or a Protestant may seem obvious, but agnostics and atheists also bring their own predispositions. Nor, if it were possible, would the apparently safe path of total neutrality avoid disaster. It is essential to empathize with the passion which is fundamental to the subject. You have to feel why it was vital to burn a heretic or gut a Catholic priest. A value-free Reformation is an impossibility.

The only safe course is to be as objective and fair to the evidence as possible, and to be transparent about one's own position. Thus I write as a Protestant with a background in English evangelical nonconformity; that is the community I instinctively understand. My broader position is that the Reformation was essentially a religious event. Not exclusively – politics, economics, and society explain much of the tragedy – but essentially so. Anything less falsifies. What is more, like any other major religious episode, the Reformation has to be placed in the ongoing context of the wider history of Christianity and Christian belief, and this makes understanding even more difficult. It poses the obscenity of Christians who claimed to be motivated by the love of God killing other Christians who claimed to be motivated by the love of God.

The change that has come over Reformation Studies in the last thirty years has shaped this book in a second respect. Until the last generation or so, the majority of Reformation scholars adopted a top-down perspective. They concentrated on major events, on theological ideas, and the impact of significant individuals. Even though many good studies of local events were undertaken, these tended to take the Reformation as a "given". Today, historians recognize the need to re-tell the story from the bottom up; that is, how the Reformation came to individuals and communities and what it meant to them. Certainly the story of Reformation theology has to be told. The great ideas do have to be explored; why people think is as important as what they think. Yet the significance of theology is marginal until we ask how new religious ideas reached ordinary man and woman, whether (and why) the ideas were or were not accepted, and how this changed lives.

In this it is vital to remember that the word "religion" covers different things. There is religion as ritual, religion as a set of ideas, and religion as a personal commitment; in other words, we must distinguish between the way churches worshipped, what people were taught to believe, and how belief was – or was not – internalized. For example, in England in 1559, the state imposed a switch from services using the medieval Sarum liturgy to services using the *Book of Common Prayer*. This tells us that ritual changed. It tells us little about what people believed, still less about their spiritual response, and almost nothing about variation between person and person: generalization is perilous. We also face a contradiction which has been at the core of Christianity since the early centuries. Is "a church" comprised exclusively of those who by conviction choose to belong – what is termed "a gathered church" – or does it represent and include the whole of the community? In practice, if not in theory, much of the West has now embraced the gathered church model. It accepts that a church consists of individuals who choose to attend and decide for themselves the nature and extent of their individual religious commitment. In the sixteenth century, reformers of all complexions certainly wished to promote individual commitment; in particular, some Protestant reformers saw that model as returning to the early Christian church. Yet over the centuries the European church had become a massive and complex structure of interlocking ecclesiastical and political machinery. Its thought patterns dominated both language and philosophy, and the ideas and concepts of society. Of course the sixteenth century does provide plentiful examples of men and women making a spiritual commitment; several thousand, indeed, were willing to die for their beliefs. But the notion that personal conviction was all that mattered cannot account for whole communities ending in one Reformation camp or another. Why England became Protestant and France did not is not adequately explained by counting conversions. Arriving at such community allegiance was a substantially political process which historians have unhappily learned to call "confessionalization".

Practical considerations also follow from a bottom-up approach. The first is length. Diarmaid MacCulloch's brilliant *Reformation: Europe's house divided 1490–1700* (2003) required over 700 pages. This book, therefore, concentrates primarily on England. The Channel was, however, better at keeping out enemies than keeping out ideas, so events elsewhere in the Western church do play an important part, and so too the religious thinking of Luther and others. Space also imposes constraints on period. The book starts with the later Middle Ages, effectively after the Black Death (1348–50), and ends over two centuries later when something like a Protestant England was, it can be argued, beginning to exist.

A further consideration is the right terms to use. Long custom has tied together the words "Reformation" and "Protestant"; for many writers they are synonymous. What, then, should we call reform movements in churches which stayed loyal to the pope? One suggested possibility is "Counter-Reformation". But that implies that the reform in those churches was essentially a reaction against Protestantism and otherwise might not have occurred. A more positive assessment sees Rome attacking the problems that had given rise to Protestantism, and so prefers the term "Catholic Reformation". This book, however, contends that the terms "Reformation" and "Counter" or "Catholic Reformation" are seriously misleading. They presume an iron curtain between Protestant and Roman Catholic, but that is only how the Reformation story ended. It did not begin like that. Division had not been inherent from the start, and to think otherwise is a distortion. This book, therefore, presents the story of a single impetus for reform, renewal, and revival in the Western church, which over time was distorted and fragmented by circumstance and personality. Terminology is used accordingly.

These considerations explain the structure of the book. The first section looks at religion in the years before the Reformation, examining the place of church worship and activity in English life, and exploring what Christianity meant at the grass roots. The second section looks at the context and the character of reformation in Europe, looking at the story overall and at some thinkers and theologians known and less well known. The final section tells the story of government pronouncements and local responses in England and what had or had not been achieved by the final quarter of the sixteenth century. The endnotes principally indicate the sources of quotations used, as well as providing helpful cross-references and explanations additional to the text. Spelling and language has normally been modernized.

In the course of writing this book, I have incurred significant debts. First to Lion Hudson, and particularly my commissioning editors, Kate Kirkpatrick and Alison Hull, for their support and forbearance with a writer who took his time. My academic friends and colleagues Fr Dermot Fenlon, Professor Peter Marshall, and Professor Robert Swanson read all or part of the manuscript and saved me from many errors. Any that remain are not their responsibility. My fellow student Beryl Shepherd provided the equally helpful perspective of a senior public librarian. Many friends, too, by their regularly expressed interest and faith in the project have encouraged me to persevere with a topic which grew steadily more complex, and not least among them, my daughter, to whom the book is dedicated.

ENGLAND BEFORE
THE REFORMATION

1

LOCATING THE REFORMATION

The most remarkable thing about the Reformation is that it still matters. It began in the early sixteenth century and powerfully influenced the history of Europe until at least the eighteenth, but its consequences are still with us. No one today, observing Ireland or for example Belgium, can have any doubt about that. The Reformation was a Europe-wide phenomenon, but the way religious issues played out was not uniform. Each country or region has its own distinctive reformation. Of nowhere is that more true than England, thanks to the relative isolation guaranteed by the Channel. What, then, was the situation there on the eve of what would be a revolution in thought and behaviour?

The National Context

The key fact about England in the early sixteenth century is best expressed by the paradox that the country was effectively twenty-five times larger than it is today. Consider communications. Instead of today's rapid conveyance of people and goods, and even more ideas, these travelled then at a walking pace. A horse was quicker, but only perhaps twice as fast because forty miles was the maximum distance an animal could reasonably be expected to cover in a 24-hour period and be fit to continue the next day. An accountant who made a routine journey from Bedfordshire to Chester in 1530 took five days for 140 miles. To move letters rapidly along a few key routes, the government maintained a relay of riders to travel at a gallop, but the non-stop record for London to Edinburgh averaged only eleven miles an hour. Only beacons could give a warning of invasion in anything like real time, though districts could be alerted by the ringing of church bells. The effect of this tempo of communications was accentuated by a population of not more than 2,260,000. That gave a density which is equivalent to the current English population having exclusive occupation of 75 per cent of the European Union.

National figures do, however, mislead. The population was not spread uniformly. Three-quarters lived in the lowlands of the south and east where the density could reach 100 per square mile and sometimes more. The high lands of the north and west averaged twenty per square mile or even fewer, and so were nationally less significant. Given the small population, much land was not occupied and a great deal was still wooded. Indeed, the country should be envisaged as almost an archipelago of cultivation in a sea of waste and woodland, provided that we recognize that waste and woodland were vital sources of raw material. The economy also varied. The north and west focused on animal husbandry, the south and east on arable. Within those broad divisions, climate and soil produced great variation. Ease of access was critical too – for example, it was no use being able to grow grain in quantity if no navigable river was accessible to move such a bulky commodity. Animals, on the other hand, could be moved on drove roads. The only nationally structured industry was the manufacture of cloth, precisely because product could be easily moved on pack animals for export through London. The effect of these local variations was to make England a patchwork of perhaps forty more or less distinct economic regions. Between these regions levels of wealth and income varied widely. Kent, for example, paid fifteen times more tax per acre than Yorkshire. Wealth was also very unevenly distributed within communities. Perhaps 40 per cent of people lived on the margin, supplementing inadequate land with seasonal wages. Only just over 2 per cent came from gentry families or better.

Patterns of society differed from region to region. For example, the south and east of Warwickshire was a countryside of long established compact villages, farming in common, socially stable and hierarchical. Even so there were exceptions. When the accountant on the way to Chester in 1531 reached the Dunsmore near Rugby he had to employ a guide. The north and west of Warwickshire was very different. In the "Forest of Arden" small hamlets were the norm, much less regulated, and peopled by individuals who supplemented the produce of smallholdings in the woodland by nail-making and other metalwork. There was a growing awareness of being English, but the everyday horizon of most men and women was the economic area they lived in. Language was not yet standardized. In 1522 a Cumberland man resident in Kent was accused of being an alien Scot. A foreigner was a person not from my area. Individuals were able to move long distances, more perhaps than one imagines – London was a major destination. They were, however, likely to be from families at least prosperous enough to fund younger sons who had no prospects at home. The other extreme would increasingly be people taking to the road in search of work, because by 1520 the population was beginning to rise. It takes time for a rural economy to increase employment by bringing more land into cultivation, and until then too many people will be chasing too few jobs. Another consequence was that England was a country of young people – 37 per cent in 1556. All this said, it remains the case that the bulk of the population was relatively static and that most people did not migrate beyond parishes near to where they had been born. Few towns interrupted this picture of a largely rural England. In the early sixteenth century only perhaps 6 per cent of the population lived in any sort of urban environment. London was the only genuine city, with a population of perhaps 60,000. Norwich was the next in size – say 12,000 – followed by a handful of regional capitals such as York or Salisbury (possibly 8,000). Many market towns failed to reach four figures and were little more than villages.

England in the fifteenth and sixteenth centuries was, thus, a very diverse country, but it was a national unit nevertheless. What we exaggeratedly call the Wars of the Roses began with the crisis of a ruler who was inadequate and ended with strong rule restored.[1] Government was already substantially centralized at Westminster. The legal systems were sophisticated and consultation mechanisms well established – most notably parliament. The laws it passed applied countrywide, as did any extra taxation it agreed to over and beyond that already enshrined in law. Other factors too affected the country generally. The population rise was the most important. Initially this stimulated the economy but, as well as putting people on the roads, from the early 1520s it began to push up prices. Increased government spending also kicked in, thanks largely to the costs of war and the preparation for war, and the governments of Henry VIII and his son Edward VI made inflation worse by destabilizing the currency.

These factors were national, but given England's wide regional differences the impact would vary considerably. Assuming the principle "one size fits all" was simply unrealistic, a consideration which would prove to be of enduring importance in the English Reformation. So too would another dimension of localism – power. England had no civil service, police force, or standing army, so who could exercise authority? The answer is that everything, from the county down to the parish, depended on the willingness of people with the clout that came from property, wealth, and community status, to support and obey the crown, gentry whom the crown could recruit as magistrates and commissioners, and parish officers chosen by neighbours. The number of such people was, however, limited, as was the effectiveness of sanctions against them. The crown could discipline individuals but not large groups, still less do without the country's "natural rulers". This meant that it was not enough for the crown to order this or that. Whether the order was effective would depend on people in each locality being in a position to enforce it and being willing to do so. Except for London and its immediate hinterland, the king was a distant figure; local considerations were immediate. Royal decisions thus were most effective when they coincided with interest in a community. Conversely, local priorities, bureaucratic lethargy, and lack of enthusiasm were hard to overcome, as was deliberate obstruction.

The Church in England

Strictly speaking, there was at the start of the sixteenth century no English church. There were two separate provinces of the Western church which answered to Rome. In the north, the archbishop of York presided over three dioceses. In the south, the archbishopric of Canterbury covered the fourteen remaining dioceses in England and four in Wales. Each province had its own Convocation [assembly], but Canterbury's was much the more important – it met concurrently with parliament. Dioceses were made up of parishes, some 9,000 in all, but varying greatly in size. In the populous south the average was four square miles or less; in the wilds of Lancashire it was thirty-three. Taken overall, the English church was wealthy. Enquiries carried out in 1535 suggest that the church owned a fifth or more of the nation's estate, giving it perhaps £400,000 a year, and that at a time when the crown struggled to raise £100,000. That is as Henry VIII saw it, but the comparison is somewhat unfair because it aggregates the incomes of thousands of individual recipients. These varied enormously. Some bishops and senior clergy enjoyed receipts on a par with the aristocracy. A minority of parish priests were comfortably off, or held more than one benefice. The majority did much less well. In 1535, one in ten of parish priests in the diocese of Coventry and Lichfield was supposed to exist on less than £5 a year, the wage of a farm labourer. Moreover, only a fortunate minority of ordained priests actually had the security of even a modest benefice. The rest of the 30,000 or so might be employed on a meagre salary to assist in a parish and/or live by conducting casual services (which also could boost an incumbent's income).

Most clerics, from parish dogsbody to the majority of bishops, were known as "seculars" because they lived and worked in the community [Latin *saeculum* = world]. A much smaller category – around 10,000 – lived in monasteries and similar restricted communities. They were known as "the religious" and as "regulars" because they followed a prescribed *regula* or rule of life and conduct. There were some 800 or so of these communities. Only perhaps 150 were for women, housing maybe 1,000 nuns. Again there was uneven distribution. The province of York had fewer than 100 houses for men and 29 for women. The rest were in the south. Of the regulars, two-thirds were monks and their principal contribution to the religious life of English men and women was continued prayer. Nuns did the same. The remainder of the regulars (say 2,500) were friars, whose houses were normally located in towns. Their prime role was pastoral work in the community.

Together, religious houses accounted for perhaps half of the total wealth of the church but there were again wide variations. Nearly one in ten (many of them friaries) had an annual income of less than £20 but the wealthiest monastery, Westminster Abbey, enjoyed nearly £4,000 a year. Indeed, of the total wealth of the religious houses, 25 per cent went to twenty-three monasteries in receipt of £1,000 plus. Again there was the north–south divide. Only three of the wealthiest abbeys were in the province of York. The number of brothers in the various monasteries differed widely too. Twelve monks was the minimum needed to ensure observance of "the rule". Some houses had three and even four times that number, but they were a minority. Some houses had fewer than ten monks. As for nunneries, most were tiny. It is, however, wrong to think of houses only in terms of the religious occupants. Except for the very smallest, they were units, sometimes significant units, in the secular economy, both locally and through their more distant estates, which in some cases were spread over several counties. The monks generally had ceased farming directly, so the nearest their distant tenants got to them was the steward or bailiff appointed to manage the properties – normally local gentlemen and yeomen. There was, of course, also a domestic staff – cooks, grooms, and the like – to cater and care, and not just for the religious. Monasteries served travellers; some educated boys and (in a limited number of cases) housed retired lay folk who had purchased a "corrody" – in effect, care and accommodation for life. Another feature of late medieval monasteries was that, in most, abbots had withdrawn from the common life into purpose-built lodgings with a large staff where they lived as one of the local gentry.

The church had its own judicial system – canon law – and its own courts. These not only regulated the behaviour of the clergy and punished all crimes committed by them but had a wide jurisdiction affecting laypeople too. Many areas of disputes with the laity came under church law – for example over the payment of tithe. Then there were moral offences, most commonly sexual misbehaviour. Church courts also had jurisdiction over borderline religious areas such as marriage, defamation, wills, and testaments. The authority of England's archbishops and bishops was perhaps more effective than royal authority since their dioceses did have local bureaucracies. They personally were substantially involved in royal service, but were able to leave their religious responsibilities to professionals who by and large ran the church machine well. But, that said, bishops were in practice not the independent authorities they were in theory, which made for difficulty when, as was not unusual, one of them sought to raise the standards and performance of his clergy. Dioceses were peppered with "peculiars". These were parishes or groups of parishes exempt from the authority of the local bishop, some answerable to authority outside the diocese, some directly to the pope, some to no authority at all. Significant numbers of the regulars were outside episcopal control, including the friars and the occupants of over a hundred monasteries. There were other forms of exemption too – for example from the archdeacon (the next figure below the bishop) – and even cases where an archdeacon was effectively free of the control of his bishop. What is more, although the diocesan supposedly had the right to ordain his clergy, he did not have control over parish appointments. This was generally in other hands – those of nobles and gentlemen or monastic houses. Hence, even if the bishop did discipline an incumbent, there was no certainty that the successor would be any different. Bishops had a further area of concern too. A diocese was an integral part of the society of its area. The bishop was a local magnate, with all that meant in terms of networking and patronage. These could bring him positive support but equally could undermine him, depending on whether his policies were or were not popular. And, when the Reformation came, that would go for his ideas as well.

2

THE ENGLISH AT CHURCH 1500

On any Sunday in the early sixteenth century, the parishioners of All Saints North Street in the city of York would be found wending their way to their parish church as they had done for generations. In the rest of England's parishes and in the local chapels in remote areas, their fellow countrymen and women were doing the same. The population of All Saints North Street was small, but the building measured only twenty-nine metres by fourteen (ninety-five feet by forty-six feet) and even that area was not all free space.[1] The eastern ends of the two side aisles were partitioned off to make at least four chapels while, as in all churches, a tall screen – solid to waist high with open arches above – divided the central section into a chancel to the east – the preserve of the parish priest – and the nave to the west, which accommodated the parish. Worshippers thus faced congestion as they entered by the south-west door, a crush only tolerable because private pews were only just coming into fashion and the custom for the majority was to stand or kneel.

Across the top of the screen ran the "rood beam", a substantial timber which supported the "rood", a large statue of Jesus Christ hanging on the cross, flanked by images of his mother, the Virgin Mary, and his closest friend, St John. In some buildings the beam supported a platform [the "rood loft"], on which the figures stood along with votive lights and possibly a small altar too. Where a church had a chancel arch above the rood, the space ["tympanum"] might be filled with a so-called "doom", a graphic painting of the Last Judgement which showed souls being conducted to heaven or dragged down into hell. Beyond the rood screen the focus of the chancel was the high altar – raised against the east wall and topped with a stone altar slab incised with five crosses to mark its consecration. It was flanked by two statues, one certainly a statue of the Virgin, and in All Saints a further statue of Mary stood beside the altar in a side chapel dedicated to her ("the Lady Chapel"). The other side chapels had their statues too – St Nicholas, St Katherine, St Thomas, and St James. The windows of the church were also crowded with appropriate sacred images. The windows of the Lady Chapel emphasized the story of the Virgin, and the window lighting the chantry of St Thomas showed Christ between the Apostle Thomas and St Thomas Becket.

The Sunday Service: The Priest

Sunday began with the presentation of the holy loaf. This was baked by households in turn and the provider processed to the high altar, recited a special prayer, and presented the priest with a candle. Then came matins, a service of series of readings and prayers, followed by the main event of the day, parochial high mass. For this, the clergy put on elaborate vestments over the "albs" [sleeved tunics] they wore every day. Once robed, the priests consecrated holy water and processed round the church, sprinkling both the altars and the congregation. Next they passed through the rood screen into the chancel, accompanied by various assistants carrying the processional cross, a sacring bell, and an incense burner.[2]

At the altar steps the service began with the clergy following elaborate texts and rubrics which specified every gesture and movement. The laity could undoubtedly smell the incense, but because of the intervening rood screen would see very little of the priest going through the opening ritual and in any case he did so facing east, i.e. with his back to them. Eventually he placed a round wheaten wafer on the communion plate or paten and poured wine into a communion goblet or chalice. Nor could much be understood of what the priest was saying; a good deal was deliberately repeated so as not to be heard and in any case (as with all church pre-Reformation liturgies), everything was in Latin.

Sunday Services: The People

While the clergy in the chancel were engaged in the liturgy, the laity was expected to engage in private devotions, such as reciting the Creed, which they were required to learn in Latin [*"Credo in unum Deum"* – "I believe in one God"]. If they had also learned the words of the Latin *Gloria* [*"Gloria in excelsis Deo"* – "Glory to God in the highest"], the *Benedictus* ["Blessed is he who comes"], and the *Agnus Dei* ["Lamb of God who takes away the sin of the world, have mercy on us"] they could say or sing them at the right places along with the priest. Also, by the sixteenth century, literate laity who could afford it might have a printed guide to the liturgy of the mass and private prayers to say at appropriate points, each accompanied with a Latin *Paternoster* ["Our Father who art in heaven"] and an *Ave Maria* ["Hail Mary"]. The less wealthy and those who could not read were expected to repeat prayers from memory or else say the "Our Lady's Psalter" – 150 repetitions of the *Ave Maria*, counted off on a string of beads in groups of fifteen separated by saying a *Paternoster*.[3]

Thus far the parish mass was a ceremony which the laity observed, not a service they took part in, but then the Latin Gospel Book would be ceremoniously brought from the chancel through the screen and held up for a cleric and none but a cleric to read. Then the priest would enter the pulpit to deliver a sermon. He would first repeat a text from the reading, translate it into English, and preach on it. How frequently sermons were delivered is hard to say. They were popular and every parish was supposed to have one every quarter. However, plague all too frequently caused interruptions, and only a minority of clergy had a licence to preach or the education to do so. Nevertheless, for the conscientious village priest who could cope with Latin but had no licence, printed helps were coming on the market. Town churches such as All Saints North Street and the other churches of York were probably better placed, because of the city's four friaries. Friars saw preaching as a main part of their vocation.

After the sermon (if there was one) the parish priest proceeded to "bid the bedes", a term derived from the Anglo-Saxon word for prayer. In the first part, the priest, speaking English, called on the people to pray for the pope and the clergy, especially those from the parish, for the king and persons in authority, for those in special need such as pregnant women, and for the family which had donated the holy loaf. Then he led prayers for the dead, especially recently deceased parishioners, and, depending on the length, recited all or part of the "bede roll", a list of past benefactors of the church.

With the bidding of the bedes completed, the priest returned to the chancel for the climax of the mass, the consecration of the wafer and the wine. This was announced to everyone by ringing the sacring bell. The priest repeated the words Christ had used at the Last Supper – "*Hoc est enim corpus meum*" ["for this is my body"] – and raised ["elevated"] the newly consecrated wafer [or "host"] high above his head for everyone to see. So too the chalice: "*Hoc est enim calyx sanguinis mei*" ["for this is the cup of my blood"]. Everyone was expected to reverence the consecrated host, and in order that people could get a glimpse of the elevation, special holes ["squints"] were provided through many rood screens. Then came the communion, when the wafer or host was eaten and the wine drunk, after which the mass ended with prayers. Only priests consumed both bread and wine – what was called "communion in both kinds". The laity were entitled to the wafer but they normally took communion only once a year at Easter or when they were dying (part of the "sacrament of extreme unction"). The nearest parishioners came to the communion at the regular Sunday mass was kissing the paxbred, a disk or board (with a sacred picture on it). The priest took this just before he consumed the consecrated elements, kissed both the cloth on which the host rested and the lip of the chalice and then kissed the paxbred, and this was taken to the parishioners to be kissed by each in turn. The mass then ended with prayer and a Gospel reading after which the loaf presented at matins was brought out, solemnly blessed, cut up, and distributed to the laity. Though an ordinary loaf, it obviously paralleled the host and, indeed, it was supposed to be the first food eaten that day.

The end of the parish high mass was not the end of the Sunday services. Masses had still to be said at each of the four or five side chapels or chantries – so named for the services chanted there. These were "low" masses without the special interruptions in the parish mass, and several could be said at the same time. Later in the day private services would be held but parishioners were again supposed to attend for evensong, which comprised Latin readings and prayers with no special lay participation.

Other Services

On the great festivals of the Christian year and on major feast days, the ceremony would be much more elaborate, particularly on the festival of the saint the church was named after; at All Saints that was 1 November. The festivals of saints to whom chantries were dedicated would also be marked. On 2 February the Commemoration of the Purification of the Virgin Mary was celebrated by a procession in the church and churchyard when everyone was supposed to take part and be given a blessed candle to protect their homes from thunderstorms. Another parish procession was held on the feast of Corpus Christi in late May or June. At Rogationtide (which fell in November) parishioners were expected to process on three successive days. The greatest season of the church year was Lent, Holy Week, and Easter. On Palm Sunday there was a procession and elaborate ceremonial and on Good Friday a consecrated host was "buried" in a symbolic tomb beside the high altar and was "raised to life" with great rejoicing on Easter Sunday to mirror the burial and resurrection of Christ.

Activity at All Saints was, however, not confined to Sundays and holy days. Where an early Tudor church had sufficient clergy it might be in almost continuous use. Each day there was a dawn or "morrow mass" for servants and workers, followed by a parish mass at the high altar and masses in each of the chantry chapels. Then there was a steady demand for particular services. There were marriages – "spousals" – children to baptize – no later than a week after birth – and mothers to "purify" or "church" – a month after delivery. The dead had to be buried and this would mean setting up the parish hearse [staging] in the church to support the coffin and saying "The Office for the Dead", part one of the funeral liturgy. Overnight a vigil would be kept and the next day the second part of the liturgy, and then the corpse was buried. In many cases, further commemorations of the deceased would take place over succeeding weeks or even years.

What this weekday activity could amount to can be gleaned from Scarborough, another Yorkshire town, two generations earlier.[4] The parish church there was holding at least one of these ceremonies (and frequently more) on 123 weekdays, and that does not include perhaps more than sixty baptisms – plus six special occasions for local guilds. There would also be occasional offices, for example a mass said for a traveller passing through.[5] Certain inns, indeed, maintained a licensed chapel to provide a morning mass for the guests. It is also the case that some parishes had subsidiary chapels where the liturgy was celebrated.[6]

Outside the Parishes

As well as the work of the secular parochial clergy, further religious provision came from the regulars. Initially these "houses of religion" had been endowed by wealthy individuals to intercede for themselves, their families, and other benefactors. Monks and nuns offered prayer communally at specified times on a 24-hour cycle ["the office"] in the chancel of the monastic church. By 1500 new foundations were rare. Instead, as we shall see, individuals purchased particular prayer packages for themselves or for deceased relatives, friends, and patrons. As for the friars, in addition to preaching, they heard confessions and augmented the work of the parishes. They were also prominent at the universities (Oxford and Cambridge) and they taught children.

One dimension of pre-Reformation Christianity which in the past has been significantly underplayed by Reformation scholars is what can be termed "voluntary religion". A minimum pattern of observance was required from all parishioners, but beyond that parishes offered scope for much variety and diversity. Pilgrimages, private masses, indulgences, names on the bede roll – none of this was regimented. The most significant example of this was a voluntary religious association under the patronage of a particular saint, variously known as a guild, brotherhood, or fraternity. These were lay controlled – which helps to explain their attraction – and varied from humble rural ones to large and wealthy organizations with significant property and members who were aristocrats. Fraternities were hugely important and hugely popular; they were everywhere – nationwide possibly as many as 30,000. Small villages might have just one, larger communities many more. Northamptonshire had over a hundred, including fourteen in Northampton itself. The City of London had over 150, say one for every 400 inhabitants – and that was in addition to craft guilds and livery companies.

People might belong to a number of fraternities and, in almost all, women as well as men could be full members. A number had community purposes. Some provided schools, almshouses, or other kinds of charity.

Others looked after public works, such as roads or bridges. The social dimension was strong too. Many would intervene where a member suffered loss or accident or mediate between brothers or act as executor. Some guilds were effectively business networks, even willing to help a brother who had got into difficulty. Most of the larger fraternities owned a guild house and income-generating property. But at the heart of a fraternity's life was lay piety. Often it would support a special chapel in the parish church, with statues and lights to burn before them; some had their own free-standing chapel. It might employ a regular priest or engage one as required. Always there was a special annual service in honour of the saint the guild was dedicated to. Every brother also knew that his fraternity would support him in death, that greatest of crises, and would pray for him.[7]

Popular Support for the Church

The importance of the church and what it offered is strikingly evidenced by the many hundreds of English men and women who put their money where their mouth was. To this day the extent of this is evident in the hundreds of surviving parish churches which were built, extended, or rebuilt in the two centuries between the Black Death and Henry VIII's rejection of the pope, many of them magnificent. Perhaps the pearl is the church of St Peter and St Paul, in Lavenham, completed in 1530 and paid for by the money which the Spring family made from the local cloth industry. But only five miles away in the same small area of Suffolk is the equally splendid Holy Trinity Long Melford, completed in 1484, and that is only three miles from Sudbury, where St Gregory's has a fifteenth-century tower and All Saints and St Peter's were each completely rebuilt in the fifteenth century. Gloucestershire presents a parallel case with St Peter and St Paul Northleach bracketed to the north by St James Chipping Campden, and to the south by St Mary Fairford, three pre-Reformation masterpieces paid for by wealthy wool merchants, and so the catalogue could go on.

The interiors of churches were likewise elaborated and beautified. We have noted the glass, the chantry chapels, and the statues at All Saints North Street. At Fairford, as well as effectively rebuilding the church fabric, John Tame (d.1500) and his son Edmund (d.1534) engaged experts – possibly even the king's own glazier – to make and install a complete and now unique display of stained glass. Other donors gave to enhance performance of the mass. In 1500, at Humberstone in Leicestershire, the wealthy lawyer Thomas Kebell provided two chalices and a specially bound mass book.[8] Over the years, gifts like that would amount to a substantial collection. In 1552 in the small village of Bluntisham on the edge of the Fens, the parish church of St John the Baptist possessed plate weighing 3.75 kg – three chalices and patens in silver and one plated in gold, inside and out, plus a pax and a pyx [container for the host], also "double gilt".[9] Fabrics were an even more common gift. Kebell bequeathed to Humberstone a cope, three sets of vestments, and two altar cloths, plus his own doublet clothes of velvet and silk to be made into vestments. At Bluntisham there were four sets of mass vestments, each for three priests, one set decorated with golden lions and two in velvet, and three of the sets had matching copes. There were two other copes of white satin, hangings in red satin for the altar, candlesticks, a pair of organs, and various bells. Clearly the parish mass at St Mary's Bluntisham was a magnificent occasion. As well as giving to beautify a church and its services, acts of devotion included benefit to the community. Relief of the poor, repairing a bridge, paving a road, or endowing a light to guide travellers or shipping – each counted. Henry VII paid for the completion of the chapel of King's College Cambridge and set up the Savoy Hospital, a dormitory for 100 of London's homeless.[10] At a time when a day's wage was perhaps 4d. [1.23 pence], Thomas Kebell left £20 to be distributed to the poor on the day he was buried, and £13.66 a year for twenty years to support scholars at Oxford and Cambridge. The York merchant Nicholas Blackburn the elder (d.1432) left £160 to be distributed to the poor and further sums for local roads and bridges; his son, Nicholas the younger (d.1448), gave All Saints North Street two stained-glass windows.[11]

In the twenty-first century, Western Europe is accustomed to churches used occasionally and services which most people find irrelevant. In the centuries before the Reformation, the church was knit into the very fabric of society, and nowhere more than in England. It is no accident that nearly half of the storytellers in the *Canterbury Tales* are linked in some way or other to the church, or that the setting which Chaucer chose to bring together a cross-section of Englishmen and women was a pilgrimage.

3

POPULAR RELIGION: OBSERVANCE

At the turn of the sixteenth century, Andrea Trevisiano, an Italian diplomat, wrote that the people of England "all attend mass every day and say many *Paternosters* in public. They always hear mass on Sunday in their parish church and give liberal alms... nor do they omit any form incumbent on good Christians."[1] The envoy had clearly watched such activity in city churches he attended, but we have to be cautious in assuming that was so in the rest of over a hundred London and Westminster parishes. Caution is even more needed with the thousands of parishes elsewhere in England, for he is unlikely to have travelled much beyond the metropolis. The pattern of church life we have observed at All Saints North Street was possibly typical, but there must also have been much local variation. In thinly populated areas such as the Pennines and Lancashire, one church might serve many square miles and have an income too small to attract able and educated priests. There, except for funerals, residents had to depend on chapels of ease and part-time chaplains. Yet even in such areas religion did matter, so what prompted piety?

The Sacraments
The Christianity of medieval liturgy and practice was focused on the seven sacraments. Men and women were believed to be sinful by nature, and in a universe ruled by an all-powerful and holy deity, they would necessarily end in hell. God, however, was also loving, and so he had provided a potential

way of escape through his Son, Jesus Christ, who died as a sacrifice to atone for sin. Yet this did not mean that salvation was automatic. Men and women had to exercise faith in that sacrifice and support their faith by being good and doing good. This they could not do alone; they needed divine help ["grace"]. That grace was mediated to the believer through the church (and the church alone), and it did so through "the means of grace" – the sacraments.

The initial sacrament was baptism, which washed away original sin, and the other six – confirmation, penance, the mass, marriage, ordination, and extreme unction – dispensed grace for both living and dying. The most revered of the sacraments and the cornerstone of pre-Reformation Christianity was the mass. It was also unique. Baptism and the other sacraments were believed to have spiritual effects, but the mass involved a physical miracle. As the priest pronounced the words of consecration, the bread and wine on the altar became the literal body and blood of Christ. Outward appearances did not change but substance did, and the miraculous process was therefore known as transubstantiation. Thus when the priest "elevated the host", he was displaying the crucified body of Christ. Likewise the chalice contained the blood of Christ, and fear of spillage explained why it could not be given to the laity. A similar reverence protected the body of Christ. On the rare occasions when the laity did eat the consecrated wafer, English custom was for a special cloth to be held under the chin to catch any crumbs and a sip of unconsecrated wine to be given to ensure that the bread had been completely swallowed.

The huge solemnity involved in receiving the physical body of Christ and the danger of taking the sacrament when "out of charity" with anyone explains why lay men and women took communion so rarely. That had the effect of shifting the focus of the mass from partaking in a symbolic corporate meal to the moment of consecration and the miracle of transubstantiation. Observing the consecrated host as it was held up by the priest was popularly known as "seeing God" and the miraculous character of the host was taught in story after story. When arson destroyed parts of St Mary's Rickmansworth (probably in 1522), the appeal for the restoration fund stated that, although the pyx had melted in which it was kept, "the blessed body of our Lord Jesus Christ in form of bread was found upon the high altar and nothing perished".[2] In a church with several altars like

All Saints North Street, masses might be said concurrently but care was always taken to stagger the moment of elevation so that observers would have several opportunities to adore the host. The belief was that devoutly hearing mass was more acceptable to God than fasting, scourging or saying the whole Psalter and more profitable than engaging the prayers of the Virgin and all the saints in heaven.[3]

Purgatory

The supreme claim for the efficacy of the mass was in assisting souls in purgatory. This was understood to be a post-mortem state in which all the deceased who were neither so sinful as to be damned nor so saintly as to be immediately received into heavenly bliss were put through a necessary process of purification. This was a belief which since the early Middle Ages had crept up on the Western church, which answered to Rome, and had been given theological form during the eleventh and twelfth centuries. It was never accepted in the Eastern church, which answered to Constantinople, but in Rome's northern dioceses, including those in England, purgatory became an overriding preoccupation. This concern for the souls of the dead developed from the church's teaching on penance, the sacrament that offered the grace of forgiveness for sins committed subsequent to baptism. Where a baptized person was genuinely sorry for such sin and made a clean breast of it to a priest, they would be given absolution and assigned a compensating penance. However, just one confession would not be enough. Human nature is fallible, and the cycle of contrition, confession, absolution, and satisfaction needed to be repeated continually, at a minimum every Easter before taking communion. Even so, everyone other than a saint risked dying with penance insufficient or inadequately performed, and thus the soul would be too sinful to pass into heaven until refined by some time in purgatory. Of course anyone guilty of mortal sin would be condemned to the everlasting torments of hell, but the disciplines of purgatory were only less horrific by being (eventually) time-limited. According to sermons preached by John Fisher, the bishop of Rochester (probably in 1520), the pains of purgatory were many times worse than the most painful human symptoms he could imagine – headache, toothache, gout, kidney stone, colic, and urinary retention – and what is more in purgatory the pains lasted a thousand times longer.[4] Fisher's point, however, was that all of this was avoidable by doing good deeds.

Indulgences

Penance and purgatory are, of course, inextricably involved in that cause célèbre of the Reformation – the system of indulgences Martin Luther attacked in the *Ninety-Five Theses*, which he allegedly nailed to the church door in Wittenberg.[5] The origin of indulgences lay in unrealistically severe penances awarded at confession in the post-Roman world and the early Middle Ages. The practice therefore grew up first of commuting penances to something more realistic and later of attaching specific measures of indulgence to particular pious activities, normally expressed in terms of days and years of remission from purgatory. But penance was due to God himself, so how was the church entitled to remit it? The answer theologians came up with was that the infinite merits of the head of the church – Jesus Christ – plus the abundant virtues of its saints had provided a "treasury of merit", a credit account which clergy could dispense to cancel out part of what the penitent owed. An indulgence which tapped that reservoir could thus be a powerful inducement to good works and acts of charity. In 1095 Pope Urban II had declared that all penance was remitted to a man who went on crusade, provided he had been through confession, and increasingly popes financed projects by offering similar plenary indulgences. The principle always was that benefit depended on the purchaser first being confessed and absolved, and so indulgences did not undermine the need for faith. Moreover, they only covered past offences and so were not "licences to sin". Nevertheless the possibility of misunderstanding and abuse is obvious.

Bishops were restricted to granting forty and archbishops to 100 days' remission but in 1521 the pope, twelve cardinals, the archbishop of Canterbury, and four English bishops combined to offer 7,500 days of pardon for donations to pay the ransom of an English knight of St John who had been captured by the Turks. Fragments of glass surviving in All Saints North Street show that at least one window promised indulgence, possibly the 26,000 years and 30 days' remission attached to devotion to Christ as the Man of Sorrows. A major development in the teaching about indulgences came about in 1476 when they were declared to be retrospectively effective for souls already in purgatory. This crucial change made it possible for the dead to receive vicarious benefit paid for by the living. What is more, although plenary indulgences could only be issued by a pope, selling them was subcontracted, eventually to pardoners who paid a fixed fee, and salesmen had every incentive to ignore the theological small print, even as far as promising to free souls from hell.

Despite the fun Chaucer had in the *Canterbury Tales* with the pardoner and his wallet "brimful of pardons come from Rome all hot", evidence of the abuse of indulgences is rare in England. However, one aspect which the church was unable to rein in satisfactorily was the attachment of indulgence to reciting specific prayers, or to praying before specific images, or to particular acts deemed pious. In 1532 a Tudor manual set out prayers to be said during mass which would produce over 100,000 years of remission.[6] If a heretic was being burned – as in the case of Nicholas Peke in 1538 – indulgence would be offered to anyone who would throw a stick on the fire. However, no one this side of the English Channel could match the archbishop of Mainz, whose collection of relics promised 39 million years of pardon.

Prayer for the Dead

The concern of an Englishman or woman to provide for their own dying and death is understandable in an age when there was little protection against illness and accident. Indeed, the death of possibly half the population in the mid fourteenth-century epidemic remembered as the Black Death must have intensified the sense of personal vulnerability, especially as outbreaks recurred over the next 300 years. To individual risk was added a moral responsibility to deceased parents, siblings, spouses, friends, neighbours, and benefactors, all as entitled to expect help in death as they had been in life. Thus the devout recitation of the "Fifteen Oes" [meditative prayers commencing "O Jesu" and ending with the *Paternoster* and the *Ave*] carried a promise of the conversion of fifteen kinsmen and the release of fifteen souls from purgatory.[7] Indulgence could also be earned by pilgrimages, and holy sites competed to offer the best remission package for "tourists". The community was enlisted too. Bidding the bedes called on the prayer energy of the whole parish and it was believed that if one of those named was in hell or already in bliss (and so in either case beyond the need for prayer) the prayers being offered would benefit the next of kin. Donating or bequeathing valuables to the church, undertaking building, leaving land to the parish to fund poor relief or money to provide candles to burn in ceremonies and before statues – all these would guarantee a place on the parish bede roll.

The obvious danger was, of course, that the pressures of life and the passage of the years could mean that prayer by the living might tail off in intensity. A long bede roll could only be read in instalments and a name might come up only once a year. Hence a wise man made arrangements in advance for specific intercessions to be continued after he was dead. Prayers could be contracted directly; Thomas Kebell left bequests totalling over £16 to ten religious foundations to pray for him.[8] Acts of charity which earned remission from purgatory had the added benefit of attracting the prayers of the faithful. Henry VII expected each of the homeless provided with overnight accommodation in his Savoy Hospital to say a prayer on his behalf and Thomas Kebell the same from the recipients of the £20 he left for the poor.[9]

Even more effective than prayers alone was the mass celebrated for the soul of the departed. In it the priest re-presented to God the sacrificial death of the Son of God for the salvation of humankind. To harness this supreme act of divine power, the elite and wealthy might leave money for thousands of masses to be said on their behalf. Henry VII arranged for 10,000 to be said immediately after his death at sixpence a time, half as much again as the going rate. What the king provided lavishly, his subjects would do to the best of their respective abilities. A popular provision for those who could afford it was a "trental", thirty soul masses said on successive days after the burial. Kebell left £16.67 for 1,000 masses to be said for his soul over thirty days, at 4d. each. Another possibility was to endow a chantry to support one or more priests in perpetuity. Henry VII did this in Westminster Abbey – funding three priests to celebrate mass for the king's soul for ever. If a chantry was financially out of the question, a priest could be individually contracted to say mass for as long as the money lasted. Kebell arranged that a priest would, every day for seven years, say the full service for the dead and a mass for Kebell's own soul and those of (named) relatives, plus specified prayers on weekdays and the Psalms of the Passion on Sundays.

The capital outlay amounted to £37.33. Individuals might also plan to be remembered on the anniversary of their death, very generally by an "obit" or an annual succession of obits – that is recitations of the Office for the Dead and requiem masses. If the expense of individual provision was too great, men and women could rely on their guild or fraternity to provide full funeral ceremonies at death and an inclusion in collective masses for brethren and sisters departed.[10] It is with some justice that late medieval religion has been described as "a cult of the living in the service of the dead".[11]

4

POPULAR RELIGION: CRITICISM

The apparent involvement of the church in the day-to-day life of ordinary English men and women during the two centuries before the Reformation poses a huge question. If the church was so entrenched in the community, how could a massive countrywide religious change have taken place within the lifetime of a single individual? Faced with excessive demands for taxation, the men of Lavenham threatened rebellion in 1525, but they did not rise in the 1540s to protect the contents of the church of St Peter and St Paul, their recently completed masterpiece. The only part of the country where religious opposition became serious was the lightly populated north, and its protests were forcibly suppressed by men from the more wealthy south. Why then did the English church turn out to be built on sand?

Through a Glass Darkly

Measuring community beliefs and attitudes is not easy in the twenty-first century, with its sophisticated sociological tools. Trying to do that for the sixteenth century is infinitely more difficult. We have first to recognize that our information is restricted to whatever interested and was produced by institutions and individuals who recorded it. The church and the clergy were by far the largest group in the "writing classes", with the result that much of what we know reflects their perspective and values. In the second place, we have to remember that among both clergy and laity, written material was principally produced by or for those with status, wealth, property, and education. Thus to tell what a bishop or a duke believed may be possible, but not the cottager and still less his wife. Moreover, information very generally survives in the form of anecdotes. In the past, this has led to students of the Reformation engaging in a kind of historical ping-pong, trading one example against another. Indeed, that pitfall is not always avoided today. All that numerous particular examples can suggest is a possibility. Equally important is remembering the existence of the "known unknowns". Given an England of over 2 million people, and perhaps 30,000 clergy, the feelings of only a tiny handful of individuals will ever be known. Generalization is impossible; the most we can hope for is a more or less educated guess.

A Corrupt Clergy?

That said, what of the traditional explanation that the medieval church collapsed because the clergy of those years were hopelessly corrupt and the nation commitedly anticlerical?

Sermons of the time frequently lambaste priests for not living up to the requirements of their calling, but complaints from the pulpit are not good evidence; preachers follow the adage that "damn braces but bless relaxes". Research, indeed, finds no evidence of generic corruption in the English church. That is not to say there were not abuses. Given the wealth of the church, some wrongdoing was inevitable. What was more, the wealth itself would seem to make mock of clergy vows of poverty, and dishonour a Christ who said that "you cannot serve God and money".[1] The clergy were the largest profession. They made up perhaps 2 per cent of the population but possibly three times that in a city like Norwich. They were ubiquitous, distinctive in dress and "tonsured"; that is, with the crown of the head shaved. Clerics were expected to be celibate but they were privileged in law and some lived very comfortably. Inevitably problems occurred. However, these were arguably no more frequent or serious than in previous centuries. Generally the church authorities dealt with scandals effectively and efforts were being made to improve standards of clerical education and behaviour. And not only was the English church one of the best regulated in Northern Europe; it had strong support from the English crown, one of Europe's most effective governments.

Anticlericalism

If the church was not institutionally corrupt, what made the English so anticlerical? Or were they? Historians argue the question vigorously. The term "anticlerical" comes from the efforts made in the French Third Republic (1870–1940) to exclude the church from public life. It is also used as a synonym for "anti-sacerdotal", hostility to the very existence of a priesthood, as found in the Spanish Civil War. In sixteenth-century Europe, especially Germany, anticlericalism, even anti-sacerdotalism, could be deep seated, but neither was significant in England.[2] From time to time friction did occur over church estates – certain monastic houses were particularly unpopular. However, as the church usually preferred to pay laymen to manage its property, relations with the tenants on its estates differed little from those of secular landlords. The same is true of the many franchises – rights of jurisdiction – which the church nominally held but which the crown increasingly kept under scrutiny (as it did with the lay lords). There is no evidence of the kind of deep economic and social hostility to church landlords which erupted in Germany in the so-called Peasants' War (1524–25). Admittedly there is no evidence either of enthusiasm to set up new religious foundations. After 1450, no new abbeys were founded. Later in the century two friaries were set up but only one thereafter.

Where parish grievances did arise, they were almost always caused by individual misconduct, not from systemic failures. For example, the parishioners of Bridge near Canterbury did repudiate their priest when the bishop's team arrived in 1511–12 for the periodic inspection. However, their complaint was that the vicar would neither provide regular services himself nor pay for a substitute and that he used his position to deny the sacraments to anyone who offended him. Bridge was not being anticlerical; the village simply wanted to get rid of the priest it had and be given a proper pastor in his stead. In other words, the criticism of priests in Tudor England was very often a call for higher standards of service. Ironically the church even invited such calls by its public stress on the need to improve clerical behaviour.[3]

It must also be remembered that the laity and the clergy were mutually dependent. The laity needed the services of the clergy, but the clergy relied on the laity for their incomes. Parochial incumbents usually enjoyed the security of an income from tithes, but the majority of priests serving as chaplains and auxiliaries only earned if lay folk engaged their services, and clergy in that position were "routinely hired and fired".[4] On occasion, and particularly with guilds and fraternities, the laity spelled out exactly what they required of the priest, to the point of specifying the liturgy itself. Indeed it can be argued that these voluntary lay initiatives in religion helped to familiarize the English with the idea that the church was a proper area for them to be involved in. For centuries, the attitude of the hierarchy had often been: "because you are lay folk, it is your business to believe that your prelates are men who do all things discreetly and with counsel".[5] When Archbishop Parker said much the same in 1571 about a bill in parliament, a spokesman for the MPs replied, "No, by the faith I bear unto God, we will pass nothing before we understand what it is, for that were but to make you popes. Make you popes who list, for we will make you none."[6]

Reputation

If anticlericalism proper is something of a red herring in the English Reformation, how much popular esteem did the clergy enjoy? Was there what might be called "soft" anticlericalism? That certainly is the case with another professional group, the lawyers. They were resented, abused, and valued in equal measure. That the clergy were regarded similarly is very probable. When the laity engaged a priest they more and more often specified that he must be "of good conversation" – that is, live an exemplary life; significantly, they did not take for granted that he would. Neither is it a sign of general respect that churchmen – dishonest, randy, or both – are stock figures in comedy. Four out of the five of them on Chaucer's pilgrimage are rogues and the whole plot of John Heywood's 1533 play *Johan Johan* is concerned with a parish priest cuckolding a parishioner. The priest assures the husband that he can prove the wife is virtuous:

> *I shall tell thee what I have done, Johan,*
> *For that matter; she and I be sometime aloft,*
> *And I do lie upon her many a time and oft*
> *To prove her; yet I could not espy*
> *That ever any did worse with her than I.*[7]

Friction with a particular cleric could lead to his whole profession being damned. There was, too, a widespread feeling that the clergy felt that they were invulnerable and would accuse even justified critics of being heretics.

More substantial evidence comes in the form of friction over clerical assertion and privilege. The most common cause was the collection of tithe. In theory the rector of a parish was entitled to a tithe [10 per cent] of everything produced and this could give rise to serious litigation. How frequent that was must not be exaggerated. In many rural communities tithe was governed by custom or compromise, and with a poor living, the incumbent had much in common with his flock, all villagers together. Cases which did arise were normally a consequence of unreasonable behaviour on one side or the other. Yet it is clear that in some places tithe disputes were becoming more frequent and intractable, probably because inflation was beginning to kick in.[8] (Most tithe was paid in kind, which gave the clergy a distinct advantage at a time of rising prices.) Clerical privileges, too, were being looked at askance, notably "benefit of clergy". This allowed any so-called "churchman" – a category which included porters and others in minor orders (i.e. below the rank of deacon) and thus effectively laymen – who was convicted of a first offence of felony to escape the gallows. Yet nothing in all of this suggests a level of hostility to the church which was sufficient to endanger it. Indeed, a parishioner critical of the church overall might very well say, "Of course, my own vicar is different."

London

There were, however, two possible exceptions to this. The first was London, England's only real city.[9] Many candidates for the priesthood from modest origins saw ordination less as a spiritual calling than a way to an income, constant employment, and social advancement, while the better born clergy felt they were entitled to the perquisites attached to high clerical positions. Moreover, priests comprised a majority of the better educated and so were the obvious people for the crown and the wealthy to recruit as secretaries and administrators. None of this was exclusive to London, but the city was where most patrons could be found and the best place for an ambitious educated priest to "put himself about". Moreover, although many London parishes paid the incumbent particularly well, the actual work in those parishes tended to be left to low paid deputies and casual employees, which meant that London was also a mecca for poor priests looking for employment.

In the confines of the city, the combination of wealthy priests otherwise engaged and poor priests looking for work made very obvious the spectacle of clergy not appearing to follow their calling. It was easy to see them as parasitic and tales of the occasional rogue priest readily grew by telling. John Colet (1467–1519), the dean of St Paul's, told his fellow clergy that heresies were "not so pestilent and pernicious unto us as the evil and wicked life of priests".[10] Paying London clergy also created special problems. The principle that the parish priest was entitled to a tithe made good sense in an agricultural context. In London, however, the difficulty of applying a rule framed as 10 per cent of produce to a money economy of wages and trading profits created a running sore. Between 1520 and 1546, over a third of the city's parishes went to law over tithe. A detailed petition by the city to the crown in 1513 or 1514 also complained of excessive charges for weddings, burials, and other services, even for keeping a name on the bede roll. A further factor was that in London the level of lay literacy was high, and although successful merchants might value the sacraments of the church they were not inclined to overvalue the status of the priest who delivered them and who in their guilds and fraternities did what he was told.

Many of these factors lie behind the famous case of the well-to-do London merchant, Richard Hunne. He had skirmishes with various clergy over several years which culminated in his being sued in 1512 for the sheet in which his baby son had been taken for burial. The canon law on such "mortuary" fees was against him but Hunne continued to resist and sought protection through the royal courts. Eventually in October 1514 he was arrested and imprisoned by the church on a charge of heresy. Seven weeks later he was found hanged in his cell. A London jury cried murder, but the church claimed suicide, condemned Hunne posthumously as a heretic, and had his body exhumed and burned. In consequence his family forfeited everything.

Anticlericalism in London hardened still further in the 1520s. Henry VIII tried to control the city more directly and made unprecedented tax demands but Thomas Wolsey, his chief minister, got the blame for both. The minister, however, was also a cardinal and the papal legate (so that effectively he ruled the English church), and he rammed home his unique authority in church and state on every occasion. Inevitably, therefore, Wolsey's high-handed treatment of the City fed the dislike of clerical pretension, and did nothing to endear Londoners to the pope whose power he represented.

Parliament

The second exception to the picture of a general accommodation between the English clergy and people was Westminster. Although the church could count on the crown for support, there is no doubt where the balance of power lay. Kings readily claimed the authority of God and religion in support of their status, but they also maintained a firm grip on the church. The crown controlled the appointment of the bishops and senior clergy; the church had to pay increasing amounts in tax; the church courts were kept under scrutiny and in their place. This was monitored by the judges and lawyers of the "common" [i.e. royal] law courts, and professional jealousy encouraged them to find increasingly ingenious ways to poach on the business of the church courts. When that happened, the crown insisted that the church give way. Its authority took precedence.

The potential for friction between the common law and the judges [the "ordinaries"] of the church's own courts was also evident in the House of Commons. A significant number of members were common lawyers by profession and many more had had some legal training. Criticism of church pretensions led to several statutes restricting church liberties. The church, for its part, did all it could to defend its autonomy and even before Hunne died, the atmosphere was tense. Fuelled by the episode, a major confrontation erupted over the exemption of clergy from the jurisdiction of secular courts. Eventually the king himself became directly involved.

The matter was papered over but Hunne was not forgotten. In 1523 his family had their property quietly restored and in 1529 London's powerful Mercer's Company (Hunne's own) petitioned parliament "to have in remembrance how the king's poor subjects principally of London, have been polled and robbed without reason of conscience by the ordinaries in probating of testaments and taking of mortuaries, and also vexed and troubled by citations with cursing [excommunication] one day and absolving the next day, and all for money".[11] Further bills to limit church abuses reached the statute book. Three years later the Commons would present a comprehensive complaint against the church courts [the "Supplication against the Ordinaries"], which played a major part in bringing about the break between England and the pope.[12]

Of course, neither London nor the House of Commons was the nation at large. London stood head and shoulders above the rest of the country in population, wealth, and economic power. The Commons represented the educated and the prosperous with a good leavening of royal officials and the clients of peers. But it was this very distinctiveness which made friction with London and Westminster so dangerous.

5

POPULAR RELIGION: CHALLENGES

The Italian visitor who was so impressed by the devotion he saw during mass in London also noticed "any who can read taking the office of our Lady with them, and with some companion reciting it in the church verse by verse, in a low voice, after the manner of churchmen".[1] However, "any who can read" is a huge qualification.

Illiteracy and Ignorance

At the start of the sixteenth century not being able to read was the norm. Illiteracy was gradually being pushed back but progress varied a great deal according to circumstances. One way of measuring is by the ability at least to sign one's name. This was greater among men than women and in towns than in the countryside; male literacy in London may have reached 40 per cent. Literacy also varied according to status and occupation. By the mid-sixteenth century most English gentlemen and merchants could manage a signature, so too about half of those classed as yeomen and a third of craftsmen and artisans. Among husbandmen [peasant farmers] perhaps only one in ten could sign and fewer than that among labourers and the poor. These figures may understate the number able to access books, because reading is a skill more easily grasped than penmanship. However, given that peasant and labouring families made up the overwhelming majority of the rural population, few of those in a village church would have been able to benefit from devotional material in English, although where a person could read and did own a primer, others might gather round to listen. As for understanding a liturgy in Latin – assuming it could be heard – that was beyond most men and women. Passages in the Latin liturgy which were repeated regularly and pronounced audibly must have become embedded in the memory but were these intelligible without translation?

Adding to the obstacles presented by illiteracy and Latin was the level of the religious instruction which the laity received. The only requirement set by Pope Innocent IV (1243–54) was that lay folk had to believe specifically that God exists and rewards the good and, beyond that, take for granted that what the church taught was true. The English church of the late Middle Ages had a far higher ambition. Lay people were expected to be able to repeat the *Paternoster, Creed,* and *Ave* in Latin, and know the Ten Commandments and the two Gospel commandments, the seven works of mercy, the seven virtues, the seven deadly sins, and the seven sacraments. Considerable effort was put into reaching this target but additional instruction is unlikely to have been general. Even if achieved, four sermons a year was a meagre diet. With parishioners often delaying their annual confessions until Holy Week or even Easter, a parish priest may not have found it easy to follow up or probe consciences in depth, although auxiliary clergy might have helped or even been recruited. All of this, of course, assumes that the priest was himself sufficiently equipped to instruct his flock. In 1551 in the diocese of Gloucester over half the parish priests did not know the author of the Lord's Prayer or were not able to repeat the Ten Commandments.[2] More importantly, the syllabus focuses very largely on factual knowledge, religious observance, personal conduct, and the consequences of immorality and negligence. Sermon material too was primarily concerned to impart information, inculcate facts, and encourage routine observance. The Christianity which the church promoted was a religion of creed, behaviour, and charity. Encouraging individual spiritual experience was not a widespread priority.[3]

Sacred Art

The church, of course, was fully aware of the problem of illiteracy. Its response was to encourage a visual presentation of the faith. Church decoration – the extensive wall paintings and stained glass found in many churches – taught the Christian stories. So did religious drama, as in the mystery plays put on by the craft guilds in a number of large towns. Yet what of the next stage, which turned information into discipleship? There were the obligatory images found in churches, supremely the rood. At Compsal near Doncaster, a verse sets out the called-for reaction:

> *Let fall down thy knee and lift up thy heart,*
> *Behold thy maker on yonder cross all torn;*
> *Remember his wounds that for thee did smart*
> *Begotten without sin and on a virgin born.*
> *All his head pierced with a crown of thorn;*
> *Alas, man, thy heart ought to break in two.*
> *Beware of the devil when he blows his horn*
> *And pray thy good angel convey thee there from.*[4]

But was an injunction to avoid the wiles of the devil an adequate spiritual response to the crucifixion, and what if you could not read? Statues of the Virgin and the saints were intended to lead the mind of the faithful to Christ, but the reputations which some images acquired indicate that they were essentially revered as sacred objects. The same was true of the supreme religious drama, the liturgy of the mass, particularly the elevation. Even the poorest parishioner should have understood that. But again the response might be veneration of the material object.[5] Archbishop Cranmer would later write scathingly of people running "from altar to altar and from sacring to sacring, peeping, tooting and gazing at that thing which the priest held up in his hands".[6] The same was true of the reserved sacrament. When taken to a sick person it was formally escorted through the streets and bystanders were expected to bow.

Religion and Society

All this said, it is important to recognize that the church in pre-Reformation England offered more than religion narrowly defined. One did not have to be devout to be engaged by the ceremony attached to the great festivals of the church. Palm Sunday was effectively a Christian rite of spring and the ceremonies of Easter Day were especially impressive. Rogationtide processions were masterminded by the church to invoke God's mercy, but were effectively fertility rites to bless the fields and a way to assert and protect parish boundaries as well as occasions for eating and drinking. Members of a fraternity did not only attend funerals. The feast day of its patron saint would be marked by the most magnificent high mass possible followed by the annual feast. In a wealthy fraternity, celebrations could spread over several days, with entertainments and guild plays.

Activities which were not specifically religious also revolved round the church. In many places Hocktide, immediately after Easter, saw on the first day a team of young men out to catch women in the street and release them for a payment to church funds, and the next day young women had their turn. May Day ushered in several weeks of special events – games in the churchyard, plays of Robin Hood, and midsummer bonfires to purge the air over the crops and to drive away plague. As with Hocktide, many of these events focused on raising money for the parish and, as a matter of course, fund-raising "church ales" were held either in the church or the churchyard. Preachers might attack "vain, stupid, profane games", but these enabled the church to appeal to the whole person. Even overtly secular business was accommodated, whether it be buying and selling, clinching deals and paying rents or, in the case of St Paul's Cathedral in London, marketing legal services.

The pre-Reformation church was, therefore, socially inclusive. It also reflected social realities. First it expressed the fact that a parish was a corporate entity. Kissing the paxbred was a gesture of accepting others and being accepted. Sharing in the holy loaf after the Sunday mass said the same. Receiving communion at Easter was popularly called "taking one's rights" and anything which interfered with that effectively excluded the individual from the community. In 1530 at Little Plumsted a few miles outside Norwich, Nicholas Tyting was refused communion because he had quarrelled with the priest. His fellow villagers found him weeping in the churchyard and one of them upbraided the rector. "How is it, Master Parson, that Tyting and you cannot agree. It is a pity that he should go his way without his rights."[7] A further layer of meaning is suggested by the fact that all involvement of the laity in the service conformed to the social pecking order. The paxbred was kissed in turn according to status, so too receiving the holy loaf and the taking of communion at Easter, and unseemly jostling was not unknown. Chaucer's Wife of Bath was "wrath" and "out of all charity" with anyone who "to the offering before her should go".[8] The Corpus Christi processions in major cities said the same. Every rank of society was represented in a proper order, with the mayor walking immediately ahead of the host. The church which expressed community also expressed hierarchy.

Another consideration was status. Thomas Kebell prefaced the elaborate provisions to promote the health of his soul with the instruction that he was to be buried "in such manner as my executors shall think appropriate for the rank to which it has pleased God to call me in this world" – certainly "laying aside all vain pomp and glory", but equally "as my executors shall think fitting for the honour of me and my friends".[9] This to twenty-first-century thinking smacks of a contradiction but not to pre-Reformation minds. Religious practice expected to reflect secular rank. In doom paintings behind the rood, popes emerge from the grave to face the Last Judgement wearing the triple tiara and so too kings wearing their crowns. Much church building and church beautifying carried the same message. The memorial brass of the Yorkshire lawyer Brian Roucliffe who died in 1494 shows him holding a depiction of Cowthorpe Church which he had built, so announcing to worshippers what they owed to him and that he was entitled to their prayers. Richard Fowler, chancellor of the duchy of Lancaster (d.1477), provided for the completion of the south aisle of the parish church of Buckingham and the erection of a new shrine to contain the bones of (the decidedly fictional) St Romwold, but with his own tomb as part of the scheme.

Rank determined whether you would be buried inside the church or in the churchyard. So too in the competition for the holiest locations within the building. Thomas Littleton, the doyen of English legal authors, prepared a tomb in Worcester Cathedral beneath the image of his patron saint, St Christopher, immediately next to the altar dedicated to the saint where Littleton's parents were "sung" for daily. Testators who owned pews might ask to be buried beneath them, so marking permanently their position in the church and the community. Those who chose to be commemorated by a less expensive memorial brass would often still couple requests for prayers and assertions of status, although Thomas Pownder, who died in 1525, may have omitted the prayers entirely in favour of recording that he was a merchant adventurer and erstwhile bailiff of Ipswich.[10] Where a chantry was founded, the priest sang mass for the soul of the founder, but the chapel itself would be designed and decorated to commemorate the importance of the founder and the status of his family. The Vernon Chantry in the parish church of Tong in Shropshire is a notable example. The founder, the courtier Sir Henry Vernon, actually lived in Derbyshire but Tong was the burial place of important ancestors and so he created a family mausoleum there, modelled on Henry VII's chantry at Westminster, with a riot of heraldry to demonstrate that the Vernon family had connections with some of the greatest in the land.

That status and family were as strong a motive for religious giving as concern for the hereafter (possibly stronger) is certainly suggested by what happened later in the sixteenth century. Fast forward a generation, and funeral monuments are equally or more in vogue, though shorn of pious petitions. In other words, family commemoration followed one fashion before the Reformation, another after it. Brasses were still installed to sound the praises of the deceased, rehearse family descent, and record benefactions. The post-Reformation prohibitions on requesting prayers made no difference at all. At Thames Ditton in Surrey, Erasmus Forde and his wife Julyan, backed by their eighteen children, knelt opposite each other across not a holy image but a coat of arms. Sculptured monuments proliferate. In Holy Trinity Stratford-upon-Avon, Shakespeare's world-famous combination of a tomb-slab and a wall-mounted bust follows the same formula as one of the medieval memorials at Tong. At Warwick, a few miles away, the chantry chapel built to intercede for the soul of Richard Beauchamp, the great fifteenth-century earl of Warwick, was annexed as a private mausoleum for the Dudley brothers, Queen Elizabeth's courtiers. At the end of her reign, Sir Gabriel Poyntz colonized the Lady Chapel at North Ockendon in Essex, not only for full size recumbent effigies of himself and his wife but for matching tablets to record himself and his wife (again) and seven Poyntz ancestors and their wives, back to 1307.[11]

Lay Belief

The pre-Reformation English parish thus endorsed the social structure, but religion struck even deeper resonances. Hearing mass brought material benefit. As the Lay Folks Mass Book said, "the worthiest thing, most of goodness in all this world, it is the mass".[12] Hence everything a man did after hearing mass would "profit and come to a good end"; even what he ate would be more beneficial. Women with child were told that to guarantee a safe delivery and a healthy baby, they should hear mass each day of their pregnancy.[13] It was also claimed that devoutly hearing mass would protect against illness, blindness, and sudden death for the rest of the day. When the auditor John Gostwick travelled from Bedford to Chester in December 1530 and every morning paid a friar to say mass, he was effectively taking out travel insurance – and he put the expense on his bill.[14]

Prayers also promised practical results. The person who uttered the "*Crux Christi*" [Cross of Christ] prayer made the sign of the cross repeatedly and called on it as a power to drive away the devil. Given the belief in a literal devil and hosts of demons bent on dragging a Christian to hell, such a prayer was to that point orthodox, but those reciting it were also assured of victory over temporal enemies, protection in battle and against thieves, and immunity from epilepsy, pestilence, thunder, fire, and water, while pregnant women could engage the power of the prayer by writing it on a strip of parchment long enough to wrap round them.[15] An even clearer example of an exorcism began with a recitation of forty-seven Greek and Latin titles and names for God, each accompanied with the sign of the cross [+] and the plea that the names would "protect and defend me from all disaster and for infirmity of body and soul, may they wholly set me free and come to my help".[16] The incantation "Holy God, Holy Strong One, the Immortal One, have mercy on us", said alternately in Greek and Latin, was "a good prayer against pestilence" [plague]. Yet how many of those who repeated "*Agyos otheos sancte deus Agyos ischyros sancte fortis, Agyos athanatos eleyson ymas*" knew Greek, or Latin for that matter, or would recognize the liturgy the words came from?[17] Even reciting a snippet from one of the four Gospels could invoke divine power. Repeating the clause "not a bone of his shall be broken" was a remedy for toothache.[18]

An easy assumption to make in the twenty-first century is that these folk beliefs were characteristic of the uneducated. After all, the great theologian St Thomas Aquinas roundly condemned superstition, divination, and the chanting of magic incantations. In the *Canterbury Tales*, Chaucer the sophisticate mocked the way the Pardoner peddled bogus relics and a sheep's shoulder bone which could turn water into a remedy for animal diseases, or if swallowed by the owner would encourage fertility in his livestock and cure any feeling of jealousy at his wife's infidelity. The jibe had a long life, for it was echoed by the dramatist John Heywood in his 1544 *The Play called the Four PP.*[19] Yet there is good evidence that the educated were not exempt from the mixture of piety and superstition. It is inescapable, even in those elite creations of late medieval piety, books of hours.

The term "hours" refers to the timing of the monastic "offices", but these books contained more than material for services. In many manuscripts, bespoke material was included at the wish of the owner. Thus Brian Roucliffe, whose brass we have seen proclaiming his generosity in church building, had a number of additional devotions copied into a large book of hours which he later specifically bequeathed to his son. Examples created for princes and aristocrats were jewels as much as books, elaborately written and superbly illustrated by the finest practitioners in manuscript illumination. Others were made for a more popular market, within the reach of men and women of moderate incomes, and that was even more the case when printing became available. All in all, books of hours were "the most popular book of the late Middle Ages", devotional primers for literate laity, the equivalent to material published for private devotion today.[20] Yet in these books of hours there are the same incantations. If a person said, listened to, or even carried a copy of the prayer *"Deus prospicius esto"* ["God be favourable"], he would not die by fire, bad weather, battle, poison, or execution and would not die suddenly – that is, without absolution for his sins.[21] An invocation which is effectively a spell against storms and thunder reads: "Jesus of Nazareth, King of the Jews, Christ conquers; may Christ reign: may Christ vindicate us, and from all thunder, tempest and every evil free and defend us. Amen. Behold [+] the Cross of the Lord, flee you enemies: the lion of the tribe of Judah, the root of David conquers."[22] Here we have not peasant credulity but what many of the laity understood religion to be.

Like the veneration of saints, charms and incantations derived from the pagan past, but despite St Thomas Aquinas they too were sanctioned by the church. The reason the church brought its bells and banners to the Rogationtide ceremonies was to drive evil spirits away from the community, and sometimes the next-door parish would object to the arrival of the demons so displaced. The new forms of devotion to Christ, which, as we shall see, marked the later Middle Ages, quickly spawned "superstitions" of their own. Arranging for five celebrations of the Mass of the Five Wounds promised deliverance from all earthly evil.[23] Repeating the Holy Name was a particular talisman against the plague.[24]

Consecrated objects ["sacramentals"] were believed to have power in themselves; they were, in technical language, apotropaic. Thus it was common to carry a fragment of the parish loaf in a pocket or pouch. Wheaten bread blessed by a prayer attributed to St Paul would cure diarrhoea. Candles blessed at Candlemas were a protection against thunderstorms. Holy water was similarly powerful. Before the Sunday mass, the priest first took salt, exorcised and blessed it so as "to become the salvation of body and soul to all who" took it. Then he consecrated water so as to be an "effectual power" to cast out demons and drive away disease. As well as being used in church, amounts of this sanctified salt water were taken by "the holy-water clerk" to the various houses in the village, where it would be sprinkled on hearths and elsewhere to drive off evil spirits.[25]

Degrees of Commitment

The overriding impression given by the pre-Reformation church is of busyness and practicality. In content it covered everything from providing for the hereafter to protection against accidents in the everyday. Indeed, a cynic might conclude that the late medieval church resembled nothing so much as a huge insurance business. But if so, how deeply committed to Christianity were English men and women in the opening years of the sixteenth century?

It is certainly possible that there were parishes where the majority of those supposed to be present at the services did attend, did worship with devotion, and did warmly support church activities. It is equally possible to envisage a parish where a comparable level of activity reflected the enthusiasm of a minority. It also seems very probable that there were those who simply took the church for granted. It and its rituals were a fact of life, so they just did what was expected. Distinguishing between these categories is rarely possible since the evidence which survives – letters, narratives, benefactions, and the rest – comes from the enthusiasts. The bored and the casual leave little trace. In Elizabeth's reign, Roger Martin wrote a moving lament for the lost beauty of the fabric and the liturgy at his Suffolk parish church.[26] However, it is very evident that the well-to-do Martin family had a proprietorial attitude to Holy Trinity Long Melford. Furthermore, trying to generalize faces the problem that religious commitment varies from person to person and can fluctuate over the lifetime of an individual. This makes it particularly difficult to rely on the wording of a person's final will and testament. That was usually drawn up when the testator was dying, so concern for the hereafter is hardly surprising: "the devil was sick, the devil a monk would be. The devil grew well, the devil a monk was he."[27] Moreover, the wording of a will seems very often to have been supplied by the scribe employed, who was in many cases the parish priest. And, once more, what evidence is there for the great majority who left no will?

One factor in the acceptance of the church is easily overlooked: compulsion. The church which claimed to be a community of the faithful also had coercive power. As well as authority in all cases concerning the clergy and over important areas of lay life, its courts had authority to deal with moral and religious offences.[28] Offenders could be summoned to attend a court and accept its judgments under threat of excommunication, and although that could be ignored, being excommunicated was a significant nuisance to anyone in trade or with property since it removed the protection of the royal law courts. What the church had no power to do was to threaten the death penalty, and that gave it no ultimate way to discipline any individuals who were religiously heterodox – for example, anyone refusing to be confessed and take communion at Easter (since 1215 the church's main test for subversion). However, in 1401 the English crown provided real teeth. Henry IV had ousted Richard II and needed endorsement by the church and the pope. This coincided with the threat of the Lollard heresy and Henry paid his debt by agreeing to the statute *de heretico comburendo* ["for the burning of heretics"], which put royal muscle behind the enforcement of conformity.[29] Where an individual had been formally condemned by the church as a heretic, they could be handed over to the crown to be executed. It was possible to avoid death by confessing and adjuring heretical belief. That, however, was not painless. It involved public humiliation and sometimes imprisonment, and in strict law there was no second chance. Even if once more penitent, a "relapsed" heretic was nevertheless supposed to be burned. Outward conformity was very much the safe option.

To ignore this, as well as the considerable variation between England's parishes and the little information we have for most of them, and instead picture a land of well-loved and well-attended churches serving rural populations of devout Christians, is to subscribe to the myth of "Merry England". We need the correction offered by A.G. Dickens: "the great majority partook amply of that mundane utilitarianism which marked mid-Tudor Englishmen of all classes and counties".[30] Some, possibly many, were barely engaged by religion. Behaviour in church was certainly not always decorous, a fault regularly targeted in sermons. A distant liturgy which could barely be heard was hardly likely to rivet every attention. People gossiped and laughed; girls were more interested in the young men than the service, and vice versa. As a mid fifteenth-century cleric wrote, "they chatter, they lark about, they kiss women, and hear no word of the service but mock the priest, saying that he dawdles over his mass and keeps them from their breakfast".[31] The need to ring a sacring bell was precisely to call the congregation to heel at the moment of consecration. Sermons were popular. Why? Instruction or entertainment? We cannot tell, and, equally, ducking out was not unknown. Others of the congregation escaped after the elevation. As for overall attendance, the cleric who complained about chatter declared that people "come to matins no more than three times a year". There is also "evidence of considerable lay absenteeism from the mass".[32] Nor do we know about those who did attend, but under community or employer pressure. The differences in the size and the prosperity of parishes make generalizing about such social control almost impossible. We may guess that the servants and tenants of the Martin family at Long Melford dutifully appeared on cue, but we have no way of knowing their private thoughts or those of the rest of the villagers. A Protestant who had been on the run in the reign of the Catholic Queen Mary noted subsequently that "there was no such place to shift in, in this realm, as in London, notwithstanding their great spying and search".[33] Powerful secular alternatives to church were on offer too – games, bear-baiting, and similar distractions. Retailers found it paid them to keep their shops open for business during service time; so did tavern keepers. In 1542, more than half the parishioners of St Giles Colchester absented themselves on Sundays and holy days, some at work, some in the alehouse and one who stayed in bed.[34] All of which is a salutary warning to bear in mind at all times: the possibility – even the likelihood – of a silent cohort of English men and women who knew little and cared less about religious niceties.

6

PRE-REFORMATION SPIRITUALITY

Anthropologists have long been aware that patterns of behaviour rarely have a single significance. Instead, layers of meaning – obvious and less obvious – pile up, one on top of another. We have seen how the church made sense of the life and death of English men and women and supported them in relevant and highly practical ways, but we would be naïve to expect that this satisfied everyone. So can anything be said about the spiritual quality to be found among England's Christians prior to the Reformation?

Scepticism

Assessing the variations in belief within the majority, conformity is anything but easy. As we have noted, observance, piety, and faith differ from person to person and even fluctuate within an individual lifetime.[1] The difficulty is particularly acute at the grass roots. Given that acquiescence in public was the safe option, it is no surprise that evidence of atheism or even agnosticism is scarce. Silence, therefore, tells us nothing either way. Alcohol elicited profanity but, tavern talk aside, scepticism about key elements of the Christian Creed was from time to time unearthed by church authorities. In 1486 Roger Browne, a Coventry man, verged on denying the incarnation, saying "that the Lord never shed his blood on earth and did not have a mother".[2] Two years later, Margery Goyt from Ashbourne in Derbyshire claimed that Christ was "not born of a virgin because Joseph was betrothed to Mary and he had sexual intercourse with her many times, so Christ was conceived of Joseph's seed, just as Margery conceived her son from the seed of her husband".[3] In 1539, Thomas Prat from Thirsk in Yorkshire admitted saying that "God never bled all his blood, for if he had bled all his blood he could not have risen again from death to life", which came perilously close to questioning the resurrection.[4]

Heresy

Such sceptics as existed were not the only Tudor people thinking unconventionally. A number of Christians insisted that the church was in need of radical reform. Emerging at the end of the fourteenth century and influenced by the Oxford theologian John Wycliffe, their criticisms were one by one rejected by the church hierarchy. Those who continued to maintain them were labelled heretics and given the pejorative nickname "Lollard" [possibly from *lollen* – to mutter, or *lolia* – weeds]. Heresy – adhering to a religious opinion contrary to accepted church dogma – was the religious equivalent of high treason. By setting private opinion against the united consensus of the faithful, the heretic was withdrawing from the Christian church and "outside the church there was no salvation".[5] Heresy was also uniquely dangerous because it could be contagious. Not only was the heretic himself destined to hell, he could take others with him. He was the religious equivalent of a dog with rabies.

Lollards were not numerous in the nation at large and had nothing like the impact which Wycliffe's teaching had 650 miles away, in the Czech-speaking lands of Bohemia. There his insights were taken up by Jan Hus, the rector of Prague University, and, following Hus's execution for heresy, his followers ["Hussites"] forced the pope to concede lay communion in both kinds and a liturgy in the vernacular. In England, by the second half of the fifteenth century Lollardy was only significant in family networks and house groups in particular localities in the south, but in those areas they might be counted by the score and even more. In parts of the diocese of Lichfield, over 400 suspected Lollards and Lollard sympathizers were detected in the three years 1518 to 1521; in Colchester some forty were detected between 1527 and 1531. The networks were also loosely linked by travelling preachers. London too had its Lollards. As elsewhere these were mostly artisans and craftsmen, but some belonged to the prestigious livery companies. The demand which came to define them was an insistence on the laity having access to an English translation of the Bible. On the Continent, vernacular translations were available but because two English translations had been produced during the initial criticism of the church that led to Lollardy, the English bishops seized on that as the litmus test for heresy. From 1409 onwards, it became an offence to possess a copy of the Bible in English, or to translate "any text of Holy Scripture into English" without permission from the bishops, or to preach in English on theological topics such as the sacraments. In 1513 John Colet was barred from his pulpit in St Paul's Cathedral, in part because he rendered the Lord's Prayer into English, and the case against Richard Hunne was that he owned a prohibited translation.

Apart from insisting on access to the Bible in English, the principal theological challenge of the Lollards was to the doctrine of transubstantiation. The views of John Reve, a glover from Beccles in Norfolk, are typical. In 1430 he confessed that he had "held, believed and affirmed that no priest hath power to make God's body in the sacrament of the altar, and that after the sacramental words said of a priest at mass there remains nothing but only a cake of material bread".[6] Other comments could be a deal more ribald. When John Athee from Egham in Surrey was assured that God by his word could turn bread into the body and blood, he replied "so he might do if he would turn it into a chicken's leg".[7] In Rye in the 1530s it was being said that "the divine service sung in the church of God is of no more effect than the bleating of a cow to her calf".[8] In 1536 the Convocation of Canterbury complained to Archbishop Cranmer that "light and lewd persons" were asking, "Is it [the host] anything else but a piece of bread or a little pretty piece round Robin?"[9] Transubstantiation simply appeared to defy common sense. A Coventry shoemaker confessed in 1511 to asking, "What can the priest make of a morsel of bread etc.? Should he make God today and eat him today and do likewise tomorrow?"[10] Another man picked up in the same Coventry trawl for heretics admitted to being taught that "God made man & not man God, as the carpenter doth make the house and not the house the carpenter"; the host was "a token or a remembrance of Christ's passion & not as the very body of Christ".[11]

The considerable effort which the church put into defending the doctrine of transubstantiation suggests that doubts about the miracle may have extended beyond the Lollards. Numerous sermon illustrations told of doubters who became convinced by the horror of seeing the host become bleeding flesh until prayer restored the safe appearance of bread. A play performed later in the fifteenth century told of a recent miracle in Spain when Jews paid a merchant to steal a consecrated host which they subjected to all the torments of Christ's passion. It bled throughout and when put to roast in an oven, the oven burst to reveal the risen Saviour, who reproached the Jews for re-crucifying him. The Jews were converted and the merchant collaborator was awarded penance and absolved. The text is connected with Bury St Edmunds in Suffolk but is known to have been performed at Croxton in Norfolk, so evidently it was toured through East Anglia.[12]

Lollards were able to attend the regular ceremonies of a parish mass without inviting challenge as to the meaning of the sacrament. The Colchester baker John Pykas even admitted that each year he was "confessed and houseled but for no other cause but people should not wonder upon him".[13] It was, however, more difficult to disguise refusal to give conventional respect to religious images. As we have seen, All Saints North Street had at least six in addition to the figures on the rood screen. Other churches could have a dozen and more; St Mary's, the parish church of Faversham, may have had thirty-five. The rood would have a light burning before it and so too the other images, the cost being met either by an individual wishing to venerate the saint or by the parish generally. Respect for martyrs and saints (with their relics) and also the Virgin Mary and the Archangel Michael had spread in the Western church by the end of the fifth century as newly converted communities translated much of their pagan heritage into Christian terms. Enthusiastically endorsed by Pope Gregory the Great (590–604), it became usual, and later a requirement, for a parish to display statues of at least its patron saint and of the Virgin. The church never taught that saints and their statues should be adored; adoration [*latria*] was due to God alone. It was, however, proper to give reverence [*dulia*] to saints in heaven and hence to honour their images. A statue would remind the viewer of the godly achievements of the particular saint while prayer to the saint would enlist not only direct material help but also their powerful intercession with God on behalf of the petitioner. Some saints had only a local following, but in England statues such as the Virgin at Doncaster and at Walsingham acquired a national reputation, while others had regional importance, such as "the Lady of the Tower" in the Carmelite friary in Coventry. Lollards would have none of this. In 1511 John Cropwell, a Coventry wiredrawer, said that he was going to offer "to an image of Blessed Mary" [of the Tower]. The Lollard Robert Hachet commented, "Ah, God help thee, thou art a fool."[14] Nine years later Hachet, now seventy, was again arrested and this time was burned to death. Cropwell's prayer might well have been:

> O most benign Mary, daughter of the father of heaven, mother of the son
> of God, spouse of the Holy Ghost, I pray thee that as the Father celestial
> of his great might and power has exalted thee in the highest throne of
> heaven, so I pray thee, most benign virgin and mother Mary, to succour
> me and help me and all my friends and to defend us from the temptations
> of our enemy [the devil].[15]

In extreme but rare cases, images were actually defaced or destroyed ["iconoclasm"]. A particularly serious incident took place in 1522 at St Mary's Rickmansworth when arsonists targeted the statues and the reserved sacrament and succeeded in ruining the chancel and the vestry, as well as despoiling the font. The culprits were never found, but in all probability were Lollards retaliating against the recent burning of two of their number. Lollards also attacked pilgrimages, relics, and shrines, denied the existence of purgatory, and generally refused to accept that clergy had any special status or unique powers.

Personal Religion

As the sixteenth century loomed, heretics were a small minority, but they were not the only English people to take Christianity with the utmost seriousness. Indeed Lollards are best understood as the radical element among many who were seeking for a more personal religious experience. Throughout its history, Christianity has been characterized by periodic revivals and consequent upheavals, and one had begun in Western Europe in the twelfth and thirteenth centuries. Whereas in earlier times much of the energy of the church had been expressed in monasticism, now the needs – and demands – of ordinary men and women came to the fore. The result was the emergence of a piety characterized by a focus on the person of Jesus

Christ ["Christocentrism"] and the climax of that would come with Martin Luther and others like him.

One outworking of this revival in England was the emphasis we have already noted on Christ's physical presence in the host. Although transubstantiation had previously been widely believed, the church only adopted the explanation officially in 1215, and in 1274 ordered that observers should bow or kneel every time the name of Jesus occurred during mass.[16] Soon we find the consecrated wafer being displayed on the altar in a box [a pyx] for people to reverence at all times, not just during mass – the body of Christ, always present with the faithful. The widespread popularity of the existing cult of the Blessed Virgin Mary might seem to cast doubt on this desire for a closer appreciation of Christ, but for the more discerning, the opposite could be true. Christ had derived his human life from his mother so there was an obvious congruence between the body born of Mary and the body consecrated on the altar. As a prayer to be said at the elevation put it:

> *I thee honour with all my might*
> *In form of bread as I thee see,*
> *Lord, that in that Lady bright,*
> *In Mary, man become for me.*[17]

Venerating Mary brought her son even closer to failing humanity. Soon devotion to the presence of Christ in the sacrament created pressure for a special day to honour the miracle and in 1264/65 the pope acquiesced and added the feast of Corpus Christi ["body of Christ"] to the church calendar. First observed in England in 1318, the feast became one of the high points of the church year to express not just individual devotion but the devotion of whole communities. Numerous guilds and fraternities sprang up to support this devotion, and both existing and new religious dramas ["miracle plays"] were also drawn to the date.

The cult of Corpus Christi focused, as did mass in a parish, on the immediacy of Christ in the host, but that did have dangers. In some minds, it could engender a fixation on the physicality of the host, not on the host in the context of a eucharist and communion. Thus one early Tudor devotional manual stated that with God present and so near to a man, "as often as he draws his breath and takes it of [from] the air, so often does he receive a special grace for his soul".[18] Other new devotions avoided this and aimed to help the believer to enter emotionally and spiritually into the experience of the Passion of Christ itself. One which was becoming increasingly popular in England was the cult of the Five Wounds.[19] This called the faithful to contemplate Christ's wounds and respond personally to each one in turn. A focus on the suffering which Christ had endured on behalf of the individual believer was also encouraged by large crosses and crucifixes placed in numerous different locations and those worn by individuals. As John Fisher, bishop of Rochester (1459–1535), put it, they were there to evoke the emotion: "O my Lord that would'st die for me upon a cross, how noble and excellent art thou, and again, how wretched and miserable am I?"[20] A cult which was even more popular than Corpus Christi was devotion to the Holy Name of Jesus. Indeed it came to rival the established cult of Mary. The New Testament text has a number of references to the power of the name of Jesus and this became the theme of an enormously successful travelling preacher, St Bernardino of Siena (1380–1444). It struck a popular chord and very soon in far away England, Jesus Brotherhoods sprang up (particularly among the elite) to fund and manage a regular celebration of the Mass of the Holy Name, in some places several times a week and even at specially designated altars and chapels. In 1494, thanks to the advocacy of Henry VII's mother, Lady Margaret Beaufort (whose clergy composed the liturgy), the pope established a feast of the Holy Name and attached to it several thousand years of pardon.[21] The focus of the devotion was the monogram IHS ["Jesus"] surrounded by the sun's rays (although the Lady Margaret set it in a crowned Tudor Rose) and again the emphasis was on "the sweetness, gentleness and accessibility of the human Saviour".[22]

For a small number of individuals, mysticism provided a private route to God. This was particularly true for women. The universities of Europe viewed reason as the way to understand the deity, but women had no access to such formal education. Instead they threw mind and imagination into experiencing God and responding to the Holy Spirit in silence and contemplation. Across the Channel, Hildegard of Bingen (1098–1179) and Catherine of Siena (c.1347–80) are the best known. England had Julian of Norwich (1342–c.1416). Her reflections on sixteen visions of the crucified

Christ are preserved in her "Book of Shewings", better known as *Revelations of Divine Love*, with its assertion that "all shall be well and all manner of things shall be well". A younger contemporary was Margery Kempe from King's Lynn (*c*.1373–*c*.1438), whose pilgrimages even included Jerusalem and whose outbursts of religious emotion repeatedly got her into trouble with the authorities. There were men too, such as Richard Rolle (*c*.1305–49), whose mystical writings circulated widely.

Self-Help

The case of Richard Rolle illustrates a further aspect of the late medieval religious revival, grass-roots fervour outside church structures, lay people whom the ministrations of the church did not satisfy, groups who were determined to seek for themselves a deeper and more personal awareness of God. The exemplar here is Francis of Assisi (1181/82–1226), who embraced poverty and worshipped Christ not as a distant deity but as "God with Us", the Man of Sorrows. His devotion reached such a spiritual intensity that Francis developed stigmata – the duplication on his body of wounds like those of Christ himself. Fortunately for Francis, his evident sanctity protected him and a majority of his followers from the excommunication which his incorrigible originality invited. Instead the pope regularized the Franciscans as an extra-parochial medicant order of "friars" [*"fratres"* –"brothers"] committed to spreading a deeper experience of faith and Christian living by preaching and hearing confessions. Other devotional movements also appeared, some of which were suspect or even suppressed as heretical, and others which were accepted by the church. An early and notable example was the Carthusian Order, which reached England in 1182. Apart from attending services in the monastery chapel, Carthusians lived effectively as hermits.

A development which remained outside the church was the emergence, particularly in the Low Countries, of individual women who remained in secular life but made a voluntary (and terminable) commitment to celibacy, prayer, and good works, especially to the poor. Soon they are found setting up "beguinages", small self-governing groups in private houses which, like the early Franciscans, decided for themselves how to order living and worship. This unregulated female initiative, though at first endorsed by the pope, was increasingly looked at with suspicion by the formal hierarchy of the church. In 1310 one of its most famous beguine mystics was burned at the stake. The next year the very name was outlawed and the women were forced to adopt more convent-like arrangements. They gradually complied and "remained a significant force in lay piety in the church during the rest of the Middle Ages".[23] There may, indeed, have been similar women's groups in Norwich, which, of course, had close ties with the Low Countries.[24] There, another lay initiative resulted in the "Brethren of the Common Life". Gerard Groote, university trained and at one time a monk, had a conversion experience and became a missionary preacher in the diocese of Utrecht. Banned for criticizing the conduct of the clergy, he set up a quasi-monastic community at Deventer where men and women were able to continue in secular work: "religion is to love God and worship him, not the taking of special vows".[25] The model was rapidly imitated in the Low Countries and the Rhineland, with an emphasis on living a life of deep Christocentric devotion which became known as the *Devotio Moderna* ["present day devotion"]. The Brethren included clergy and laity, and married couples and children could be equally involved; often houses were answerable to urban corporations rather than church authorities. From the middle of the fifteenth century, texts associated with the *Devotio* were circulating in England. One which was translated at the behest of Lady Margaret Beaufort was Thomas à Kempis's *De imitatione Christi* [*The Imitation of Christ*], a devotional classic which is reputedly the most widely translated Christian book, apart from the Bible itself.[26] The corporate communities of the *Devotio* seem not to have crossed the North Sea but, in contrast, solitary Christians – anchorites who lived in a cell and hermits who travelled about – seem to have been more prominent in England than on the Continent.

As well as the clear commitment to Christ which was demonstrated in patterns of devotion, there is a miscellany of material which documents the prayer life of serious medieval Christians. Evidence for this survives in a wide variety of sources, from devotional manuals to jottings in account books, and the occurrence of the same prayers in source after source must argue that they were in common circulation. At the moment of the elevation of the host a recommended prayer was:

May you be loved, King; and may you be blessed, King; and may you be
thanked, King, for all your good gifts. Jesus, my delight, who spilt your
blood for me and died upon the rood, you give me grace to sing the song
of love for you.[27]

A prayer to be learned for one's deathbed began:

Sweetest and most loving lord, my Lord Jesus Christ, God's own dear
son. For the honour and virtue of your blessed Passion admit and receive
me among the number of your chosen people. My saviour and redeemer,
I surrender all of myself fully to your grace and mercy, do not forsake me.
To you Lord I come; do not reject me.[28]

And, if a person's own prayer was inadequate, the Virgin Mary and the
saints stood ready to expedite inadequate intercessions.

O heavenly senators and clearlights [sic] and judges of the world, holy
apostles and evangelists, St Peter, St Paul [etc.] with all other disciples
of our Lord Jesus Christ and specially Saint N… whom I serve and have
chosen to be my advocate and to pray for me. I beseech you all humbly &
with my very heart to pray to your master our Lord Jesus Christ for me.[29]

Images on the souvenir cards which were sold at pilgrimage sites also fed
devotion and so too bede rolls for private use which interspersed prayers with
sacred pictures – Henry VIII owned one when he was still Prince of Wales.[30]

Denial of an English Bible

Although in late medieval England a flourishing devotion focused on the
sufferings of Christ and on a personal spiritual experience of him, it faced
one great barrier. There was no ready access to the Bible in English. Copies
of the Lollard Bible did exist – indeed the number which have survived
despite the risk demonstrates how strong demand was. But the text was
not generally accessible. In any case it had been translated – not always
very exactly – from the "Vulgate", the standard Latin Bible produced in the
fourth century, notionally by St Jerome (c.345–420). It was also in a medieval

English which was rapidly being superseded. Thus where a translation from 1534 renders James 2:13 as "For ther shalbe iudgement merciles to him that sheweth no mercy, & mercy reioyseth against iudgement", the Lollard equivalent is: "For whi dom with out merci to hym that doith no mercy but merci aboue reiseth dom".[31] Deprived of something more available and better than the Lollard text, the late medieval religious revival in England was fatally stunted. It was left to feed on works such as *The Golden Legend* – one of the earliest texts Caxton selected for printing and one frequently republished. It consists of over 250 lives of saints (largely invented) and some discussions of holy days in a typically allusive medieval manner. How real the longing was for something better is shown by the reception London gave to conduct books for "simple souls", dealing with confession, prayer, and the life of Christ, but these only came on the market in the 1530s.

The bishops would not lift the 1409 prohibition on vernacular Scriptures. English men and women were to be allowed no free access to the Bible, only to the Bible as mediated by the church. According to John Foxe, one of the Coventry women executed in 1520 went to the stake for possessing the Lord's Prayer, the Creed, and the Ten Commandments in English.[32] Small portions of the Bible were allowed in the vernacular in books of hours, and sermon texts were translated, but all that the bishops would countenance for the devout generally was Nicholas Love's English version of St Bonaventura's *Meditationes Vitae Christi* [*Meditations on the Life of Christ*]. This purported to be a harmony of the four Gospels and was republished at least six times between 1484 and 1525, which again clearly demonstrates the hunger the English had for more than *The Golden Legend*. Indeed, it has been claimed that Love's text went "a long way towards satisfying lay eagerness for knowledge of the Gospels".[33] Yet purchasers of Love's book would have been quickly disillusioned. All they had brought home was "a mixture of paraphrase of some basic events and very free comment".[34] The text begins with fantasy – a lengthy account of a debate in heaven about man's salvation, initiated by the angels. Then follows material (nearly as lengthy and just as bogus) on "the manner of life of the glorious Virgin Mary before the Incarnation of our Lord Jesus Christ".[35] Similar fiction dominates much of what follows, a good deal involving Mary and the conversations she supposedly had with Jesus Christ. It describes the "Sermon on the Mount" as containing "all the perfection of Christian living", but reduces that to the *Paternoster* and a meditation on poverty, plus a mention of fasting.[36] Omission of the lengthy (and crucial) controversies and parables of Holy Week is excused because "it were long process to treat in special all these matters".[37] Despite this, space is found for a fictitious prayer by Mary which prevented further mutilation of Christ's crucified body and for two equally invented pages describing how Mary was the first person Christ appeared to after the resurrection "as it may be reasonably trowed [believed]" and the talk that ensued.[38] Love's book might conceivably have provided a minimum stimulus to meditative imaginings, but as a substitute for the Gospels it was tendentious and worse than inadequate.[39] And, of course, even if the *Meditations* had been a genuine paraphrase of the Gospels (such as those produced after the Reformation), it would still have covered less than half of the New Testament. Whether the laity knew of the Epistles is highly doubtful, although the Wife of Bath did have an idiosyncratic take on St Paul's teaching about marriage.

The refusal of the English bishops to sanction a vernacular Bible was deeply ironic. It tied the hands of establishment reformers such as Colet (and the young Thomas More). The dean might adopt a new plain style of biblical preaching, but all but a tiny minority of his hearers had no means to follow this up. The bishops' policy was a monstrous "own goal". In the middle of the fifteenth century, printing would arrive in Europe and soon after would come a radical breakthrough in biblical studies. From that point on the traditional English church was hopelessly on the defensive. The only way for ordinary folk to access the life and teaching of Jesus Christ was to risk breaking the law.

ACROSS THE CHANNEL

7

PRINTERS AND SCHOLARS

Printing by the use of movable metal type began in Germany in the early 1450s when Johann Gutenberg published the Bible which bears his name. By 1471 presses were in operation in a dozen or more locations in Europe and by the end of the decade in upwards of a hundred, including four in England. The impact of printing was profound. For the amount a professional scribe would charge to produce a single manuscript copy, a printer could produce some 300, so more books became available more quickly and more cheaply.[1] One staple activity of the early presses was printing Bibles in the local vernacular and by 1490 these were available in all the major Western European languages, except English.

Textual Authority
The consequence of printing was not only greater availability; there was a new concern for accuracy. Copying by hand inevitably meant errors. Setting type did too, but printed pages could be proof-read to produce a corrected text, which would, of course, be the same in every copy. That in turn raised the question of authority. If two printers each issued a particular text, how could anyone know which was the more reliable? The problem was particularly acute with the basic early Christian documents which were ancient manuscripts, with all the transmission risks that implied, to say nothing of the problems in translating from the original Latin, Greek, and Hebrew. Scholarly textual criticism therefore became an essential tool.

It is here that the fifteenth-century breakthrough in biblical studies was so vital. It was an aspect of the wider intellectual movement which historians label the Renaissance ["Rebirth"]. The first signs of this appear in thirteenth/fourteenth-century Italy in new attitudes to the texts first from Latin and later Greek antiquity. Renaissance ideas are sometimes called "humanism", but it is vital not to confuse this with modern "humanism". The latter is a philosophy that affirms the dignity of man without reference to God. In late medieval and early modern Europe, humanism referred to "humane studies". These were liberal subjects – literature, ideas, politics – studied through the Latin and Greek classics. Universities, by contrast, were dominated by a study of theology and law. Humanism is a complex phenomenon which has spawned a huge literature, but the element relevant to biblical studies was the turn from the Latin then in everyday use – Europe's business language – to classical Latin and Greek in pursuit of both elegance and effectiveness of communication ["rhetoric"]. This led to the preparing of modern editions of the classics (and the search for more) and so to the development of the very principles of textual criticism which biblical studies needed for evaluating and editing early Christian texts. One of the first casualties was the "Donation of Constantine", a supposed grant by the emperor Constantine the Great (306–37), which gave Pope Sylvester I (314–35) much property and authority over the Roman empire. In the 1430s and 1440s three scholars, the Italian Lorenzo Valla (c.1406–57), the German Nicholas of Cusa (1401–64), and England's Richard Pecock (c.1392–c.1459) demonstrated independently that the Donation was a later forgery. The "diplomatic" [i.e. style, language, context] is all wrong for the fourth century. Another famous casualty was the popular *Golden Legend*: "unworthy of God and Christian man".[2] The scholarly concern to establish the best text also led to editions of the early Christian writers [the Fathers] which replaced the collections of extracts which had been the principal material available hitherto – some very much distorted. The most significant texts were those of Augustine of Hippo (354–430), and the appearance of volume eleven of his collected works in 1506 marked the completion of sixteen years of effort. But more important by far than reliable texts of the early Fathers would be a modern edition of the Bible itself, to replace the Latin Vulgate which was centuries old.

A Modern Bible: Jacques Lefèvre d'Étaples

In producing the Vulgate, St Jerome had used early Greek manuscripts for the New Testament, but for the Old Testament he relied primarily on the Jewish Greek translation ["the Septuagint"], though he made gestures towards the Hebrew original. One of the first humanists to apply critical methods ["sacred philology"] to Jerome's work was again Lorenzo Valla. His work on the Greek New Testament texts demonstrated that the Vulgate contained serious errors. The next generation of humanists took this much further, two scholars in particular: Jacques Lefèvre from Étaples in Picardy (c.1455–1536) and Erasmus of Rotterdam (1466/69–1536). Lefèvre, an ordained priest, studied at the University of Paris and later taught philosophy and mathematics there, interrupted by some years travelling in Italy. His initial interests were in mysticism and in editing and commenting on the works of Aristotle. He then moved to sacred philology and in 1509 published *The Fivefold Psalter* [*Quincuplex Psalterium*]. This printed four early translations of the Psalms side by side (including the Vulgate) with a fifth column presenting his own Latin version authenticated by reference to the Hebrew text, the first Bible translation to do so in more than 1,000 years. In 1512 came an even more significant Bible text, a *Commentary on the Epistles of St Paul*, which set the Vulgate text alongside a revision by Lefèvre based on the original Greek, plus substantial editorial material. As well as dealing with textual issues, this discussed the substance of the Epistles verse by verse.

As we shall see, Lefèvre's comments in both the *Fivefold Psalter* and the *Commentary* were radical, but what perhaps was even more important was his approach to the Bible itself. The passion he and other humanists had for the classics made them want to step over the texts handed down by medieval scholars and grasp the originals; the slogan was "*ad fontes*" – "back to the fountain head". In that spirit, Lefèvre brushed aside the established way of interpreting Scripture through allegory, metaphor [tropology], and mystical meaning [anagogy]. What mattered was the literal sense. However, by "literal" Lefèvre meant more than the surface meaning; it was the meaning as understood spiritually through the guidance of the Holy Spirit: "the literal sense and the spiritual sense coincide".[3] The method was widely welcomed and later reformers would adopt it as their own. As well as this principle of exegesis [Bible interpretation], Lefèvre moved steadily to the conviction that for a Christian the Bible was the only authority, a position which reformers would call *sola scriptura* ["scripture alone"]. Medieval theologians accepted "that scripture was the sole material base of Christian theology", but with the vital proviso "only as interpreted by the faith of the church".[4] A minority of scholars went further and asserted that in themselves church traditions had authority – the so-called "unwritten verities". Against both positions, *sola scriptura* held that the Bible was self-authenticating – in other words, that one passage could be interpreted by another – although there was generally a recognition that evidence from the early Fathers deserved respect. Thus when in 1522 Lefèvre published a Latin text of the Gospels [*Commentarii initiatorii in Quatuor Evangelia*] the preface declared that "the word of God is sufficient... all else on which the word of God does not shine is as unnecessary as it is superfluous".[5] Then next year came his French translation of the New Testament, claiming "that men and their doctrines are nothing, except insofar as they are corroborated and confirmed by the word of God".[6] In 1524 came a French translation of the Psalms "so that men and women who speak and understand this language might be able to pray to God with greater devotion and feeling".[7] The French authorities stepped in to block Lefèvre in 1525/26 by prohibiting Bible translations.[8] He thereupon switched to Antwerp printers to issue the whole of the Old Testament in 1528 and a complete Bible in 1530. Lefèvre's translation work was also important outside France, particularly in England where French was the second language at the court of Henry VIII.

A Modern Bible: Erasmus of Rotterdam

Jacques Lefèvre d'Étaples enjoyed a considerable reputation, but it was surpassed by the most prominent Renaissance scholar of the day, Erasmus of Rotterdam. Educated in a *Devotio Moderna* school before becoming a monk, Erasmus became the supreme humanist and famous as the finest writer of classical-style Latin in the whole of Europe. So good was he that effectively he became a professional author, subsisting on the proceeds of his work and the patronage of the good and great who were desperate for the cachet he would bring them. He had won his reputation by work on secular classical texts but, it is said, became interested in the problem of biblical philology in 1499 on his first visit to England, having heard John Colet preach at Oxford and expound Scripture in the plain literal style which Lefèvre would later promote. Erasmus studied to improve his Greek and began working on an edition of the works of St Jerome. Then he discovered Lorenzo Valla's notes on the errors in the Vulgate. He published the notes in 1505, and in 1516 came his greatest achievement – an edition of the New Testament in Greek, with notes and his own Latin translation.

The importance of the first New Testament translation to depend on the original Greek is self-evident. However, what drew particular attention to Erasmus's text was that it effectively demolished passages of the Vulgate which supported key church doctrines. The most significant was how to translate the Greek word *"metanoeite"*, the verb used in the Gospels to express the response which both John the Baptist and Jesus Christ urged on their hearers. Jerome had translated this as "do penance" [*"poenitentiam agite"*]. Erasmus now showed that the verb meant "come to your senses" or "repent". This change threatened the very basis of the sacrament of penance and the whole penitential system of the medieval church.[9] John and Jesus had not been calling people to undergo a church ritual but to have a change of heart. The sacrament of marriage was a parallel case. St Paul had described it as a *"musterion"*, which Jerome had translated as *sacramentum*, the Latin term for a guarantee in law or the initiation ceremony of a legionary. Erasmus (following Valla) showed that the word simply meant "mystery". Then in revising his text for a 1519 edition (which received papal endorsement), Erasmus introduced a change that challenged the position of the Virgin Mary. According to the Vulgate version, the angel Gabriel greeted the Virgin Mary with the words: "Hail, full of grace" [*"Ave gratia plena"*]. That made Mary the greatest contributor to the treasury of merit after Christ himself.[10] Erasmus corrected the translation to "highly favoured" [*"gratiosa"*]. His commentary went even further, demolishing texts which had been interpreted allegorically to prove that after the birth of Christ Mary continued a virgin to the end of her life. He was, he said, prepared to accept the claim as a truth espoused by the church but not on the basis of the text. Even more sensitive was his omission of the one sentence in the Vulgate in use in 1516 that gave unequivocal support for the doctrine of the Trinity, viz.

there are three who give testimony in heaven, the Father, the Word [Jesus Christ] and the Holy Spirit.[11]

His decision was entirely valid since the words were a scribal comment which had become incorporated in St Jerome's original around the year 800. However, Erasmus rashly agreed to reinstate the verse if it existed in any Greek manuscript and had to eat his words when shown a Greek text from about 1520. Despite that faux pas, his edition of the New Testament text embodied the then best philological principles and was arguably the single most important cause of what became the Protestant Reformation. It was not the only factor, but it is hard to see how change would have come without the "word of God" in the hands of the people.

Erasmus's text was rapidly followed by new translations of the Bible into many of Europe's languages. In 1521 Martin Luther translated the New Testament into High German, and the Old Testament followed. The following year, a Flemish New Testament was published and the complete Bible appeared in 1526. New Testaments appeared in Danish and Swedish in 1524 and 1526 respectively. An Italian Bible was published in Venice in 1532 by which time, as we have seen, Lefèvre's complete French translation was in print.[12] As for Erasmus, he not only continued to improve his New Testament text, but began preparing paraphrases of the various books, beginning with the Epistles and then the Gospels. Necessarily these were in Latin to ensure Europe-wide circulation, but translations quickly appeared in French, German, and Czech. But not in English, thanks to the entrenched opposition of the country's bishops.

8

EUROPEAN ANXIETIES

Anyone approaching the story of the Reformation has to peer through the mist of more than 500 years. Even more important, they also have to peer through a fog of historical tradition. For centuries the word "reformer" has been synonymous with "Protestant", despite the word "Protestant" only being coined in 1529 and then to describe a specific German group which protested on a specific issue. Not for decades would "Protestant" pass into general European currency. What is more, organized denominations which would come to be called Protestant are not found before the mid 1540s. Thus the name which past historians and controversialists have bequeathed to us is an anachronism. Yet time has so embedded the term in common use that today it is very difficult to avoid calling Luther, Zwingli, etc. "the reformers". Indeed this book will from time to time surrender to just that compulsion. But it is vital to remember the distortion this involves. Confining the term to "Protestants" creates an artificial divide between "reformers" so-called and individuals who were just as enthusiastic for revival but who are fitted by history into a competing – and equally anachronistic – Catholic box. Nor, as we have seen, can the distortion be avoided by calling those people "Catholic Reformers" since that presupposes a rival reformation which was Protestant. Far more satisfactory than a "Protestant Reformation" and a competing "Catholic Reformation" is avoiding adjectives and speaking simply of "Reformation". Only events and the passage of time split the Christocentric revival of the fifteenth and early sixteenth centuries into a schismatic wing which rejected papal authority, and a non-schismatic wing which gave priority to church unity, even if that meant settling for less in the way of change.[1]

What makes the fog around the Reformation even thicker are the myths which rival confessions generate. On the Roman Catholic side, a common assumption is of the one, holy, catholic, and apostolic church assailed by error – the picture conjured by Pope Leo X of Luther as "the wild boar from the forest" who seeks to destroy God's vineyard.[2] That assault (the story continues) ushered in a time of great trial, but from it that supposedly one true church emerged to continue its divine destiny, stronger, purified, and often, as the church had been in its first centuries, strengthened by persecution. Martyrs also vindicate the Protestant story, most compellingly in the pages of John Foxe's monumental *Book of Martyrs*. Indeed, one Protestant narrative – there are several – tells of a false medieval church sunk in error except for a persecuted remnant of the faithful which endured through the centuries. Then by the intervention of the Holy Spirit in the life of Martin Luther, the saving gospel burst on a needy world. Another Protestant scenario depicts the Reformation as a great missed opportunity. Although the medieval church was in desperate need of reform, elements in it – especially at Rome – were unwilling to accept God's intervention, and hence the one unified Western church had to fragment. Denominations too have their subtexts. Presbyterians claim a monopoly of the name "reformed" because of what they see as the refusal of Luther and other Christians to go the whole way with the Holy Spirit. Among Anglicans, a widespread myth is of a Church of England deliberately created to be both Catholic and reformed. For religious radicals, the Reformation is depicted as a time of struggle against established religion, whether Catholic or Protestant, until – again through the fires of persecution – believers as individuals became free to follow the leading of God.

Setting aside these Reformation myths and half-truths, a good starting point is to observe that the late medieval church was anything but monolithic and united. That was probably how it appeared locally to most of the laity but theology was astonishingly diverse. There were, perhaps, as many as nine identifiable "schools" of thought, which were often associated with particular universities or faculties or with particular religious orders. What they had in common, despite such differences, was methodology. They followed the highly detailed and logical approach known as "scholasticism" with the aim of achieving a rational justification for religious belief. Their source material was the Vulgate Bible (as standardized at Paris in 1226) together with such texts as were available of the writings of the Fathers of the early church and later thinkers. Inevitably exploration spilled over into doctrine, ideas became radical and debates fierce. At one stage, the followers of St Thomas Aquinas were expelled from the University of Paris because they denied that the Virgin Mary was herself conceived without sin. The reason this scholastic ferment flourished unchecked was that church authority had become paralysed. The papacy had spent seventy years away from Rome, under French domination at Avignon, followed by a further thirty years of internal division (to say nothing of the subsequent pressures of Italian politics and the attractions of the Rome of Bramante and Michelangelo). Attempts were made to establish church councils as an alternative to papal authority, but these had been undermined by successive popes and proved abortive.

How to Be Saved

The most contentious issue among church thinkers was the part which human decision played in a person's salvation. We have seen how the late medieval church taught that men and women are saved by the sacrificial death of Jesus Christ, but that they have to play their part. They have to exercise faith and do good works, supported by the grace of God ministered through the sacraments of the church. Yet while penance, purgatory, and sacramental grace were taught to parishioners, scholars had questions. Might not the cycle of penance, good works, and purgatory imply that salvation was in fact earned; that an individual became righteous in the sight of God by his or her own efforts (the technical term is "justified")? In the fifth century a scholar named Pelagius had advanced that view and been demolished by St Augustine, but many late medieval academics, possibly a majority, were attracted to the opinion, although with a crucial modification. They agreed that Pelagius had been a heretic – no human effort could actually make a person righteous – but argued that God had nevertheless promised – made "a covenant" – that he would accept the person who did his or her best. "God will not deny his grace to whoever does what lies within them" – in other words, anyone who rejects evil and tries to live virtuously.[3] They pointed to the analogy of a ruler who in an emergency issued lead coins but assigned them a higher notional value, promising to redeem them later with gold and silver coins at that higher value. The modern equivalent would be paper money, which is intrinsically worthless but its value is what the state prints on it. Human effort, the theologians said, is of little value in itself (like the lead or paper), but God graciously credits it for more than it is worth. Hence men are not saved because of the merit of their lives, but human effort – "doing what lies within you" – does play its part in their salvation.

Other scholars took a different position. They looked to the writings of St Augustine and repudiated the "covenant" idea as a clever deceit. Human beings, Augustine had argued, can do nothing to save themselves. Sin is an intrinsic defect which corrupts even the best deeds and intentions. Men and women cannot reach even a leaden standard. Only God can effect a rescue, and that he has provided through the life, death, and resurrection of his Son Jesus Christ. Men and women are saved by God's unmerited gift of salvation in Christ. Augustine's view removes the burden of human effort and offers salvation by grace. However, with it comes a terrible corollary. If nothing human beings can do has any influence on God's decision to save them, whether they will in fact be saved must depend exclusively on God choosing to do so ["divine election"]. That means that their eternal destiny is predestined.

This scholastic debate is, of course, the context of Martin Luther's protest. Born in 1483, the eldest son of a mine-operator, he was educated at the University of Erfurt with an eye to a career in law, but after being terrified in a thunderstorm he entered an Augustinian monastery and began to study theology. In 1508 he was invited to lecture on moral philosophy at the newly established University of Wittenberg and in 1511 was appointed professor of biblical studies there. His first lectures (1513–15) were on the Psalms and these show that the thirty-year-old Luther then followed the majority view on justification.

The doctors of theology rightly say that God gives grace without fail to whoever does what lies within them.[4]

God had made "a testament and a covenant with us" that he would justify anyone who came to him in humility, and this could be relied on because of the "righteousness of God" ["*iusticia Dei*"], the fact that God treats every individual fairly and impartially.

The Evangelical Alternative

Schoolmen debating the niceties of the doctrine of salvation ["soteriology"] were a world away from humanist scholars concerned to establish the Bible text and make it better known. The intention of Lefèvre and Erasmus and those like-minded was to deepen spiritual life within the church by promoting a direct encounter between the individual and the words of Scripture. The Greek word for "gospel" is *euangelion*, so those involved are generally described as evangelicals. This description must be understood to mean no more than a shared attitude of mind and definitely not any agreed doctrinal position. The early decades of the sixteenth century were, in Lucien Febvre's telling phrase, a period of "magnificent religious anarchy".[5] It was only as the implications of the newly accessible Bible were explored that seismic issues erupted. What authority did Scripture have, and what authority belonged to tradition? How should the eucharist be understood? What did the Bible say about baptism? Did the clergy have a special status? What was the nature of the papal office, and how did that relate to the mind of the church expressed in a general council? It was only in answering these and other questions that confessional divisions emerged. It is this evolving process which, for example, explains how Thomas More was evangelically inclined in his twenties but died a martyr for Rome in his fifties. And how Anne Boleyn could insist on the priority of the Bible but spend the last night of her life revering the blessed sacrament.

The Evangelical Gospel: Erasmus

Erasmus understood the challenge of Scripture as having two aspects. Negatively, it was essential to sweep away the obstacles presented by low standards among the clergy and superstition generally, a conviction which lost nothing from his experience in Italy of the decadent churchmanship of Julius II's Rome. Typically he turned to satire and had all Europe laughing at his 1511 bestseller *The Praise of Folly* [*Stultitiae Laus*], which pilloried one group of society after another and clergy most of all: theologians, monks, friars, and all grades from priests, bishops, and cardinals up to the pope himself. In 1513 he returned to that target in a bitter satire on the recently deceased Julius II, *Pope Julius barred from Heaven* [*Julius Exclusus*]. It ends with St Peter, the gatekeeper of heaven, saying that he was "not surprised that so few reach here, when pests like this sit at the helm of the Church".[6] The positive half of Erasmus's message was the call to men and women to follow what he called "the Way of Christ" ["*philosophia Christi*"], the conscious imitation of Christ by a life of piety and discipline informed by Holy Scripture. As he wrote in 1503 in *The Weapon of the Christian Soldier* [*Enchiridion Militis Christiani*], his very popular handbook for Christian living:

> *If you approach the scriptures in all humility and with regulated caution, you will perceive that you have been breathed upon by the Holy Will of God. It will bring about a transformation that is impossible to describe… Man may lie and make mistakes; the truth of God neither deceives nor is deceived.*[7]

The whole purpose of his New Testament translation was to make Scripture as widely available as possible. "Christ", Erasmus declared:

> *wishes his mysteries to be published as widely as possible. I would wish even all women to read the gospel and the epistles of St. Paul and I wish they were translated into all languages of all Christian people, that they might be read and known, not merely by the Scotch and the Irish but even by Turks and Saracens. I wish that the husbandman may sing parts of them at his plough, that the weaver may warble them at his shuttle, that the traveller may with their narratives beguile the weariness of the way.*[8]

On other occasions he added prostitutes and pimps to his list.[9]

Erasmus, however, did not move in the world of husbandmen and weavers – or, one hopes, pimps. He was an academic and clearly had no idea that the readers of his New Testament text would not be satisfied with his cool vision of the *philosophia Christi.* Or rather he dismissed the danger: "should we keep the bee from the flower because from time to time a spider comes out of it?"[10] Conservative churchmen disagreed and said "I told you so". Letting untrained minds loose on the holy text was inviting trouble, and the more so given the revisions made in humanist Scripture translations. In 1525, the Carthusian monk Peter Coousturier (alias Sutor), at one time the prior of the Sorbonne [the popular name for the theology faculty of the University of Paris] made a full-blooded attack on lay access to the Bible, vernacular commentaries, and paraphrases. His book, *Concerning Bible translation and damnable new interpretations* [*De tralatione bibliae et novarum reproatione interpretationum*], insisted that none of these novelties were necessary for salvation – indeed they were probably harmful. The laity, he asserted, were simple and incapable of understanding Scripture. That was reserved for those who led the spiritual life (i.e. clergy). The understanding of the laity would be superficial. They would fail to grasp the deeper interpretative meanings of the texts, arrogantly assert the right to debate the mysteries of faith, and, perhaps, form conventicles – meetings outside church control – where heresies could flourish. In particular, the new translations were the vehicle for erroneous teaching.

> *If in one point the Vulgate were in error the entire authority of Holy Scripture would collapse, love and faith would be extinguished, heresies and schisms would abound, blasphemy would be committed against the Holy Spirit, the authority of theologians would be shaken, and indeed the Catholic church would collapse from the foundations.*[11]

Even Thomas More, Erasmus's English friend and fellow humanist who had initially welcomed and defended the Greek New Testament, was by 1529 reduced to saying that an episcopally approved English Bible would be a splendid idea but it could disturb simple Christians. Thus it should not be on general sale but be made available by diocesan bishops to selected readers. Four years later he was extolling the outright ban.

The classic instance of the life-changing impact of Erasmus's New Testament is the testimony of the Cambridge academic Thomas Bilney. In 1516 "Little" Bilney, as he was fondly known, bought a copy of the newly published Erasmus text, attracted, as he said later, by its fine prose idiom. But instead of improving his Latin style, the New Testament revolutionized his Christian life:

> *I chanced upon this sweet sentence of St Paul in his first epistle to Timothy and first chapter. "It is a true saying and worthy of all men to be embraced that Christ Jesus came into the world to save sinners of which I am the chief and principal". This one sentence, through God's instruction*

*did so exhilarate my heart, being before wounded with the guilt of my
sins, and being almost in despair, that even immediately I seemed unto
myself inwardly to feel such a comfort and quietness as I myself would
not discern and judge, in so much as my bruised bones leaped for joy.*[12]

In 1519 Bilney was ordained and went on to be licensed to preach the
religion of the heart in the diocese of Ely. He was arrested in 1527, charged
with heresy – little more than denying the efficacy of prayer to the saints,
objecting to images, and scorning pilgrimage – and he was forced to recant
and imprisoned for over a year in the Tower of London. Released but
tormented at the thought that he had betrayed his principles, he began
open-air preaching and handling copies of Tyndale's now available but
banned English New Testament. Quickly rearrested as a relapsed heretic,
Bilney was burned at the stake in August 1531.

The Evangelical Gospel: Jacques Lefèvre d'Étaples

Jacques Lefèvre d'Étaples was older than Erasmus and his influence was
largely confined to France, but the two knew each other and were friends.
They always expressed great respect for the other's scholarship, which
did not mean that when they differed either of them pulled any punches.
Yet although often paired – Martin Luther called them "great princes of
learning" – neither was the clone of the other.[13] Pinning Erasmus down on
anything other than points of philology was always difficult. Martin Luther
would accuse him of "wanting to compare everything and affirm nothing".
In essence he was a Christian sceptic.[14] He was satisfied with probability
and willing on contentious issues to accept the authority of the church and
tradition – as we have seen with Mary's perpetual virginity.[15] This dislike of
being dogmatic meant that as Reformation controversies became sharp and
sharper, Erasmus was reviled on all sides as an incorrigible fence-sitter.

Against this, Lefèvre's conviction that Scripture was the one authority
made him willing to accept the implications of what he read and to change
his ideas accordingly. In consequence, he went where Erasmus wouldn't
go, and in many respects he, rather than Luther, is the herald of the
Protestant Reformation. While Luther was still teaching that God would
give added value to good deeds, Lefèvre's 1512 commentary on St Paul's

Epistle to the Romans explicitly stated that it is impossible for men "to be saved of themselves and their good works".[16] Human effort has no part in justification.

> [He] *who keeps the works of the law throughout his life… is still not justified, still not the possessor of that righteousness from which he is able to have eternal life; for it is God only who provides this righteousness through faith and who justifies by grace alone unto life eternal.*[17]

As Lefèvre pointed out, the promise of paradise to the penitent thief who was crucified beside Christ makes that conclusion inescapable: "he was justified by faith alone" [*sola fide*].[18]

> *It is by faith that anyone is justified, so that we may see that justification is the gift and grace of God, and not something owed [i.e. a bargain made] by him.*[19]

The sacrament of penance – "the method of confessing sins which now prevails" – was a distortion: "the death of Christ is sufficient for the remission of all sins as often as we turn to him in repentance and true faith".[20] As with Luther a few years later, Lefèvre took time to work through the full implications of justification by faith – but it is clear that he had, several years ahead of the German reformer, embraced the great Reformation watchwords: "'by grace alone' [*sola gratia*], 'by faith alone' [*sola fide*], and 'to God alone the glory' [*soli Deo gloria*]".[21] In 1525, in a text which Anne Boleyn's brother would specially translate for her, Lefèvre could write that "Jesus Christ died for our sins… accordingly we owe nothing more for our sins, since Jesus Christ has made satisfaction and paid the price for us".[22]

9

THE CHALLENGE TO
AUTHORITY

The story of early reform, especially in France and England, shows that
Bernard Cottret was right to say that the demand for the Bible created the
Reformation, not vice versa.[1] However, what changed Martin Luther from
a teacher at the minor (and very new) university at Wittenberg in Saxony
into a religious prophet who shook sixteenth-century Europe was not better
Bible scholarship. It was rebellion against established religious and political
authority. This is not to say that Luther ignored the new textual work on
the Bible. Far from it. He knew the work of Lefèvre and Erasmus, and
from 1509 set himself to learn Greek and Hebrew. He was active when the
university decided to abandon scholastic theology in favour of courses on
the Bible and the Fathers of the church. In his own lectures he adopted the
new literal approach to the study of Scripture. Nonetheless, Erasmus's New
Testament did not bring to Martin Luther the immediate enlightenment
which it did to Thomas Bilney.

The *Ninety-Five Theses*

Luther was thrust onto the European stage because a Dominican friar
arrived selling a papal indulgence. The reigning pope, Leo X, was determined
to revive the seventy-year-old programme to rebuild St Peter's Basilica in
Rome, and in order to raise funds had proclaimed a plenary indulgence.[2]
That would only have been met with the usual German grumbles about
interfering Italians if it had not been for the problems of the German

princeling Albrecht of Hohenzollern. In 1513 he was elected archbishop of Mainz, and a year later archbishop of Magdeburg. Church law forbade such doubling up and the 24-year-old Albrecht was, in any case, under age. On two grounds, therefore, he had required a papal dispensation, and to pay for that had borrowed 21,000 ducats from the Fugger banking house. To cover the repayments, the pope agreed that half the proceeds of selling the indulgence in north Germany should go to St Peter's and half to Albrecht (i.e. the Fuggers). Johann Tetzel, the friar chosen to implement the plan, was the crudest of salesmen, ignoring the link between indulgences and penance and announcing that "as soon as the coin in the coffer rings, the soul from purgatory springs".[3] He is said to have displayed a price list of various sins and claimed that the pardons he sold could absolve even a man who "had committed an impossible sin and violated the Mother of God".[4] The elector of Saxony refused to let Tetzel enter his territory, so the friar set up as near as possible and attracted many of Luther's Wittenberg parishioners. Several scholars had already expressed doubts about indulgences, but this first-hand experience scandalized Luther. From early April 1517, when Tetzel arrived, he spent several months examining the theology of indulgences and by the autumn had made up his mind. The church's teaching and practice was in error.

The accepted way to test any new scholarly conclusion was to hold a formal academic disputation and on 31 October Luther informed the university of his readiness to debate a series of propositions – the famous *Ninety-Five Theses* – and sent a copy of them to Archbishop Albrecht. The lasting impression which the *Theses* give is of judicious moderation. They only become sharp when handling Tetzel's sales talk and when reporting the blunt questions asked by the laity, such as, "why does not the pope empty purgatory, for the sake of holy love and the dire need of the souls that are there if he redeems an infinite number of souls for the sake of miserable money with which to build a church".[5] Luther referred to the pope throughout with respect, and wrote as though the pontiff was ignorant of the way indulgences were being promoted. Nevertheless, he was not just saying that indulgences were being mishandled; he was questioning their very legitimacy.

It was the implications of that challenge as well as the threat to the coffers of the Fuggers and the pope which explains why the *Theses* were so dangerous. Luther accepted that the church had the right to impose penances to regulate and discipline human behaviour in this life, but denied that it had any power beyond that. "The pope… cannot remit any penalties other than those which he had imposed either by his own authority or by that of the Canons [church laws]."[6] The very idea that such "canonical" penalties had any relation to the penalties of purgatory was "quite evidently one of the weeds" which sleeping bishops had allowed to grow up in the church.[7] Thesis no. 6 went even further – questioning the pope's power to forgive:

The pope cannot remit any guilt, except by declaring that it has been remitted by God and by assenting to God's remission; though he may grant remission in cases reserved to his judgement.[8]

If Luther was right, the pope, or rather the church, possessed no power to influence the fate of souls in purgatory other than by prayer.[9] This undermined the whole penitential structure of the church and declared "The Treasury of Merits" a myth.[10] Luther had recovered the apostolic understanding of forgiveness as between the individual and God. The institutional church could no longer affect salvation. Rome was marginalized. There were social implications too. If the living could not influence the destiny of the dead, the basic *raison d'être* of Europe's thousands of fraternities was cut away. Even more, if the layman did not need to be absolved by a priest, what of the relationship between them? Academic questioning by an unknown professor in one of the most insignificant of Europe's universities threatened an avalanche.

Luther himself did not precipitate it. He did not know of his archbishop's financial interest in Tetzel's success, but Albrecht immediately recognized the threat posed to both himself and the pope. Within weeks, a copy of the *Theses* was on the way to Rome with a request to Leo X to silence Luther. Quickly though the archbishop acted, it was too late. Someone who had read the *Theses* had sent them to the printer. The criticism of indulgence-selling struck a chord with the German people, who deeply resented the flow of money to Rome, and copies both in German and the original Latin poured off the presses. Tetzel raised the temperature still further by publicly defending his actions and calling for Luther to be condemned as a heretic. Tetzel's fellow Dominicans wrote in his support, claiming that even questioning indulgences was heretical because it questioned the pope's authority. Then Johann Eck, a heavyweight theologian from the University of Ingolstadt, initiated a pamphlet war with Luther.

There was now no chance of holding a judicious academic dispute. In Rome, proceedings were commenced against Luther for questioning the authority of the pope and in August Leo X ordered Luther's arrest as a notorious heretic. Luther then appealed to Duke Frederick, the elector of Saxony and the founder of his university, asking to be tried in Germany. Meetings with a papal legate took place at Augsburg but they came to nothing. Luther wanted to talk doctrine, the legate insisted on obedience to Rome, whereupon Luther fled back to the safety of Wittenberg. Convinced by his experiences that he had now to choose between loyalty to what he saw as the truth and loyalty to his church superiors, he drew up a formal appeal over the head of the pope to a general council of the church.

Justification by Grace through Faith

By this time Luther had experienced a spiritual conversion – what scholars call his "Tower experience" ["*Turmerlebnis*"]. In 1515 he had moved from lecturing on the Psalms to lecturing on Paul's Epistle to the Romans. This was the New Testament letter on which St Augustine had based his teaching that "justification" – acceptance by God – came by God's unmerited gift of salvation in Christ to those men and women he had chosen. By early 1517 at the latest, Luther had abandoned his earlier view that God would graciously respond to puny human effort. Augustine was right: a man can "neither will nor do anything but evil".[11] Nor was this only an academic conclusion. Luther had tried to live by the principle of "doing what lies within you" and had failed miserably. All he could expect from a righteous God was rejection. He wrote later:

Although I lived a blameless life as a monk, I felt that I was a sinner with an uneasy conscience before God. I also could not believe that I had pleased him with my works. Far from loving that righteous God who punished sinners, I actually hated him.[12]

Yet, in spite of his despair, Luther continued to wrestle with St Paul and St Augustine, and his thinking about indulgences helped him to recognize the reality that God wanted to save sinners.[13] Yet how was that possible? What could reconcile a God who was righteous with a sinner who could never be righteous? The answer hit him as he read verse 17 of the first chapter of Romans: "As the Scripture says, he who through faith is righteous [*justus*] shall live."[14]

Luther realized that Paul was not using *justus* to describe the perfect standard human beings had to meet. "He who through faith is righteous shall live" meant that God was ready to justify fallible humans as an act of grace. All that was needed from them was faith in God's promise that he would justify them. "By grace are you saved through faith."[15] Faith was not assent to creeds; it was individual commitment. God wasn't looking to men and women for impossible efforts at virtue; he was looking for trust. And the result was to unite the individual with Christ. "Faith is a wedding ring."[16] Not that a man could decide whether or not to believe. That would allow the notion of human merit to sneak back in. Faith was not a matter of human decision. It was the gift of God. But because faith unites believers with Christ there was no question of God expecting men and women "to do what lies within them"; everything had been done for them by Christ. Luther's despair and self-loathing vanished. As he described it later, he immediately felt "as though I had been born again, and as though I had entered through open gates paradise itself".[17]

From Academic to Heretic

All this was personal to Luther. What gripped public attention was the ongoing indulgence issue. This came to a head in June 1519 in a debate at the University of Leipzig. Others were involved, but the principal contestants were Luther and Eck. In his writings against Luther, Eck had focused on the issue of church authority, and this was the line he took in the debate. He elicited from Luther the admission that he doubted the divine origin of the papacy and held that the Bible was the supreme authority, not church councils. Eck responded that Luther was another Jan Hus, who had been condemned as a heretic in 1415.[18] Luther responded honestly but incautiously: "I am sure of this, that many of Hus' beliefs were completely evangelical and Christian"![19] Eck seized on Luther's replies as proof that his adversary was out to destroy the church and he devoted the rest of his life to discrediting Luther. He attacked him in print, succeeded in having parts of the reformer's writings condemned by the theologians at the University of Cologne, and took an active part in moves against him at Rome. These led in June 1520 to the papal bull [decree] *"Exsurge Domine"* ["O Lord, arise!"]. This cited forty-one errors supposedly held by Luther and condemned them as "heretical, offensive, erroneous, objectionable to pious ears, misleading to simple minds and contrary to Catholic teaching".[20] He was given until December to come to heel.

Luther had never set out to challenge the church and all the while remained a monk loyal to his monastery, but his treatment in 1518 and 1519 and the continuing barrage of traditionalist criticism convinced him that more was now at stake than errors over indulgences. The church was refusing to face up to truth. As well as publishing numerous pamphlets in both German and Latin, he launched a direct attack on the pope in the vernacular *Address to the Christian Nobility of the German Nation*, which appeared in the early summer of 1520. This asserted not only that Rome's jurisdiction had become corrupt, but that the clergy were a venal interest group. Their claim to be different from the rest of humanity was bogus and their object was to exploit a laity which knew no better. The nobility – and that included the emperor – had a God-given duty to put things right.

A few months later *The Babylonish Captivity of the Church*, Luther's second great manifesto, appeared. Addressed to the clergy (in Latin), it dismissed four of the sacraments as having no biblical authority: confirmation, marriage, holy orders, and extreme unction. It argued that communion in both kinds should be given to laity as well as clergy, and rejected the hypothesis of transubstantiation. Even more radically, Luther asserted that the mass was not a sacrifice and that it conveyed no power. Christ's body and blood were, in a mysterious way, certainly present physically in the bread and wine, but as the material sign of God's promised forgiveness in Christ. And since the mass was not a sacrifice, the special power and identity of the priesthood was a delusion. All Christians were priests, and clergy were effectively laymen appointed to provide a service – they were ministers.

Hardly was *The Captivity* in the hands of booksellers before Luther published the third of his key writings, *The Freedom of a Christian*. In this he made a first attempt at dealing with the difficulty that "justification by grace through faith" could appear to remove all incentive to moral living. After all, if the way in which you behave has no relation to your fate in the hereafter, why keep the Ten Commandments? Luther's response was that justification did indeed free the Christian from any compulsion to earn credit by his or her good deeds, but it did not end there. It commenced

the process of becoming godly, not health but getting well, not being but becoming, not rest but exercise. We are not now what we shall be, but we are on the way.[21]

In any case, justification was not a zero-sum game. It had cost Christ everything and the only possible response to being justified was one of love towards God which resulted in righteous living. And to nail his colours irrevocably to the mast, Luther climaxed the year by publicly burning the pope's bull, along with the books of Johann Eck and the books of canon law which enshrined the church's jurisdiction. On 3 January 1521 a second papal bull was promulgated, finally excommunicating Luther.

At this point Charles V, the Holy Roman emperor, stepped in. The Empire was a political umbrella which covered the dozens of states, cities, and dignities that comprised the geographical Germany. An emperor was elected and so did not have the independence of authority enjoyed by, say, the hereditary rulers of England and France. But he still had an overall jurisdiction in Germany and was also something of a figurehead for Western Christianity. Recently elected, the young Charles was concerned to have good relations with the pope and to fulfil his Christian responsibilities, but he had to avoid alienating powerful German interests. The Turks were threatening his Austrian lands and he needed help. Moreover, the bargain Charles had struck to get elected had included a promise not to outlaw anyone without a hearing, and the groundswell of popular support meant that Luther could not be silenced quietly. The emperor, therefore, did not outlaw him immediately as the pope demanded. Instead he agreed with Luther's protector, the elector of Saxony, that the monk should appear under safe conduct at the forthcoming meeting of the Imperial Diet [assembly] at Worms and be given a formal hearing.

On Wednesday 17 April 1521 the famous confrontation took place. Charles governed Spain, Italy, and the Americas, as well as Germany, Austria, and the Low Countries, so Luther faced the most prestigious ruler in the world, backed by the authority of the pope and flanked by the ruling princes of Germany. He was brought in to confront a table piled with books and immediately asked whether the books were his and if he would repudiate what he had written. Luther was, it seems, overawed. He acknowledged the books were his but asked for time to consider the demand to recant. The following afternoon nervousness was over. He said that he would apologize for any excessive vehemence in his writing and if he could be shown from the Bible that he was wrong, he himself would burn his books. That reply was dismissed as unclear and Luther's response has rung down the ages:

> *Since your majesty and your lords demand a simple answer, I shall give one without horns and teeth. Unless I am convinced by the testimony of Scripture and evident reasoning, I continue convinced by the Sacred Scripture I have cited – for I believe neither solely the pope nor the councils, for it is evident that they have erred often and contradict one another. My conscience is captured by the Word of God. Thus I cannot and will not revoke, since to act against one's conscience is neither safe nor honest.*[22]

It is hard to imagine a more uncompromising assertion, but political pressure nevertheless forced Charles to agree to further talks. Luther, however, continued to insist that his understanding of Scripture was correct and that he would only accept the decision of the general council of the church if it agreed with the Bible. To Charles's later regret the safe conduct was honoured, but on his way back to Wittenberg Luther was abducted on the orders of Frederick of Saxony and placed in protective custody. On 8 May the emperor signed the edict declaring Luther an outlaw.

10

MAGNIFICENT RELIGIOUS ANARCHY

In the Protestant calendar, the nailing of the *Ninety-Five Theses* to the church door in Wittenberg on 31 October 1517 marks the start of the Reformation. Yet Jacques Lefèvre had anticipated Luther's key doctrine of justification by faith alone by several years, and the *Ninety-Five Theses* made no mention of it. Moreover the issue of justification was, as we have seen, a bread and butter topic among Europe's theologians. Why then should what began as a spat between competing religious orders – Luther the Augustinian monk against the Dominican friar Tetzel, with Eck the academic joining in – have ended where it did? Politics in the church and the Empire were one factor. They turned Luther's academic objections to indulgences into the defiance he offered to the Diet at Worms. Another ingredient was his direct appeal to German feeling: "we should drive out of German territory the papal legates with their faculties which they sell us for large sums of money. This traffic is nothing but skullduggery."[1] Another factor was humanist biblical scholarship. The implications which that carried for reform (as exemplified by Erasmus) provided an immediate entry for the issues Luther posed. Printing played a crucial part too. This still new technology carried Luther's ideas far and wide – perhaps a million tracts by 1524 – and even more the news of his stand against authority. But above all, interest in Luther's message is explained by the current hunger for religious revival. Except for that market, few titles would have reached the booksellers.

In the changed world of the twenty-first century it can be difficult to appreciate why Luther's contribution to the justification debate seemed to be what so many were looking for. That his views attracted scholarly attention is unsurprising, but why did it strike a chord in people who were neither academically educated nor theologically sophisticated? The answer is that the message of "justification by faith alone" was supremely simple. It promised freedom. First, freedom from a Christianity of obligation. It was not necessary to be as introspective as Luther to welcome escape from the moral tyranny of having to "do what lies within you". Second, Luther's message promised freedom from dependence on the church's claimed monopoly of grace. Instead of acquiring merit through devout liturgical observance and a repeated cycle of confession, penance, and absolution, the believer could rely solely on God's promise. Of course, freedom from the tyranny of good works carried its own lifestyle implications – hence Luther's *Freedom of a Christian* – but there was a qualitative difference between a faith of personal commitment and responding to a church popularly understood to jingle the keys of heaven and hell.[2]

Not Luther Alone

It is, on the other hand, important not to see the story of the Reformation as the story of Martin Luther. He may have tossed a large stone into the pool but almost immediately it was followed by a shower of other stones, each creating ripples which intersected and mingled. Responses varied from locality to locality, particularly among the independent German cities. There were significant reformers outside Germany and even those in Luther's immediate circle were perfectly ready to think and publish for themselves. Modern scholars trying to decide how much particular writers or developments or regions owed to Luther all too often end in uncertainty. One has also to remember that thinking was ongoing as individuals changed and developed their ideas and argued one with another. Thus although Luther attacked indulgences in 1517, he insisted in 1519 that the existence of purgatory was undeniable, and only "ditched his belief in purgatory around 1530".[3]

Five principals deserve our attention. Jacques Lefèvre again, Luther's young friend Philipp Melanchthon (1497–1560), Huldrych Zwingli from Zurich (1484–1531), Martin Bucer from Strasbourg (1491–1551) and John Calvin at Geneva (1509–1564).

Jacques Lefèvre we have already met.

Philipp Melanchthon came from a prosperous urban family from Bretten, near Karlsruhe, which had links with prominent humanists. Something of a prodigy (the University of Heidelberg turned him down for a master's degree because he was only fifteen), Melanchthon began publishing at the age of seventeen and in 1518 was appointed professor of Greek at the University of Wittenberg. There he came under the influence of Luther, whose work he progressively systematized, and Melanchthon's influence was crucial in what ultimately became the Lutheran Church.

Martin Bucer was born thirty miles south of Strasbourg and at the age of fifteen joined the Dominican order as a novice. He became interested in humanism and met Luther. In 1521 he secured his release from the Dominicans, began to preach reform, and soon had to take refuge in the tolerant city of Strasbourg. He became the major figure in the city's religious life, and in 1540 became superintendent of all its churches. Bucer, as we shall see, was the ecclesiastical statesman most determined to keep the church united: "Flee formulae, bear with the weak. While all faith is placed in Christ, the thing is safe. It is not given for all to see the same thing at the same time."[4]

Huldrych Zwingli came from a small Swiss village, twenty miles south of Lake Constance. He studied at various universities, including Vienna (a centre for humanist scholarship), and, after some years as a village priest, was appointed in 1518 as "People's Priest" at the Grossmünster, the main church of the large and powerful city of Zurich. He welcomed Luther's writings (he was six weeks younger) but dated his own enlightenment to 1516 and always claimed that he "did not learn the teachings of Christ from Luther, but from the Word of God".[5] Erasmus had a strong influence on him – in 1516 Zwingli journeyed to Basle to meet him – and Erasmus's *"philosophia Christi"* shaped much of his subsequent thinking, not only at a personal level but even more its application to society. Concern for the community was a very live issue for the Swiss because in 1499, after generations of conflict, they had finally got free of their overlords. Zwingli secured much of north-eastern Switzerland for reform, but his attempt to make advances politically led to war and he was killed at the second Battle of Kappel.

John Calvin belonged to a younger generation. Born at Noyon in northern France, he studied arts and some theology at the University of Paris, followed by civil law, first at Orléans and then at Bourges. Back in Paris, his growing interest in religious reform got him into trouble and in 1533 he left France for the safety of Basle. There he devoted himself to writing the *Christianae Religionis Institutio*, a title commonly translated as *The Institutes of the Christian Religion*, but better understood as *A Training in the Christian Religion*. The book appeared in May 1536, six chapters long, but Calvin continued to write and rewrite, and by the final 1559 edition, six chapters had become eighty. The importance and influence of *The Institutes* can scarcely be overstated. In the next two centuries it became a key international reformist text, except in areas loyal to Luther. In 1536 Calvin made a brief visit to Noyon, but returned via Geneva. The city (not at that time part of Switzerland) was experiencing a somewhat chaotic reformation led by Guillaume Farel, a pupil of Jacques Lefèvre, and Farel badgered Calvin to stay and help. Their efforts to establish some form of religious order were fiercely resisted and they were expelled. Calvin took refuge in Strasbourg, where Bucer put him to serve as pastor of the French-speaking congregation in the city. He continued to work on *The Institutes* but then, out of the blue, he received an invitation to return to Geneva, where both politics and religion had gone from bad to worse. Initially he turned the city council down but after resisting for a year gave in. He remained at Geneva for the rest of his life, training missionaries to export reform (particularly into France), and achieving some success in his efforts to establish a godly civic community.

Exploring the way these thinkers differed is not plain sailing, and attempting to reduce their often prolix complexity to a few words risks distortion. Even so, the effort is essential if we are to understand events even in far away England. There were four principal areas of debate: (1) justification by faith; (2) how good works related to justification; (3) what the eucharist was, and how (if at all) Christ was present; and (4) the doctrine of predestination.

Justification by Faith

The issue on which there was general unity was justification by grace through faith, but there were substantial differences of substance and emphasis between the individual reformers.[6]

Jacques Lefèvre d'Étaples was accused by Luther of not fully "articulating" justification by faith, but this was because the Frenchman expressed it differently. He was just as convinced that faith was God's gift and "everything is given us and pardoned in Jesus Christ alone if we have faith in him".[7] "He who trusts in works trusts in himself and leans on a cane which breaks... by grace alone can we be saved."[8] But where Luther saw God rescuing the helpless sinner, Lefèvre saw God lavishing love beyond measure: "the death of Christ atones for our sins and not only ours but for the whole world and even for an infinity of worlds".[9] "Jesus Christ and his word is our life, our salvation, our redemption, our glory, our faith, our hope, that is to say our all, nay more than all. It is an all which is infinite and incomprehensible."[10]

Zwingli rarely mentioned justification. This was not because he thought that human effort did play a part in salvation. Early Swiss reformers were less concerned with the individual conscience than with the moral consequences of the gospel for the individual and society. Zwingli's conviction was that the authority of Scripture was absolute and must, therefore, reveal God's specific will for Christians and the church: "whenever we give heed to the Word, we acquire pure and clear knowledge of the will of God and are drawn by his Spirit and transformed into his likeness".[11] On the first Sunday in Lent 1522, in Zwingli's presence, a dozen men defied the Lenten fast by eating sausage, and a fortnight later he preached a sermon extolling Christian freedom. This was not Luther's freedom from the damning effect of a moral law he could not keep. Zwingli's freedom was freedom from human dos and don'ts in order to follow the true law of God. The tract he published a month later pointed out that the Bible said nothing about meat in Lent. Man made rules like that obscured the true laws of God. The city council tested the issue by calling a public disputation. This in itself was a radical step, a community asserting that it, not the church hierarchy, had the right to order religion. Held in January 1523, the debate was very one sided:

the bishop only sent observers and Zwingli duly triumphed. Zurich ruled that the Bible was henceforward the only permitted source for Christian teaching in the city.

The Relation between Justification and Good Works

The problem was twofold: "how can a holy God accept men and women while they are still sinful?" and "why live a moral life if behaviour has no relation to destiny in the hereafter?"

Until **Luther,** Augustine's answers had satisfied the church. Justification was a single process involving both acceptance through God's grace and moral improvement. Luther argued otherwise. The Christian was justified because Christ's victory over sin was credited ["imputed"] to him, but he was still a sinner. He was at the same time *"justus et peccator"* [righteous and a sinner]. Objectors said that encouraged "antinomianism": if you can count on God to save you, why change? Do whatever you like. Luther nevertheless insisted. Justification had not even the slightest connection to good works.[12] Those were essential, but only as the *consequence* of justification. That formula – justification first and moral change next – became hugely important for subsequent Protestant thinking.[13]

Jacques Lefèvre was initially confused. His assertion that "if we do not perform good works when we have the opportunity of performing them, we lose the grace of justification" simply reinstated good works as essential for salvation.[14] Later he was more on target: "works are the sign of a living and fruitful faith. But the absence of works is the sign of a useless and dead faith."[15] By 1522 Lefèvre was reaching towards the solution Luther had adumbrated, a distinction between "justification" – being declared righteous – and becoming righteous – what would later be labelled "sanctification". By 1527 he was clear that good works sprang from faith.[16] "God operates the will and the energy and the action and the performance."[17]

Martin Bucer reached much the same conclusion in the 1530s. However, to get there he proposed what he called "double justification".[18] First, justification from sin was required, then a second stage, "the justification of the godly". That involved responding with the aid of the Holy Spirit to the moral demands of the gospel and the example of Christ. This causal link between justification by faith and moral living shut the door on antinomianism because if anyone was living immorally that showed he could not have been justified from sin in the first place. Bucer felt this solved the problem, but others believed that it was too contrived.

Philipp Melanchthon built on Luther's insight that justification consists in Christ's righteousness being imputed to the sinner.[19] He focused on the fact that in the New Testament, "justification" is a legal ["forensic"] term denoting a verdict of acquittal handed down by a judge.[20] It did not indicate actual guilt or innocence, simply the judgment given. Thus the person justified by faith was not becoming righteous, he was declared righteous. And what made that "forensic" justification possible was the imputation of Christ's righteousness.[21] Beginning to behave morally – "sanctification" – was, as Luther had argued, an entirely separate process. Justification was the visa guaranteeing entry into eternal life; sanctification was the journey there.

John Calvin advanced the simplest and most satisfactory explanation of the link between saving faith and moral living. Luther had shown that when God gives faith to an individual, the result is union with Christ and that brings justification. But, Calvin argued, union with Christ does not end there. It persists and initiates a process of becoming like Christ ["regeneration"]. God's grace works through faith to produce moral living in the Christian, just as it did to justify him.

The Eucharist

At first sight it may not seem entirely obvious why holy communion should have become the issue in the Reformation which it did. After all, it was simply a matter of obedience to the command of Christ found in the New Testament. The problem was that the medieval church had made it very much more than that. The reformers could not find support for the hypothesis of transubstantiation in either Scripture or the early Fathers. They were equally unhappy with a liturgy which talked of the priest "sacrificing

Christ" for the salvation of the living and the dead. How could that square with justification by faith?

Thus far reformers were agreed, but what should replace traditional teaching was another story. On that they were divided more frequently and more fundamentally than on any other issue.

Luther, as we have seen, denied that the mass was a sacrifice and insisted that what was present on the altar was bread and wine. However, he was adamant that Christ's body and blood were in a mysterious way physically present in the bread and wine.[22]

Jacques Lefèvre once again anticipated Luther. In 1512 he said that the mass was not a sacrifice, other than a sacrifice of praise. Christ's one sacrifice is "more powerful than innumerable offerings infinitely repeated" and the mass is a "remembrance and recollection" of that sacrifice.[23] On the question "How is Christ present in the sacrament?", Lefèvre seems to have believed (as Luther) that this was true materially. "The appropriation of his body and blood is the most profound uniting of Christ with those who receive him and the closest binding of his ineffable love to us."[24] On the other hand he said that the eucharist contains no "mystery other than the remembrance effected by the presence of the body and blood formerly offered… which is all sufficient for salvation".[25] Above all he stressed the role of faith. "The sacrament does not effect anything without faith", but the believer "is incorporate with [Christ] by the holy communion of faith of which the sacrament is the sign".[26]

Huldrych Zwingli took a different position, which reflected the particular importance he placed on respecting the silences in Scripture.

> *The essential and corporal presence of the body and blood of Christ cannot be demonstrated from the Holy Scripture. The mass as now in use, in which Christ is offered to God the Father for the sins of the living and the dead, is contrary to the Scripture, a blasphemy against the most holy sacrifice, passion and death of Christ, and on account of its abuses [is] an abomination before God.*[27]

The body of Christ was not materially present in the consecrated bread and wine. By saying "this is my body", Christ had meant "this represents my body". The person who received the bread and the wine was not receiving Christ's body literally, but declaring his or her allegiance to Christ and the community of the faithful. Along with this understanding (which was shared by others in Swiss reforming circles), Zwingli drastically changed the way eucharistic services were ordered. Instead of the traditional elaborate ritual around an altar, Zwingli presided at a table covered with a linen cloth, with the bread and wine in wooden bowls and cups which were taken round the congregation by helpers.

Luther's response was to label Zwingli and those of like mind as "fanatics". Zwingli responded by mourning Luther as a fallen Hercules: "you would have cleansed the Augean stable… if you had not taught the body of Christ was supposed to be eaten in the bread".[28] Politics then intervened. The German princes who favoured Luther were coming under significant pressure from the emperor to conform. At the Diet of Speyer early in 1529, they had "protested" against the decisions of the conservative majority, so giving rise to the term "Protestant". Talks about self-defence then began, and in an attempt to cement unity among the leading reformers, Philip, landgrave of Hesse, called a conference at his castle of Marburg. Luther drafted fifteen articles expressing the reformed understanding of Christianity and unanimity was reached on all but one: the eucharist. Even on that, five of the six paragraphs at issue were agreed. But on the nature of Christ's presence there was no meeting of minds. Luther chalked on the table, "This is my body" and refused to budge.[29] All that could be done was to record the impasse and the need for each side to display Christian charity.

Martin Bucer's opinion was near to Zwingli's. The sacrament was an external sign to which the believer responded in faith and so "ate the body of Christ" spiritually. Melanchthon agreed with Luther that the sacraments of baptism and the eucharist existed to provide a material demonstration of God's gracious promises. Initially, too, he agreed that Christ's body and blood are "truly and substantially present" in the bread and wine. However, in 1536, he and Bucer were able to agree on the Wittenberg Concord – a formula defining the eucharist which Luther eventually endorsed. The agreement said that Christ's body and blood are truly and substantially present and received "with", not "in", the bread and wine.[30] This was too much for Zurich, but it did allow the cities of South Germany to come in under the protection of the German Lutheran princes. Bucer later decided that he had conceded too much, but Melanchthon too had further thoughts. He began to say that Christ's body was "truly presented" in the bread and wine and was "with", not "in", them and also that they were "exhibited" rather than "distributed" to communicants – revisions which were much to Luther's annoyance.[31]

John Calvin rejected Luther's view that the body and blood of Christ were in some way objectively present in the bread and wine. He was equally critical of Zwingli's reductionist view that the eucharist was a reminder of Christ's death and nothing more. A sacrament was, Calvin agreed, a physical sign, but it was a sign of a spiritual reality, and the sign and the reality could not be separated. Hence Christ's presence was real but spiritual, and the purpose of the bread and wine was to unite the believer with Christ. Lutherans rejected this, but in 1549 Calvin and Heinrich Bullinger (Zwingli's successor at Zurich) were able to agree a common formulation in "the Zurich Agreement" [*Consensus Tirgurinus*]. Purists on each side raised their eyebrows, but the language of the *Consensus* became the accepted basis for the eucharistic position of Europe's non-Lutheran reformed churches.

Predestination

The doctrine of predestination has its origin in certain passages in the letters of St Paul (endorsed by St Augustine) which describe those who are saved as "elected" [chosen by God].[32] That can be understood in two ways. "Single predestination" envisages God choosing from the totality of sinful men and women those who are to be saved. The rest he "passes over"; that is he leaves the consequence of their sin to take its course. An analogy would be a mass poisoning. Those who receive the antidote will live; the rest will die, but die from the poison. "Double predestination" envisages God electing each individual for either salvation or damnation. Both sides, however, agreed that election was in no way affected by God's foreknowledge of how a person would eventually behave. Many also held that as God was supreme, it was impossible to resist his call.

Luther seems largely to have agreed with Augustine. Since a man can do nothing to save himself, his destiny depends exclusively on whether or not God decides to save him, and it was impious to undertake any further "investigation of the divinity".[33]

Lefèvre held that "the election of God is most effective and powerful" and "men shall be saved by the grace and will of God, not their own".[34] On the other hand he did not accept that God's call was irresistible.

Melanchthon initially accepted Luther's view: "Since all things that happen, happen necessarily according to divine predestination, our will has no liberty."[35] Over the years, however, he became concerned that this came very near to fatalism. He continued to believe in predestination but preferred to say that those who were saved were called by God and allowed to respond.

Zwingli became firmly committed to "single predestination", largely as a consequence of a brush with death in 1519 when he caught the plague. The "Tower Experience" convinced Luther that God had declared him righteous; Zwingli's near fatal illness accounts for the subsequent prominence of divine sovereignty in his thinking. In *The Plague Song* [*Pestlied*] he wrote:

> *Do as you will*
> *For I lack nothing;*
> *I am your vessel*
> *to be restored or destroyed.*[36]

Again Augustine was the mentor. The will of Augustine's deity was absolute, unchallengeable, and could not be resisted. The reasons why God decided who should be saved were mysterious and "arbitrary"; that is, not influenced by anything or anyone else.

The distance Zwingli had travelled from Erasmus became evident when in 1524 Erasmus launched a direct challenge to Luther's (and therefore Zwingli's) assertion that humans are incapable of helping themselves. In *Concerning the Freedom of the Will* [*De Libero Arbitrario Diatribe sive*

Collatio] Erasmus argued that although the initiative in salvation lay with God, human reason also played a part. Men and women were able to influence their own eternal destiny. Zwingli rejected this in his *Commentary on True and False Religion*, published the following March. Luther too responded in 1525, fiercely insisting in *On the Bondage of the Will* [*De Servo arbitrio*] that it was impossible for man to reach God's standards: "Whatever he does of good is the work of God in him, for man is a donkey ridden now by God and now by the devil."[37]

Martin Bucer differed. "Double predestination" was the only correct view. God consigns individuals to hell as well as to heaven. His sovereign decision is that some are to be saved and so are endowed with true faith; the rest are "destined to doom".[38] Moreover, men and women had no right to question God's decision or his action in making the damned deaf to the gospel. Everything was subject to his unfettered will.

John Calvin too taught "double predestination". Despite his heavy reliance on Augustine, he insisted that God does not let men go to hell by default.

> *Scripture clearly shows, we say, that God once established by his eternal and unchangeable plan those whom he long before determined once for all to receive into salvation, and those whom, on the other hand, he would devote to destruction.*[39]

To many, the views of Calvin and Bucer seemed – and seem – harsh and unacceptable, but they were trying to resolve a problem. Why did some listeners respond to hearing the gospel but many did not? Free will could not be the answer since humans could do nothing to help themselves. Nor could they frustrate the sovereign wish of God to save them. The only explanation of the limited response must be that God wills this human blindness. Calvin refused to ask how or why, arguing that it was sinful to speculate about God's motives. What mattered was that the truth of predestination was essentially positive. It offered to those who did respond the assurance of being specifically chosen by God: "Here is our only ground for firmness and confidence."[40] To an extent the *Thirty-Nine*

Articles of the Church of England took the same line, asserting that God's promises must be received "as they be generally set forth" in Scripture and that reflecting on predestination and election could be "full of sweet, pleasant and unspeakable comfort to godly persons". On the other hand it downplayed the doctrine, warning that for the curious to wrestle with the doctrine might thrust them into "desperation".[41]

11

THE WIDER CONTEXT

Grappling with the ideas of leading thinkers is daunting, but unavoidable
if the Reformation is to be understood. The approach does, however,
have major pitfalls. Significant individuals who for one reason or another
have attracted limited scholarly attention are easily overlooked and so
too key events.

Individuals

Heinrich Bullinger

The Reformation figure who has been most underestimated is arguably
Heinrich Bullinger (1504–75). His importance went far beyond the
agreement which he made with Calvin on the eucharist, vital though
that was.[1] He came from a village a few miles west of Zurich and was
the son of a priest. Entering the University of Cologne in 1519 at the
height of the furore which followed the *Ninety-Five Theses*, he undertook
a systematic study of Luther's ideas and decided that they faithfully
reflected the Bible and the Fathers of the early church. Bullinger then
came under the influence of Zwingli and, after the Battle of Kappel, the
city of Zurich appointed him to succeed his mentor at the Grossmünster.
There on the first Sunday he "thundered a sermon from the pulpit that
many thought Zwingli was not dead but resurrected like the phoenix".[2]
Quickly chosen to monitor the other clergy of the city, Bullinger saved
Swiss reform by separating it from politics. He was also a major theologian,
as is increasingly being realized. The Second Helvetic [Swiss] Confession

which he worked up from a personal confession of faith was adopted by the non-Lutheran churches in Switzerland, Scotland, France, Poland, and Hungary. He also wrote the first treatise on covenant theology (not to be confused with medieval ideas of covenant). This argued that God had promised his grace to humanity and that humanity in turn has to follow his precepts. Hence baptizing babies had a community significance, and civic authority had a religious justification. Developments of the covenant idea became hugely important over the next two centuries in both Europe and the Americas. Bullinger also became the patriarch of Protestant Europe. He worked tirelessly to encourage good relations between all reformers, including Lutherans, and his 12,000 surviving letters are a monument to his achievement. Add to that numerous books and pamphlets, and Bullinger's total output exceeds those of Martin Luther and John Calvin combined. Indeed, in England he was much more influential than Calvin and in 1586 the archbishop of Canterbury, John Whitgift, ordered all non-graduate ordinands to secure a copy of Bullinger's famous *Decades* and each week read one of its fifty sermons.

Events

The Peasants

We left Martin Luther spirited away into protective custody following his confrontation with Charles V. He spent ten months in the elector of Saxony's Wartburg Castle writing furiously. His principal achievement was translating the New Testament into German, amplified with explanatory prefaces and notes which set out his new understanding of the gospel. However, back in Wittenberg, a senior academic colleague, Andreas Karlstadt, had begun attacking clerical celibacy and the ritual of the mass and trying to turn the priesthood of all believers into a reality. Newcomers, too, had arrived claiming to experience direct inspiration by the Holy Spirit and asserting that the bread and wine at the eucharist were symbols, in no sense the body and blood of Christ. Baptizing babies was also called into question. Karlstadt then triggered a widespread destruction of sacred images where Luther had only attacked pilgrimages to shrines offering miracles.

The first news of the upheaval brought Luther hot foot from the Wartburg. He insisted on infant baptism because it brought everybody under church authority. Despite having rejected transubstantiation, he asserted that the body of Christ was physically present in the eucharist. As for sacred images, these were to be kept for "recognition, for witness, for commemoration, for a sign".[3] This brought matters under control but worse was to follow. Spreading like wildfire, his ideas and especially his protest were helping to produce socio-religious turmoil through much of Germany. Significant numbers of clergy led attacks on the mass which had enslaved them as well as their parishioners. Individual towns introduced reforms as each saw fit. Many nobles imposed religious change in their estates. Some imperial knights – a group already in political and economic decline – felt justified in attacking wealthy clergy. Especially subversive was Luther's emphasis on Christian freedom. Monks and nuns abandoned their vows. Then in late 1524 rural strikes and armed protests flared up over much of the country and escalated into the so-called Peasants' (better "Tenants'") War.

Similar protests had occurred from time to time, but that of 1524–25 was far more extensive, seeming to reflect the coming together of economic and social grievances with attitudes derived from the Reformation. The outbreak was very much aimed at clerical landlords.[4] The first three of the Twelve Articles drawn up by the peasants from Swabia [overlapping modern Baden-Würtemberg and Bavaria] were religious – calling for the right to elect the parish priest, the use of tithe locally for the priest and the poor instead of being alienated to distant abbeys and monasteries, plus an end to serfdom "considering that Christ has delivered and redeemed us all by the shedding of his precious blood, the lowly as well as the great".[5] The peasants also appealed to Luther, but their call for relations to be regulated by "divine law" hints at links with Zwingli, as does the frequent targeting of religious images. Luther, responded with an *Admonition to Peace* (April 1525), which laid the blame for the "rebellion" squarely on "you princes and lords and especially you blind bishops and mad priests and monks", but reminded the peasants that "the governing authorities are instituted by God".[6] The parties should, he said, accept arbitration. Then a short and risky trip, which he took to reason with the peasants, convinced him that anarchy was abroad and in a follow-up pamphlet, *Against the Robbing and Murdering Hordes of Peasants*, he urged repression: "this is the time of the sword, not the day of grace".[7] Luther's timing was bad. His call to "smite, slay and stab, secretly or openly, remembering that nothing can be more poisonous, hurtful or devilish than a rebel" was published only days before the rebellion collapsed and so appeared to justify the vengeful bloodbath by the emperor and the princes which followed; the death toll may have reached 100,000.[8] The pamphlet damaged his reputation at the time and has done so since more than anything other than *On the Jews and their Lies*, which he wrote towards the end of his life.[9]

The Anabaptists

In Saxony Luther was able to stabilize religion, but in Zurich Zwingli was far more exposed because of his emphasis on discovering and following the law of God. The first of the divine laws which attracted attention was the prohibition in the Ten Commandments on "making graven images". Enthusiastic citizens began to attack religious statues. In 1524, to prevent this getting out of hand, the city had recourse to another disputation which led to the controlled removal of images by the civic authority. Other applications of the principle "scripture alone" were not so amenable to good order. In particular, study of the New Testament quickly revealed that the apostolic norm had been to baptize believing adults, not newborn babies. In obedience to this, in January 1525, a small group of Zurichers first baptized themselves and then recruited others. As all had been baptized as babies, enemies labelled them "anabaptists" – twice baptizers – though they, of course, asserted that what had been done to them as infants had not been baptism at all. Converts were won particularly in villages to the south and east of the city and by Easter hundreds were involved.

To many twenty-first-century Westerners, the choice between baptizing newborn babies and baptizing adults seems a matter for the family or individual concerned and no one else. Quite the opposite was true in the sixteenth century, where there was general acceptance of the dictum of St Cyprian (d.258) that "outside the church there is no salvation".[10] The rite which removed the taint of original sin and made a person a member of Christ's church was baptism – hence the alternative term "christening". But if adults only could be baptized, children who died before maturity did not belong to the church and would go to hell. Even more important, membership of the church and membership of the community were two sides of the same coin, so christening was effectively the shared initiating experience of the whole community. Adult baptism was, therefore, fundamentally divisive. Moreover, if believers' baptism was, as the New Testament suggested, the original rite of admission to the church, "anabaptists" could claim to be the only true Christians and so rightly dissociate themselves from an existing church which was in error. Not only would that put paid to Zwingli's concern to nurture a society obedient to the laws of God, it would challenge the newly asserted right of the city council to regulate religion. The Zurich anabaptists were arrested. Most recanted but in 1526 four were executed by drowning. The remainder were expelled, much as Luther's radical critics had been expelled from Saxony.

Anabaptist emphasis on the authority of Scripture might suggest that they were a tight-knit dogmatic group. Far from it. The Bible means different things to different people and a minority even ended up as Unitarians – that is, they denied the doctrine of the Trinity. Membership was voluntary and groupings appear, disappear, and fluctuate bewilderingly. Every hand was against them – "Protestant" as well as "Catholic" – and they made up the overwhelming majority of martyrs to the Reformation. Anabaptists were often no more than a tiny minority, but three strands can be detected. An influential group of Swiss anabaptists met in 1527 near Lake Constance and agreed on what became known as the Schlietheim Confession. Their object was probably to distinguish themselves from wilder opinions, but what they decided was radical enough. Adult baptism was agreed to be mandatory, so too a memorialist understanding of the eucharist. Pastors were to be elected and other evidence reveals that gatherings ran on congregational lines and shared resources. Believers were to separate themselves from society, which meant taking no part in civic affairs and having nothing whatever to do with the use of force, not only in war but also in supporting law and order. Particularly destabilizing was their refusal to swear oaths, since the threat of divine punishment for oath-breakers was almost the only sanction society had to enforce contracts and obligations. Eventually the Swiss anabaptists were driven to take refuge in the relative safety of Moravia along with another strand, the anabaptists of South Germany. Among these, so-called Hutterites developed a rigorous communal lifestyle and in the third quarter of the century may have numbered as many as 30,000. But soon Moravia ceased to be safe and over the next two centuries survivors of these anabaptist groups were driven from place to place through Eastern Europe until finding eventual refuge in North America.

It was the third stream, those in North-Western Europe, whose behaviour accounted for – and in many eyes justified – the paranoia about anabaptists which came to dominate the mind of the sixteenth century. Strasbourg expelled the sect but only after Bucer had tried sweet reason. Indeed, in the 1530s he successfully brought the anabaptist community in Hesse back to conformity. However, in the Low Countries, the evangelist Melchior Hoffman won many converts to a form of anabaptism which expected the imminent arrival of the Apocalypse [God's final triumph]. In contrast with the rest of the Holy Roman Empire, what is now the Benelux was under the direct rule of the Habsburgs, and they began persecuting fiercely. The victims decided to take refuge across the border in the episcopal city of Münster where reform was being preached. They were stopped by force and in desperation tried to seize control of several Dutch towns. The emperor responded by ordering all anabaptists and those harbouring them to be executed – the women by being buried alive. By then Hoffman was in prison in Strasbourg, but important figures among his followers (the "Melchorites") reached Münster, gained control, and proclaimed the New Jerusalem. Thousands from Friesland and around – many disillusioned by Luther's "betrayal" of the peasants – flocked to the city to be baptized and wait for the end of the age. In April 1534, the bishop joined forces with Lutheran nobles and cities to besiege Münster. Within the walls, more steps were made to inaugurate the new society. Those who refused re-baptism were expelled. Property was declared to be common. Women heavily outnumbered men and were thought to be in need of both protection and control, so polygamy was made mandatory. The leaders, headed by a Dutch tailor, Jan Beukels [John of Leyden], lost all connection with reality. He lived in luxury, took sixteen wives, and proclaimed himself king of the world. Finally, after eighteen months the city was betrayed to the bishop and his allies and resistance ended in another bloodbath. John of Leyden and two of his main supporters were publicly tortured to death. As for the survivors, a rump turned to terrorism, others to mysticism and inner enlightenment. The largest group was rescued by the clandestine ministry of a former country priest, Mennon Simons. These Mennonite communities – quietist and pacifist – survived continual Habsburg persecution but found eventual tolerance later in the century with the establishing of the Dutch Republic. Despite that, the stench of Münster remained. In the words of Heinrich Bullinger, "God opened the eyes of the governments by the revolt at Münster and, thereafter, no one would even trust those Anabaptists who claimed to be innocent."[11]

Consequences

The upheavals of the 1520s and 1530s threw into stark relief the naivety of the evangelical leaders. Their assumption had been that, as in the New Testament parable, the yeast of biblical renewal would work from within to leaven the whole church. No one had any thought of schism; the object was reform. But now with rebellious peasants and anabaptist dissidents, it became obvious that the fermentation of ideas could not be allowed to continue uncontrolled. The freedom of Christ was too heady a brew to be available without discipline. And with the traditional church power structures in disarray, the only recourse was to secular authority. The result was what historians refer to as the "magisterial Reformation", reformation dominated by kings, princes, and city councils. We have already seen this at work in Zurich, but one of the clearest examples was in Strasbourg.

There Martin Bucer stressed that "nobody should live for himself alone, but for his neighbour" and like Zwingli sought a godly fusion between the church and the community.[12] Nevertheless the city councillors kept a tight hand throughout and although a majority slowly came to favour reform, with the exception of one outburst of image-breaking, friction was avoided. By May 1524 there was agreement that the mass would no longer be celebrated in Strasbourg's parishes, but the magistrates were determined on social and religious inclusiveness and for the next five years insisted on mass being provided at the cathedral and three collegiate churches. Similarly, images and side altars were retained until 1530 before being removed in an orderly fashion. A similar deferring to the city council was seen when Bucer began devising a new church order. His object was to encourage active faith in the laity which would result in concern for the spiritual and physical well-being of the community. That meant imposing standards, but the city council would never agree to these becoming mandatory. Lay wardens were appointed for each church to monitor offences or absence from communion, but when Bucer called for enforcement he received only warm words from the councillors. His structure was the model from which John Calvin developed the presbyterian system at Geneva, but Calvin too was never allowed a free hand – despite John Knox's famous description of the city as "the most perfect school of Christ".[13] In Germany the areas which followed Luther retained the old structure of dioceses and parishes, but again they were very much under the control of the local secular authority. In 1555 this was formalized when the Holy Roman Empire adopted the famous principle of *cuius regio, eius religio* ["whoever governs determines the religion"]. Religious identity thus became politicized. It can, indeed, be argued that the rulers of Lutheran and Catholic Europe exploited this to help create stable ideologically coherent states with well-disciplined subjects – in historians' jargon a process of "confessionalization".

12

SPAIN, ITALY, AND FRANCE

In telling the story of the Reformation it is easy to end up concentrating on events in Germany and the parts of Europe that would ultimately reject the authority of the pope. Indeed, so dominant is Luther and everything which comes after, that this is almost inevitable. It can, however, result in reformation elsewhere being overlooked. One such area was the Mediterranean, led initially (although briefly) by Spain.

The Reformation in Spain

The history of medieval Spain is very different from the rest of Western Europe. For most of the period, the country was split between Muslim states in the south and crusading Christian territories to the north, which eventually became the joint kingdoms of Castile and Aragon. Perhaps thanks to the psychology of this long confrontation (the *reconquista* only ended in 1492), the Spanish church underwent considerable reform in the fifteenth century, in both administration and discipline. A leading figure was the Franciscan Ximénes de Cisneros (1436–1517), who with strong royal support became the country's dominant ecclesiastic. In, for example, his own Franciscan Order he enforced obedience to the rules on poverty, celibacy, residence in a parish, and weekly preaching. Other religious orders received parallel treatment and a number of friars and monks fled the country with their wives. Arguably these reforms inhibited the anticlericalism which was a factor in encouraging more radical questioning elsewhere. Potential critics of the church had also to reckon with the state inquisition ["the Tribunal of the Holy Office"] which the Spanish rulers had (with papal permission) set up in 1481, initially to police the orthodoxy of the thousands of Muslims and Jews forced by the *reconquista* to convert to Christianity.

Despite this firm grip in both church and state, Spain did experience stirrings of the Christocentric revival. Those involved became known by admirers as *alumbrados* ["enlightened ones"]. They appear to have been mystics who focused on the parts of the Bible available in Spanish and on works from the north such as *The Imitation of Christ* by Thomas à Kempis. Inevitably, some became interested in Erasmus and Luther and this confirmed the Inquisition in its suspicions of this non-church initiative. In 1525 it suppressed the *alumbrados* – which is part of the reason we know less about them than we would like. One person linked to this Spanish spiritual revival was a convalescent Basque soldier, Íñigo López de Loyola [Ignatius Loyola] (1491–1556). He, like Luther, underwent a conversion experience. In the course of this he was introduced to Ludolph of Saxony's *Life of Christ* (a probable source for his own later *Spiritual Exercises*) and to *The Imitation of Christ*. Loyola re-envisioned himself as a soldier for Jesus, but in sixteenth-century Spain "go it alone" inspiration was dangerous and, having been identified as an *alumbrado*, in 1528 he made himself scarce and went to Paris. Another suspect *alumbrado* was Juan de Valdés, the twin brother of Charles V's secretary. He wisely took refuge in Italy a year later.

Italian Reformation

In Italy, Valdés found a groundswell of Christian renewal unhampered by inquisitors. Reformed religious orders were being set up, such as the Capuchins [reformed Franciscan friars]. Even more promising were the new lay brotherhoods or confraternities, a form of group initiative which had long been a feature of the Italian religious scene. One such was set up in Venice by Gasparo Contarini, a Venetian nobleman who underwent a spiritual conversion in 1511, which he was later able to recognize as the awareness of being justified by faith. He met Valdés soon after he arrived and introduced him to Henry VIII's cousin and critic, Reginald Pole. Pole too had had a conversion experience and become convinced of justification by faith. Valdés settled in Naples and around him grew an evangelical circle which included several noblewomen and leaders of religious orders such as the Capuchin friar Bernardino Ochino and the Augustinian abbot Piermartire Vermigli [known later in England as Peter Martyr]. The group and those like-minded became known as *spirituali*. Their keynote was grace through faith, and Valdés strongly embraced the doctrine of predestination. The writings and ideas of German and Swiss reformers also circulated generally, especially in the societies of northern Italian cities and related networks of nobles. In 1534 Alessandro Farnese became pope as Paul III, with an interest in reform and reunion. Italians who were convinced of the truth of justification by faith came to prominence at the papal court. Several were made cardinals, including Contarini and Pole. Contarini persuaded Pope Paul to set up a reform commission and in 1541 the pope sent him to the Imperial Diet at Regensburg with authority to talk with the Lutherans.

Influential voices in the Lutheran camp were equally horrified at the prospect of the schism in Western Christendom becoming permanent. At the earlier diet held in Augsburg in 1530, there had been high hopes of some reconciliation with the traditionalists on the basis of a conciliatory presentation of the fourteen points agreed at Marburg.[1] The emperor was attracted by the possibility of unity, but in the end the hardliners among his advisers won the day. Nevertheless Bucer (in particular) refused to take no for an answer. An opportunity came in 1536 when the archbishop of Cologne, Hermann von Wied, set out to reform his archdiocese. Initially this focused on traditional issues but in 1539 the archbishop invited Bucer and Melanchthon to help him draw up a more radical programme. Agreement was reached on justification and with the arrival of Contarini at Regensburg, reconciliation looked a real possibility. But it was not to be. Political interests in Germany and outside did not want agreement. Contarini could not compromise on transubstantiation and the Lutherans refused to say that it was necessary to confess to a priest. Luther himself disowned the negotiations and Contarini's efforts were rejected by a majority of the other cardinals; the support he had relied on from Reginald Pole failed to materialize.

Despite the failure, the ever hopeful Bucer continued to work with the archbishop of Cologne for several years. The formula he drafted included almost the complete reformed programme: justification by faith, only two sacraments (baptism and the eucharist), communion in both kinds, a vernacular liturgy, and an end to priestly celibacy. Von Wied and the provincial Diet accepted, but not Cologne Cathedral, and the emperor stepped in to block the change. In April 1546 the archbishop was excommunicated and resigned his offices. For a time in Italy too, efforts continued to keep evangelical reform alive. A number of the bishops remained open to the emphasis on faith and encouraged their clergy in the conviction that this was fully compatible with Catholic doctrine. In 1540 Loyola's group was recognized as the Society of Jesus, at that stage without the hostility to Protestants which characterized it later. Jesuits were told to speak with Lutherans "familiarly on those topics which we have in common and avoiding all contentious arguments in which one party might seem to beat the other".[2] Giovanni Morone and another reformer were made cardinals in 1542 and he was appointed with Pole as a co-chairman of the council which the pope had called to meet at Trent [north-west of Venice, now Trento] in the hope of uniting the church. Pole's circle was responsible for the hugely popular tract known as *Beneficio di Christo*. It was taken in large measure from Calvin's *Institutes*, with some help from Bucer, and reputedly it sold 40,000 copies in the Venetian Republic alone.

Yet, as in Germany, the tide in Italy was setting against reform. The influential Cardinal Giovanni Carafa mobilized bitter opposition against Pole and other *spirituali*, whom he saw as crypto-Protestants. Death happily saved Valdés. Contarini was arrested and died in custody. Morone was attacked. Ochino chose Switzerland rather than obey a call to Rome and he was soon followed by Peter Martyr. Their flight helped Carafa persuade the pope to set up a Roman Inquisition, with Carafa as one of the Inquisitors-General: "Even if my own father were a heretic, I would gather wood to burn him."[3] When at last the council began in December 1545 at Trent, there was a pitiful Protestant attendance. Carafa's influence prevailed and its decrees were specifically directed to rule out compromise. No *sola scriptura*: authority was declared to reside in the Bible *and* tradition. *Sola fide* similarly: justification involved faith *and* good works.[4] Pole withdrew, pleading sickness. Yet even then there was a glimmer of hope. In November 1549 the pope died and Pole was nominated. Carafa thereupon accused him of heresy and that swung opinion sufficiently for him to lose by two votes – although Pole's refusal to canvas did not help. The Council of

Trent had ended its aggressively traditionalist first session in 1547, but a brief reassembly in 1551–52 completed the work with a decree confirming transubstantiation as the most appropriate term to express the truth of Christ's real presence in the eucharist. In 1555 Cardinal Carafa himself became pope and, intent on imposing papal authority, he left the council suspended. Instead he mounted a new attack on those he saw as Protestant quislings, in particular Pole (by that time safely in England) and Morone (whom he imprisoned).

Reform in France

Attempts in France to reform within existing church structures faced a different situation to that in Italy and had a different outcome. The country had a strong centralized monarchy and a sophisticated (if complicated) legal system, while the Paris theologians could claim to be the intellectual leaders of the Western church. The best documented episode of reform on the ground involved Jacques Lefèvre d'Étaples. We have seen how his writings anticipate much of the early Luther. From 1523 he became involved in a campaign to put evangelical reform into practice. This was in the bishopric of Meaux (twenty miles east of Paris) at the invitation of the bishop, Guillaume Briçonnet, who gave Lefèvre direct responsibility for encouraging revival in the diocese. Copies of his vernacular New Testament were distributed free but his (and the bishop's) focus was on the pulpit and an active preaching campaign. It was probably to help less able priests to preach that in 1525 he produced the *Epistles and Gospels for the Fifty-Two Sundays of the Year* (*Épistres et Évangiles pour les Cinquante et Deux Sepmaines de l'An*), each passage accompanied by an explanatory homily. The bishop saw all this as quite distinct from Luther, although he had to step in on two occasions when he thought reformist preachers were going too far. Indeed in 1523 he issued fierce denunciations of Luther for undermining church order and discipline, and he specifically endorsed prayers for the dead, belief in purgatory, and the invocation of saints.[5] Yet Lefèvre clearly did not feel restricted. The *Épistres et Évangiles* show that by then he had abandoned the cult of saints along with purgatory and had reduced priestly authority to expounding the Scripture.[6] What made the crucial difference between the acceptable Lefèvre and the unacceptable Luther was that his homilies "were in no way intended to be schismatic".[7] Insisting on reform within existing church structures meant that he was not forced, as Luther was, to repudiate papal authority. Indeed, he endorsed it:

All ecclesiastical dignities and orders should obey the holy monarch..., as he is the supreme priest.[8]

Despite this, the Paris theologians began proceedings against Lefèvre, claiming to find forty-eight errors in the *Épistres et Évangiles*, most of them damnable heresies, including justification by faith alone and a denial that good works are necessary for salvation.[9]

Briçonnet and Lefèvre were able to resist the pressure, thanks to the support of the king, Francis I, and especially his sister Margaret, queen of Navarre. It was not that the king was soft on heresy – far from it. But there was little clarity as to what heresy was or was not. The Sorbonne was only a single voice. As in Italy, evangelicals could claim that what they taught was entirely orthodox. Moreover Francis was proud of his reputation as a patron of scholarship and was not persuaded that humanism and heresy were one and the same. Politics and self-interest muddied the waters even further. The attack on Briçonnet's preaching programme was promoted by Franciscans who resented losing their monopoly of the local pulpits, and the Sorbonne saw the issue as a further opportunity to demonstrate that it was not a tool of the crown. Then in February 1525 came sudden change. Francis I was captured by Charles V and imprisoned in Spain. His mother Louise became regent and her hostility led Lefèvre and others like-minded to find safety in exile. It was at this point too that Cousturier published his diatribe and the authorities banned vernacular Bible translations.[10] Owners of Lefèvre's *Épistres et Évangiles* were ordered to hand them in. The following year saw all this reversed. Francis was released and called Lefèvre back to become the royal librarian and tutor to the king's four-year-old son, Charles – posts intended to allow him to push forward his work on the French Bible.[11] However, the experiment at Meaux was not revived.

The crisis of reform in France came some nine years later. On Sunday 18 October 1534, Parisians awoke to find "placards" [broadsheets] displayed in several public places, attacking "the horrible, great and insufferable abuses of the papal Mass".[12] The city became hysterical. Alarmist rumours of a "Lutheran" threat were fed by news of similar "placards" appearing in five other towns and in the royal apartments at Amboise. Paris immediately held an expiatory procession and searched for the culprits, who were promptly executed. In January Francis ordered a second even more solemn procession and took part himself, along with the court and anybody in Paris who was anybody. The day ended with more burnings and the burst of persecution lasted until May.

The placard was the work of a French pastor in exile at Neuchâtel, but copies had had to be smuggled across the border and distributed locally. That clearly shows that reform in France already existed as a network and was being influenced by Swiss Protestants, an influence which would grow as Calvin's Geneva supplied first literature and from the 1550s trained pastors. But the "Affair of the Placards" has a wider significance too. It demonstrates that the eucharist had replaced justification by faith as the key religious issue. We have seen how at Marburg it had already divided Lutherans from those who held Swiss views on the sacrament (nicknamed "sacramentaries") – and how at Regensburg it would wreck agreement with Rome.[13] What had begun as an evangelical consensus for revival within Western Christendom was now hopelessly split over the nature of the eucharist.

Despite France now having the definition of heresy it had lacked, there was no immediate move to exploit it. The king's attitude did indeed harden but it was not until 1540 that the royal courts were ordered to take over heresy presentments from the more lenient church tribunals. Royal justice was able to score some significant individual successes but had little other effect because the majority of reformers continued to work under the cover of conformity – the pattern pioneered by Jacques Lefèvre d'Étaples. There is ample evidence of priests and friars preaching reformist sermons, often to large crowds, and also conducting private sessions for prayer or study of the Bible. Schoolmasters too were prominent. Most were able to escape from prosecution by a minimum conformity to tradition – continuing to hear confessions and consecrate the eucharist – although some clerics surreptitiously modified the liturgy to bring it more in line with reform.[14] Calvin was fiercely opposed to such occasional conformity, likening it to the Jewish leader Nicodemus, who consulted Christ under the cover of darkness. But the choice he offered between going into exile and refusing to attend mass with the consequences which would follow met the response from Paris "that it is easy for you to preach and threaten over there, but that if you were here you would perhaps feel differently".[15] For most, "Nicodemism" was the positive route. It only ceased to be so under Francis I's son, Henry II, who encouraged a surge in persecution which at last weeded out the occasionally conformist evangelical clerics. By then, however, reformist numbers were sufficient for some to risk setting up illegal conventicles, and many more were emboldened when Henry II died suddenly in 1559.

Roman Catholicism Revitalized

The initial anti-Protestant definitions of the Council of Trent and the victory of conservative forces at Rome had ended the hopes of reformers who sought religious revival within a united Western church led by the pope. Such evangelical ideas as did linger on among a number of senior Italian clerics were finally eradicated by the Inquisition in the 1560s.[16] However, once Carafa was gone, Trent was recalled in 1562 to resume its work. The agenda in the new divided Europe was now the future of that part of the church which had adhered to Rome. A programme of root and branch reform was initiated to achieve an imposing, educated, active, and closely supervised clergy, resident in every parish. Ordination was regulated, and dioceses were instructed to set up seminaries to provide clergy training. Lifestyle and morals were prescribed for everyone from cardinals and bishops to candidates for the priesthood; celibacy ceased to be an ideal and became mandatory. The laity too were regulated. Ignorance was countered by issuing a standard catechism. Local custom gave way to a uniform Latin liturgy, which nevertheless required a greater participation of the laity "about the altar of the Lord".[17] Rules prescribed lay attendance at mass and confession. Allowing permission to receive communion in both kinds was reserved to the pope. The presence of a priest was declared essential for a valid marriage. Church music too was simplified and regulated. The sale of indulgences was prohibited and rules now governed the cult of saints and the veneration of images. Teaching about purgatory was regulated and an index of prohibited books was issued to protect the faithful from error. The religious orders too were reformed, with stronger central authorities.

Despite the somewhat sordid politics which had surrounded the council and bedevilled it to the end (not least over the competing authorities of the pope and the bishops), it had produced a matrix within which regulated devotion could be nurtured and provisions for a disciplined clergy and a managed and instructed laity, which would remain effective and unchallenged for centuries. This was not the culture of the Christocentric religion of the heart for which evangelicals had longed for half a century or more. Hierarchical controls now restricted lay religious initiative. But within those clerical controls, Council of Trent ["Tridentine"] Catholicism did leave room for the individual to achieve a Christocentric focus.[18] As with what we must now call Protestantism, Trent has to be seen as something salvaged from the religious revival which had gripped fifteenth- and sixteenth-century Europe. The downside was competition and conflict. With the rift in the Western church permanent, the Society of Jesus added "defence of the faith" to its objectives and with the other revived institutions in the Roman obedience set out to reconquer lands lost to the Protestants. Edmund Campion, the most attractive of the first English Jesuits, would write:

My charge is, of free cost to preach the Gospel, to minister the Sacraments, to instruct the simple, to reform sinners, to confute errors – in brief to cry alarm spiritual against foul vice and proud ignorance.[19]

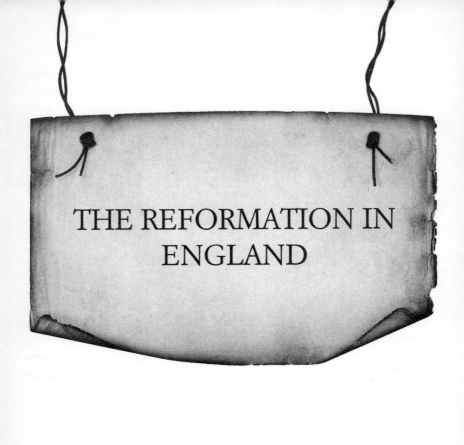

THE REFORMATION IN ENGLAND

13

ENGLAND: BEFORE THE STORM

The story of the Reformation in Europe is of a wished-for religious revival which was shattered by interests of authority and power, and split further and further apart. In England in 1520, the indulgence crisis in Germany had yet to come to the attention of ordinary men and women. Other than the presence of the Lollards, nothing threatened the unity of those who sought reform and a closer union with Christ. It was a unity soon to be fractured on the English side of the Channel too.

The Establishment

Among the voices insisting that church life had to be revitalized were those of senior ecclesiastics and academics. One of the most prominent was John Colet, dean of St Paul's.[1] A noted pastor and a preacher who expounded the plain text of Scripture, Colet, so Erasmus said, devoted his "entire energies to winning [Londoners] for Christ".[2] He had studied in Italy and France and was convinced that reform would come through Christian humanism.[3] The way to holiness lay through the true perception of Scripture, and that perception came by grace. By recovering the primitive message of the Bible, modern scholarship would chart the path to renewal. An equally committed reformer was John Fisher, bishop of Rochester. Indeed, Erasmus had originally planned to dedicate the 1516 New Testament to him, "a man who to great uprightness of life adds varied and abstruse learning".[4] Although Pope Leo X was later substituted as the dedicatee, Fisher's immediate response to the publication (despite being aged forty-seven) was to arrange for Erasmus to teach him Greek; about the same time he started to learn Hebrew.

Colet's closest friend was Thomas More but they were only part of a significant circle of Christian humanists. Their mentor was Erasmus, who made three visits to England and whose influence has been described as "immense".[5] It was on the first of these that he met John Colet and had been impressed by his "new literal" approach to the Bible text.[6] Erasmus spent much of his longest visit (1509–14) at the University of Cambridge, where he had another tight circle of influential sympathizers and where he did much of the work on his Greek New Testament. During these years John Fisher was chancellor of the university and deeply involved from 1511 in the foundation and development of St John's as a primarily humanist college. In public only Hebrew, Latin, and Greek were allowed to be spoken (officially!). In 1517, with royal encouragement, Cambridge established a lectureship in Greek. Oxford was much stonier ground. In 1516 Bishop Richard Fox had established Corpus Christi as a humanist college and also public lectures on Greek, theology, and rhetoric [i.e effective communication]. The theology lecturer was instructed to concentrate on the early Fathers and this precipitated a major confrontation with the other colleges, who believed this threatened their existing scholastic curriculum. The result was a serious attempt in 1518–19 to suppress the teaching of Greek at Oxford, which was defeated by the personal intervention of the king (prompted by Thomas More).

Men like Fisher and Colet had a high view of the authority and responsibilities of the priesthood and insisted that reform had to start with the clergy – hence the importance of the new educational curriculum. John Longland, the future bishop of Lincoln (1473–1547), declared: "our true predecessors, both monks and secular clergy, led a holy and hard life, we a much easier and softer one, we who have stained [the church's] pristine beauty and devotion with worldly desires".[7] In a famous sermon to the Convocation of the archdiocese of Canterbury in 1510 or 1511, Colet called for a personal and moral transformation in the clergy to be achieved by implementing existing standards and structures. Disentangle the church from the secular world, and with a new moral authority reform of the laity would necessarily follow – a recipe we have seen adopted by the papacy at the Council of Trent.[8] Many clerics, however, saw attacks like this as undermining their authority. When Longland tried to discipline Lincoln, he came up against significant vested interest. So did Colet when he attempted to revise the statutes of St Paul's Cathedral.

Later in the century (and subsequently) Protestants claimed Colet as a forerunner. They were wrong – he belongs with Erasmus and his *philosophia Christi*. But it is easy to see why they thought that. His focus was on the letters of St Paul. He had little time for scholasticism and engaging in excessive confession. He was "unorthodox in opinion and less than discreet in expression".[9] He failed to say mass each day, and had little time for pilgrimages, cult images, and relics. He was critical of religious communities and, when he founded St Paul's School in London, he was careful to place it under the control of the Mercers' Company. His proclamation of Pauline Christianity handed an obvious weapon to his critics, and in 1513 he was even temporarily barred from preaching and threatened with a heresy charge. John Fisher, on the other hand, would never have been linked with later Protestantism. He was a rarity in England – a bishop who was trained in divinity – and was the country's one internationally renowned theologian. Like Colet, Fisher was a famous preacher, but he valued the schoolmen as well as humanists, and his emphasis was on reform by reviving the church's sacramental and penitential practices. Indeed, as we shall see, when later he encountered Luther's writing (Colet by that time was dead), Fisher's response was to attack vehemently a heretic who was despising the authority of the church and ecclesiastical tradition.

Heresy, indeed, was the one issue on which reformist clergy saw eye to eye with traditionalists. Although Colet shared the contempt Lollards had for image worship and pilgrimages to the shrines of saints, he took his part in one and possibly two purges. Indeed, with the turn of the sixteenth century, harassment of Lollards accelerated markedly. For example, between October 1511 and March 1512, nearly eighty witnesses and suspects were investigated in Coventry, some many times. At least forty-eight of them were forced to abjure their errors, one was burned at the stake, while eight of those who survived would be arrested and burned in 1520.[10] Clearly, despite a century of repression, Lollardy was continuing to meet a spiritual need outside the church establishment. But why the acceleration of persecution in the years around 1500? The answer is not obvious. The sources are very patchy and the interrogation records we depend on most of the time only give one side of the story. Some historians take the view that the increased tempo of enquiries indicates that far from just surviving, Lollardy was reviving. This would certainly be of a piece with the increasing lay involvement in religious activity we have noted.[11] Another possibility is that more police activity was simply a consequence of efforts, like Longland's at Lincoln to reform and reinvigorate the Cathedral chapter. Fear could be a factor too. Ever since the appearance of Lollardy, church leaders had been anxious not to lose control over popular piety. Increasing lay initiatives in religion could have reinforced that fear, while lay self-help might even seem to undermine the claim of the clergy to be special. In such an atmosphere, behaviour which previously would have been ignored might well come under scrutiny.

Luther Reaches England

Although educated circles in England soon learned of Luther's 1517 protest, they were little affected by it. In March 1518 Erasmus sent Thomas More a copy of the *Ninety-Five Theses* and Thomas More apparently welcomed it as a further call for the church to put its house in order. It was More whom Erasmus probably had in mind when in May 1519 he told Luther: "You have many in England who think the best of your writing, and amongst them are some great men."[12] In the course of the debate over Greek at Oxford, More again mentioned Luther favourably. The German monk was just the latest ally in the European battle between the advocates of new humanist scholarship and traditionalist scholastics. Henry VIII's comment, so Erasmus told Luther in 1519, was only that "he could have wished that you had written certain things with more prudence and moderation. That is also the wish, my dear Luther, of those who wish you well."[13]

That the English response to Luther's writing was notably relaxed is confirmed by the sales ledger of John Dorne, an Oxford bookseller, for the year 1520. Early in the year there were some purchases of Luther's contentious 1518 tract *Concerning the Power of the Pope* [*De Potestate Papae*]. Written to answer the accusation that he was *ipso facto* a heretic for questioning the pope's authority, it anticipated his *Address to the Christian Nobility of the German Nation*. Luther wrote:

> *If the Romanists continue in their madness, nothing else remains but that the emperor, kings and princes proceed with arms against this pest of the land and no longer try to settle the matter with words but actually use the sword.*[14]

There was another flurry of sales in and after October, but over the year the Oxford sales of Luther were minimal. Even the news that the pope had declared Luther a heretic and ordered his books to be destroyed had little effect apart from rumours and complaints about heretics in the German merchant community.

Luther Attacked

Early in 1521 all this changed. The king himself began to write a book attacking Luther. Called *The Assertion of the Seven Sacraments* [*Assertio Septem Sacramentorum*], it was complete by the end of April and with Henry's name on the title page, became a European bestseller. But why this sudden rush to take up the cudgels against Luther? Foreign policy was a major consideration. In the latest twist in European diplomacy it suited the king to demonstrate that England (i.e. Henry VIII) was on the pope's side against the French. A second factor was pride. The king of France was called "The Most Christian King", the ruler of Spain was known as "The Catholic King". For years Henry had been angling for a label of his own and he included a firm endorsement of papal authority in the *Assertio*. Might that tip the scales? Yet neither international manoeuvres nor tuft hunting entirely accounts for the king becoming personally involved. Henry VIII was a man who normally hated having to write, but in this case there is no doubt of his direct input (although he did have help from Sir Thomas More and others). The explanation is almost certainly that the king had been shown a copy of Luther's *Babylonish Captivity*. It arrived at the turn of the year and when Henry read it he was profoundly shocked; so shocked that he decided he must refute it himself. What appalled the king was the book's onslaught on the mass.[15] The heart of Henry VIII's faith was an absolute conviction that every mass he heard was a miraculous sacrifice which directly aided his eternal salvation – and he heard mass every day, sometimes more than once. In other words, the *Babylonish Captivity* attacked the very belief Henry lived by. The *Assertio* did not focus on the mechanics of transubstantiation, but was adamant that by a miracle the bread and wine became Christ's physical body and blood, and that this body was sacrificed by the priest. Until his dying day, that was the focus of Henry's Christianity and it coloured all his thinking. In 1538 he would personally interrogate John Lambert about the eucharist:

King: "Tell me plainly, whether thou saiest it is the body of Christ or no."

Lambert: "Then I deny it to be the body of Christ."

King: "Mark well, for now thou shalt be condemned even by Christ's own words: 'Hoc est corpus meum' ['This is my body']".[16]

When Henry's book was nearing publication, it was launched in a dramatic public ceremony on 12 May. Dressed in cloth of gold, Cardinal Wolsey, the lord chancellor and papal legate, led the archbishop of Canterbury, the papal nuncio [envoy], foreign ambassadors, thirty-six bishops and abbots in their mitres, several peers, and other dignitaries on horseback from Westminster, a mile and three-quarters through the city of London to St Paul's Cathedral. There he blessed the company, Archbishop Warham preached, and then the great and good went outside to sit on specially constructed staging. The papal bull condemning Luther and his writings was proclaimed. Bishop Fisher preached against him. Wolsey waved a manuscript of the *Assertio* to demonstrate royal approval and a bonfire was made of Luther's books. All this was watched by a crowd of spectators, but it is hard to tell what they made of it. Fisher's sermon concentrated on the authority of the church and its councils and warned against Luther as a typical heretic, carried away by his own opinion. He also explained two of Luther's principal ideas and the case against them, thus putting justification by faith alone and the doctrine of *sola scriptura* into English for the first time ever. Ironically, his hearers went away knowing more of Luther than when they came. Thomas More would make the same mistake in 1523 when his first book against Luther not only set out More's own argument but, alongside it, copious extracts from the book he was attacking. For those too far away to hear what Fisher said in the sermon, the text was soon made available in print.

The St Paul's spectacle gave English diplomacy the intended propaganda boost. In October the pope awarded Henry his title, and English monarchs have been "Defenders of the Faith" ever since. It also marked the point when the leaders of reform in England moved towards a more defensive position, effectively ending the hope of an uncontentious religious revival – twenty years before Christians in Europe gave up![17] Yet domestically the St Paul's event had no lasting impact. Wolsey apparently took the view that the Lutheran threat was external. Henry wrote to German princes to urge further action against Luther, and English writers launched Latin pamphlets against him. But at home, Wolsey was happy to accept advice and simply ban the import and translation of Luther's works for fear of "great trouble to the realm and Church of England" as in Germany.[18] As for heretical works in Latin, these could only be coped with by academics, so the papal bull was promulgated at Oxford and Cambridge, along with the requisite bonfires of books. But there was no follow-up. Wolsey was told that Oxford was "infected with Lutheranism and many books forbidden by Wolsey had obtained circulation there", but there is no record of any more being found.[19] Perhaps John Dornes's stock had already gone on the fire. It was, in fact, Cambridge which seems to have had the greater initial interest in religious developments abroad. There the White Horse tavern acquired the nickname "Little Germany" because a number of academics met there to discuss the latest ideas of the Continental reformers. We know very little about who attended. Some were ultimately convinced that Luther was in the right, but more may have come out of academic interest.

14

ENGLAND: THE FIRST DECADE

The establishment expected that the steps taken in 1521 would be enough to keep Continental heresy from spreading to England, but they were wrong. The evangelical pressure could not be halted. And one man above all was responsible: William Tyndale.

William Tyndale

Tyndale was born about 1494, probably in Gloucestershire. He studied at Oxford. In 1515 he graduated MA and was ordained priest. He then began to read for degrees in theology (a postgraduate study) and was horrified to discover that this involved no study of the Bible. Within months Erasmus's New Testament came on the market. This would change Thomas Bilney (as we have seen), and it probably turned Tyndale's mind to the challenge of producing an English translation. We next hear of him as a tutor back in Gloucester, perfecting his translation skills and getting into trouble by attacking clerical abuses and advocating Scripture for the people. Then, armed with specimen translations of Greek and Latin classics, Tyndale went to London to get permission and financial support. He pinned his hopes for a Bible in English on the bishop of London, Cuthbert Tunstall, who was a humanist who had helped Erasmus with his Greek New Testament. But Tunstall turned him away and Tyndale realized that if a bishop with that pedigree would not support him, he would get nowhere if he stayed in England. On the other hand, there were London merchants who approved of his ambition and with their support he went abroad in 1524, settling first at Cologne.

William Tyndale was an exceptional linguist and may have begun his work in London. Nevertheless it is remarkable that his New Testament translation was in press less than eighteen months after leaving England. What was planned was a good-looking quarto volume with a prologue, notes, and woodcuts, and a print run of 3,000. By then Tyndale had definitely thrown in his lot with the Lutheran camp. The prologue was an adapted and significantly expanded version of the preface to Luther's 1522 New Testament; two notes in three were also taken from Luther. The printing had possibly got as far as the end of Mark's Gospel when news of it reached John Dobneck, a prominent anti-Lutheran writer who used the same printer. He informed the Cologne authorities, and Tyndale and his helper William Roy, an erstwhile Franciscan friar, had to get out in a hurry and take refuge in the Rhineland city of Worms (which favoured reform). Fortunately they were able to take with them a quantity of the completed pages.[1] These were prepared for sale and sent into England, but by then Dobneck's news was known in London, and Cuthbert Tunstall was prepared. The bishop had recently reminded the book trade of the ban on importing Lutheran books and he does seem to have succeeded in confiscating much of the consignment rescued from Cologne. Only one partial copy survives. William Tyndale had, in fact, played directly into the bishop's hands. The dependence of the prologue and notes on Luther did certainly nail Tyndale's colours to the reformist mast and announce his determination to bring the truth of justification by faith to his countrymen. Yet the obvious Lutheranism confirmed belief in the link between the vernacular Bible and heresy. The threat of Lollardy had brought about the ban in 1409; blatant Lutheranism now blackened the printed text. The next printing (Worms 1525–26) would let the New Testament speak for itself – no prologue, no notes – but the damage had been done.

The Contraband Trade

The arrival of the 1525 Cologne printing changed the problem facing the English authorities and made it infinitely more difficult. Keeping out and – failing that – discovering and burning banned academic works in Latin was no longer adequate. A torrent of New Testaments threatened, which would make Scripture accessible to any person who could read English. A new policy focusing on the diocese of London was urgently agreed in January 1526 (with royal approval). It envisaged synchronized raids on booksellers and stationers, a public ceremony at St Paul's (as in 1521), and booksellers forced to give financial guarantees for good behaviour. In the event, Sir Thomas More's raid on London book importers was strikingly incompetent – a preliminary visit was made the day before the detailed search, so, predictably, only a handful of suspect books was discovered. A follow-up raid in Cambridge early in February found nothing either. Dr Robert Forman, the president of Queens' College, tipped off the White Horse group. As for arrests, it seemed that the only culprits to be paraded at the planned spectacular on Sunday 11 February would be four contrite German merchants. Then at almost the last minute, Wolsey learned that the previous Christmas Eve, Robert Barnes, the prior of the Augustinian friars at Cambridge and a leader of the White Horse group, had preached a fiery sermon attacking church abuses and particularly the bishops and the cardinal. The university had tried to hush this up, but Wolsey had Barnes arrested on Tuesday 6 February and brought to London. There he was interrogated by the cardinal and forced to recant his heresies. Barnes therefore became the star exhibit at the Sunday spectacular, marching round the bonfire along with the four German merchants, each carrying a faggot to show that he had only just escaped being burned himself. Bishop John Fisher again gave the sermon, repudiating Luther in greater detail than before.

Fisher's address was quickly put into print, including a promise by the bishop to meet and discuss with doubters in private. The remarkable offer appears to have been genuine, and for the next four years major heresy trials were avoided in favour of private persuasion, especially of university students, the group most vulnerable to Lutheran ideas. On the other hand, as an effective move to prevent Tyndale's translation spreading, this second St Paul's demonstration was irrelevant. After arriving at Worms, Tyndale had taken less than a year to oversee the printing of a replacement New Testament. This time the work was complete, octavo [pocket sized], and it was soon being smuggled into England, possibly even arriving before the St Paul's ceremony. We have no statistics for the number imported, but the trade was clearly significant. As well as Tyndale's output, a printer in Antwerp cashed in with a pirated edition of 3,000 sextodecimo [half-size] copies, which were even easier to hide. His brother paid for 1,500 of these and successfully imported 500. Not all, of course, got through. In November 1526 the English ambassador had alerted the authorities in Brussels and "many hundreds" of Testaments were reportedly burned in January at Antwerp and elsewhere.[2] Still they kept coming. In May 1527 the archbishop of Canterbury tried a different tack. He bought up as many copies as he could, only to discover that this simply financed production. Later in the year, a consignment of no fewer than 3,000 copies went to Scotland.

The details we have of the smuggling are sparse and come from suspects interrogated under oath and desperate not to incriminate themselves or others. However, it seems that the unbound sheets were concealed in bales of cloth or consignments of blank paper and moved down the Rhine and across the Channel along with innocent merchandise. Identified by secret marks, the illegal material was removed and sent for distribution. Judging by the arrests, ship captains were as aware of the trade as the merchants who financed it. The next stage, getting the consignments into circulation, involved many different people. Even when Robert Barnes was confined as an abjured heretic he was able to supply a copy to two Lollard customers. In the summer of 1526 Wolsey and the bishops threatened "further sharp correction and punishment" for the keepers and readers of "untrue translations".[3] In October, Bishop Tunstall claimed in a famous sermon that he had found 2,000 errors in Tyndale's work which was spreading "pestiferous and most pernicious poison" throughout his diocese.[4] An obligatory book burning followed, but nothing stopped the flow. The most detailed account we have of the process of distribution comes from arrests made the following year. The mastermind then appears to have been once again the president of Queens'. According to Thomas More, Forman purchased the consignments.[5] Sales at Cambridge were managed by a sympathetic stationer in the town. The London end was run from the church of All Hallows Honey Lane, where Forman was the parson. Sales there were handled by a local schoolmaster, while Thomas Garrard, Forman's curate at All Hallows, ran bundles into Oxford.

The Market

Who then was buying? More says that "young scholars of the universities" were Forman's specific target. Academics too. Several of the Cambridge White Horse group had been recruited to staff Wolsey's new college at Oxford (now Christ Church), and they bought. So did individual clerics, for themselves and for others. Thomas Garrard supplied the abbot of Reading with a number of volumes, no doubt for trading on. Foreign printers saw the opportunity and soon the contraband included works by Luther and the Continental reformers, and propaganda in English such as Tyndale's *Parable of the Wicked Mammon*, his working up of a piece by Luther which spelled out justification by faith. Further Tyndale Bible translations followed – parts of the Old Testament in 1529 and 1531, and in 1534 a revision of the New Testament (this time with a prologue). Other books in English came from a handful of reformers who had also fled to the Continent when the country was getting too hot for them. Contraband books sold well at the Inns of Court in London where practising lawyers lived and numerous young gentlemen trained. Sir Thomas More's brother-in-law at the Middle Temple became a reformer and died in prison. James Bainham, also of the Middle Temple, told his accusers:

> The truth of holy Scripture was never, these 800 years past, so plainly and expressly declared unto the people as it hath been these six years.... the New Testament now translated into English does preach and teach the word of God, and that before that time men did preach but only that folks should believe as the church did believe.[6]

He was burned at the stake in April 1532.

The Forman/Garrard operation seems particularly well oiled but there were others in the field too. Richard Bayfield was executed in December 1531 and interrogations show that he had been able to land three consignments in just over a year. The first was imported via Colchester, with part despatched from there and the remainder taken to London, some for sale and some to be sent further. His second consignment came up the Thames to St Katherine's by the Tower. Bayfield was arrested in possession of the third, which he had landed in Norfolk and was taking to his London bookbinder (who was also arrested). He was accused of handling at least fifteen banned authors, including titles from Switzerland and the Rhineland which rejected both the doctrine of transubstantiation and Luther's claim that Christ's body was miraculously present in the eucharist.

Thanks to the link between reformist literature and trade, "heretical" ideas spread easily from the Continent through ports and along commerce routes. The bishop of Norwich grumbled that it was "merchants and such that hath their abiding not far from the sea" who kept and read "these erroneous books in English".[7] Traders could readily place orders in Antwerp for New Testaments. Thomas Hitton (who was burned at Maidstone in 1530) had for several years worked as an agent abroad. Crews trading into German ports came back with first-hand accounts of Lutheran congregations. It is no surprise, therefore, that evidence of early reformist opinions can be found in a coastal arc from Hull to Sussex, with an emphasis on Suffolk, Essex, London, and Kent. From this a spoke ran up the Thames Valley with links into Coventry and into the Cotswolds. The latter was a cloth-producing area and it is possible that reform particularly attracted workers in industry. The connection with trade also accounts for evidence of reform along the Severn. That young people especially were drawn in is well attested – probably half of the population was under twenty – and particularly in London where incomers were in the majority, many free of family ties. But even a family near at hand did not guarantee immunity from reformed ideas. Thomas More bitterly attacked Luther and Tyndale only to find that at Lincoln's Inn his own son-in-law was dabbling with Luther's *Babylonish Captivity of the Church* and *The Freedom of a Christian*.

The Place of Lollardy

However great the interest in reform among certain groups, it is obvious that even with commercial links, New Testaments and other reformist literature together could only reach a minority of those who could read, let alone those who could not. In a number of places, books were backed up by reformist sermons, but only where a preacher would take a risk, and some were arrrested. Others sailed close to the wind and escaped or had powerful protectors or, like the followers of Jacques Lefèvre, promoted reform under the guise of orthodoxy. Even so, impact was again necessarily limited. The principal way heterodox ideas were disseminated must have been personal connection – family, village, alehouse, trade, and such like – and this brings into focus the possibility of a link with England's existing dissidents, the Lollards.

John Foxe's monumental work, *The Acts and Monuments of the Christian Church*, provides much of the evidence for these years, but Foxe had an agenda. He was anxious to present Protestantism as the true historic Christianity, not the new-fangled religion its opponents said it was. Lollardy exactly suited his purpose: "Lollards were Protestants before the name." Whether Foxe was right to posit an influential link has been hotly disputed among experts. There are clear parallels between some of the beliefs of Lollards and the beliefs of reformers. Indeed, it is often hard to tell from interrogation evidence which side of the line a suspect falls. The Colchester Lollard John Pykas spent 4s. on buying a copy of Tyndale's New Testament from London and travelled to Ipswich to hear Thomas Bilney.[8] An individual who seems to support Foxe's case is the London haberdasher John Tewkesbury. Perhaps as early as 1512 he belonged to a Lollard cell, but in 1529 was discovered affirming justification by faith and in possession of two of Tyndale's tracts and a copy he had made himself of Luther's *The Freedom of a Christian*. On that occasion he abjured, but re-offending brought him to the fire in 1531. Yet Tewkesbury is a rare example of a Lollard demonstrably turning Lutheran, and we know it was thanks to a specific preacher: Thomas Garrard.[9] A stronger case for accepting a significant link between Lollardy and later reform is emerging from recent research into the way dissent continues in particular groups of families over a couple of centuries. This is the case in the Chilterns – a reformist heartland, as we have seen.[10] There the same families provide suspect heretics in the early sixteenth century and Baptists and Quakers in the mid-seventeenth. Similar cases can be found in parts of Essex and Suffolk and in London.

What is harder to say is how widespread such continuity was between Lollardy and later do-it-yourself Protestantism. Lollardy was strongest in the countryside; reformist ideas principally took root in the towns. Lollards appear to have been largely self-taught; reformers are found among the formally educated. Furthermore, the extent of doctrinal overlap can be overstated. Most of those prosecuted in the 1520s were accused of the usual Lollard heresies, and showed no familiarity with justification by faith. On the key question of the eucharist, Lollards were opposed to the early reformers in England, most of whom, like Robert Barnes, accepted the doctrine of the real presence. A small but growing number of reformers (especially in London) did disagree with Barnes but they were influenced not by Lollardy but by Swiss and Rhineland understandings of the eucharist. Their standard bearer was John Frith. Initially a refugee from the 1527 Oxford purge, Frith joined Tyndale and published a highly effective demolition of the arguments for purgatory put up by Thomas More and John Fisher. More issued a warrant for his arrest and Frith was picked up in 1532 during a brief visit to England. While in the Tower he continued to write, including an influential treatise refuting transubstantiation which was published after he was sent to the stake in April 1533.

So how far did Lollardy pave the way for the Reformation? The debate is still open, but arguably that has been too black and white. There is much to be said for accepting that evangelical reform did reach a new clientele but was, in the right circumstances, also capable of melding with Lollardy. A Lollard might obviously welcome the New Testament in English, but why should he abandon his pattern of covert devotion? Would he not see reformers as converts to the light and would they not learn from him? In 1530 Nicholas Field, a Londoner, met with ten men in Hughenden in Buckinghamshire. He "expounded to them many things", attacking pilgrimages, prayers to the statues of saints, saints' days and fasting – typical Lollard targets. However, he also "read a parcel of Scripture in English to them" – undoubtedly Tyndale – and passed on his experiences of religion "beyond the sea in Germany". His assertion that the "sacrament of the altar" was "a typical signification of Christ's body" could suggest that he may even have visited the Rhineland or possibly Switzerland.[11] Lollard literature overlaps with reformed literature. Individuals own both. Traders sell the old alongside the new. Tyndale himself put probably two Lollard texts into print after modernizing the English. If it is right to see Lollardy and reform in a symbiotic relationship, the contribution of earlier Lollardy to the English Reformation was preparative. This is clear in places of high Lollard infection such as Colchester, where it helped to create the town's "less traditional religious culture".[12] Elsewhere, although most people can have known of Lollardy by name only, even that would suggest that there was an alternative to the religion they had been brought up in. The vast majority of the country might be orthodox, but England was already multi-faith. The reformed message came in to expand that alternative.

Persecution

As is evident from six burnings in two years (Hitton, Bilney, Bayfield, Tewkesbury, and Baynham, plus an Exeter schoolmaster, Thomas Benet), the policy of quietly reasoning with alleged heretics did not long survive the fall from office of Cardinal Wolsey in October 1529. His successor was Sir Thomas More. Since assisting the king with the *Assertio Septem Sacramentorum*, More had increasingly been put in the role of public apologist for traditional religion, but as he rose in importance politically, so he had been able also to take active measures against heretics. Now lord chancellor, he had his chance to purge England thoroughly. He wrote to Erasmus: "I find that breed of men absolutely loathsome, so much so that, unless they regain their senses, I want to be as hateful to them as anyone can possibly be."[13] Allied with a new bishop of London who was equally persecution-minded, More made London booksellers his immediate target. Four were publicly humiliated for selling Tyndale and other heretical titles, forced to burn their books and put in the pillory. Prominent Londoners accused of sympathizing were imprisoned. Most of those interrogated either abjured or lied to protect confederates, a tactic which only confirmed Sir Thomas in the belief that reformers were moral lepers. As for the stubborn who refused to yield and went to execution, "after the fire of Smithfield, hell doth receive them where the wretches burn forever".[14] More could not understand that men he disagreed with could stand by their consciences and see dying as a witness to the gospel. Of the actual executions, More was involved in the preliminaries to three and in the case of Bilney he published what can only be called a cover-up (as he did for the Hunne case retrospectively). Frith died after More had resigned as chancellor in May 1532, but since Sir Thomas had arrested him, that probably counted as another of his successes. If so it was the last in these early years of the English Reformation. Politics was taking over.

15

HENRY VIII AND THE REFORMATION

With Henry VIII personally attacking Luther in 1521 and giving support to the efforts to keep England free of Continental heresy, nothing can have seemed less likely than a reformation in England made by royal initiative. In Spain, France, the Low Countries, and elsewhere, the state came down on the side of tradition and threw its lot in with the Council of Trent. In England, the state attempted to exploit religious innovation and in large measure succeeded.

The King's "Great Matter"

The seeds of a royal involvement in religious change had been sown in England long before Luther's *Theses* set Germany alight. Henry's elder brother Arthur had died in 1502, five months after marrying the Spanish princess Katherine of Aragon. In 1509, following a great deal of diplomatic manoeuvring, Henry VIII married the widow. The church had very strict laws to prevent intermarriage, so before the wedding could go ahead, the pope (Julius II) had to give special permission ["dispensation"] for the king to marry his sister-in-law. Sadly, Katherine then had a series of miscarriages, stillbirths, and neonatal deaths, and only a daughter, Mary, survived to maturity. Without a son, Henry – and his subjects – faced a great danger. The English expected to be governed by a king: no woman had ever ruled the country. What is more, if Mary were to be the heir to the throne she would need a husband of equivalent status, which meant a foreign prince. Property in a marriage went to the husband, so England faced the risk of becoming the overseas colony of a European state. Katherine was nearly six years older than her husband and by the early 1520s she was past having children. The need for Henry to marry again and have a son became imperative.

Popes were generally sympathetic to important figures with family problems. The church did not permit divorce, but there were complex legal grounds on which a marriage might be declared null and void. Henry's conscience, however, did not allow him to look for a legal loophole. He knew he was a devout Christian, so why had God not listened to his prayers for a son? In the Old Testament Henry found – or was shown – the answer. The book of Leviticus chapter 20, verse 21 says: "If a man takes his brother's wife, it is impurity… they shall be childless." Julius II had given approval for Henry and Katherine to marry, but a pope could only dispense church law. This verse of Leviticus was God's law. So Julius II had had no power to approve Henry's marriage to his brother's widow. Henry had not realized it at the time, but his union with Katherine had been void from the start. The lack of a son confirmed it: "they shall be childless". On that ground, in 1527 Henry asked Pope Clement VII to annul the marriage. To his surprise, the pope would not help. Clement's reaction is, nonetheless, understandable. Charles V, the emperor who had confronted Luther, was the political power in Italy and the pope had to get along with him. But Charles was Katherine of Aragon's nephew and fiercely proud of his family. Clement was also inclined to Katherine's view that Henry was being silly and would eventually come to his senses. In any case, Henry was asking the papacy to repudiate what had been settled law for two decades. The evidence also was disputed – Katherine insisted that it was the marriage with Arthur which was void because it had never been consummated. Henry's biblical argument was suspect too. Did "childless" really mean "son-less"? And did not another Bible passage – Deuteronomy 25:5 – lay down that "when brothers reside together, and one of them dies and has no son… the husband's brother shall… take her in marriage"? Surely what the Leviticus text applied to was not remarriage but adultery. Despite the obstacles, Henry went ahead on what became known as his "Great Matter". At first he pressed the lawsuit. Then he commissioned a Europe-wide search for precedents to prove that Julius II had acted *ultra vires*, while at the same time making threats against the papacy and bullying the English church. Eventually in 1533, frustrated by what he saw as six years of papal intransigence, Henry took unilateral action. He defiantly remarried, had the English church declare his union with Katherine null and void, and legislation was passed to break all ties between England and the papacy.[1]

The radical nature of that action is hard to exaggerate. Henry VIII shared the sixteenth century's deep reverence for legalities, and when he first approached the pope in 1527, he had no doubt that Clement alone had the power to annul his marriage. His subjects had thought the same. But as part of the search for precedents, a team of scholars in England (mostly clerics) had been set to trawl through "sundry old authentic histories and chronicles".[2] Research into these "legends" (as we would now call them) came up with the remarkable and radical conclusion that originally the church had been subject to the king, and that his authority had subsequently been usurped by the pope. Henry, not the pope, had all the time been head of the church in England. This discovery was reported to Henry in 1530, but many further months elapsed before he was willing to act on it. In the first place, there were practical political problems – how could the king proceed to reclaim his powers? Only the arrival of a brilliant politician, Thomas Cromwell, broke the negative hold on royal policy of Thomas More and other conservative politicians and churchmen. Cromwell engineered a coup which forced the church to accept that Henry was head of the Church of England – known as "the Supplication against the Ordinaries". More resigned as chancellor, and legislation to end the pope's power could follow. The second obstacle to the radical solution – and much the more important of the two – was the fetters round Henry's mind. All his life he had revered the pope as the head of Christendom. He had defended him against Luther. Could he really throw off a lifetime's convictions and go it alone? To bolster his nerves someone much more intimate than Cromwell was needed, and that person was the woman he wanted to marry, Anne Boleyn.[3]

The Head of the Church in Action

What has all this to do with the reformation of belief? "Not much," the older histories will say. Henry VIII continued believing what he had always believed – all the royal supremacy amounted to was "catholicism without the pope". It is indeed correct that Henry continued to believe in transubstantiation and refused to believe in justification by faith alone, but that only demonstrates that achieving the royal supremacy made him neither a sacramentarian nor a Lutheran. What it did do was effectively make Henry the pope in England, and progressively thereafter he presided over drastic changes in the country's religion. This is most evident in the steady undermining of that central concern of the pre-Reformation church: purgatory and masses for the dead. Given the close link between the pope and indulgences, the split with Rome had of itself brought them into question, but thereafter the doctrine was specifically and repeatedly talked down. Henry also used his power as "Supreme Head of the Church in England" to determine doctrine on three occasions: in *The Ten Articles* (1536), The statute of Six Articles (1539) and finally, in 1543, *A Necessary Doctrine and Erudition for Any Christian Man*, otherwise known as *The King's Book*. This set out

> *the principal articles of our religion as whereby all men may uniformly*
> *be led and taught the true understanding of that which is necessary for*
> *every Christian man to know.*[4]

None of these formulae survived Henry for long, but his enduring legacy was approving the publication of the Bible in English. Tyndale's work of translation had been ended abruptly when he was lured by a trick from his safe house in Antwerp. In October 1536 he was strangled and his body burned, but he died with a great shout: "Lord, open the king of England's eyes."[5] Two years later every parish in England and Wales was ordered to obtain an English Bible "of the largest volume" (i.e. for public reading). This was carefully not linked to Tyndale since the king hated him for opposing the divorce, but the approved text – *The Matthew Bible* – included all Tyndale's work, with the missing Old Testament books supplied from Matthew Coverdale's 1535 Bible (which was not Hebrew based). In 1539 a large folio edition – the *Great Bible* – was published, with a frontispiece showing Henry distributing "the Word of God" to both clergy and laity.

Royal Motives

It is easy to see why Henry VIII broke with Rome when Clement VII refused to annul his marriage to Katherine, but that does not explain how he came to exploit his "headship" as he did. Of course removing the pope meant that a local management for the church had to be set up and Henry took that God-given responsibility seriously. Yet apart from the need to run the church machine, why did he not maintain "catholicism without the pope" until it suited him to end the schism and restore normal relations with Rome? There are two answers to this. In the first place, Henry was dissatisfied with the church. There were political grievances. Since at least the time of the Hunne affair, he had been hypersensitive about the church invading his royal space. He was also convinced that much of the monastic wealth had been filched from the crown. In the second place, he also had issues over doctrine and organization. He had sympathized with Erasmian criticisms of the church and been in favour of a future "safe" translation of the Bible into English, and he seems to have had little time for pilgrimages, relics, and shrines. The royal supremacy put him in a position to reform the English church as he himself thought fit, and that Henry proceeded to do. Over the years, the king's ideas of what needed to be done continued to develop, with the result that through the rest of his reign reform was both ongoing and variable.

The second factor in Henry's reforming is that to a significant degree he depended on people around him. This is not to say that he was a puppet. He was no fool, he had his own convictions and prejudices, his foot was always poised over the brake in case change threatened order and stability, his was ever the final voice. Yet despite this, he also looked to others for ideas, information, and implementation. In the trauma of his "Great Matter", traditionalists such as Bishop Fisher had backed Katherine publicly, as Thomas More had secretly; William Warham, the archbishop of Canterbury, and many of the leading clerics had resisted Henry's claim to be supreme head. This meant that the king was left to listen to evangelicals who wanted to see the church reformed. In particular, three people: Anne Boleyn, Thomas Cromwell, and Thomas Cranmer.

16

EVANGELICAL
INFLUENCES

Anne Boleyn

Anne Boleyn, according to a hostile observer, had intelligence, spirit, and courage, but the secret of her influence is that she and Henry VIII were in love. A king was expected to marry a foreign princess in order to support foreign policy; for his emotional needs there were mistresses. Henry broke that rule. Anne was captivating, elegant, and sophisticated and, for only the second time in 500 years, an English king courted an Englishwoman because he wanted to marry her.[1] In the summer of 1527 Anne agreed, provided Henry's first marriage had been annulled, and despite the strain of the ensuing six-year wait, the two had an almost modern companionate relationship, which lasted to within days of her arrest in May 1536.

Anne Boleyn came from an aristocratic family deep in royal service. Her diplomat father sent her in her early teens to be "finished" abroad, mostly in the court of Queen Claude, the wife of Francis I of France. This was a huge career opportunity because the French court was one of the most prestigious in Europe. Henry VIII tried to compete, but the English court was not in the same league. With Claude, Anne trained to be the perfect royal attendant, but Claude's court was also alive with the evangelical reform associated with Jacques Lefèvre d'Étaples and with the king's sister Margaret of Angoulême.[2] Anne embraced this reformist spirit for herself, possibly even having a conversion experience. Her faith was

Bible-centred. She made a special study of the Epistles of St Paul and was familiar with the doctrine of justification by faith. That France inspired this is beyond question. Anne used Lefèvre's French translation of the Bible. She had evangelical books brought over from France. Her brother George was like-minded and the gifts he gave Anne included a presentation translation of Lefèvre's *Epistles and Gospels for the Fifty-Two Sundays of the Year*.[3] Anne's relationship with Henry emboldened other evangelicals at court such as John Dudley (the future duke of Northumberland) and William Butts, the king's physician, who brought promising Cambridge clergy to her attention.

Anne was in direct touch with reformers across the Channel and offered England as a refuge in the persecution which followed the "Affair of the Placards".[4] Her commitment to the Bible also made her sympathetic to those attempting to make an English translation available. After the Honey Lane smuggling ring was exposed she wrote in support of Dr Robert Forman.[5] Later she intervened on behalf of Richard Herman, a supplier of New Testaments to the smugglers. Wolsey had had him expelled from "the house of the English merchants" at Antwerp, but in 1534 Anne pressed for "this good and honest merchant" to be reinstated because his offence was

nothing else, as he affirms, but only that he did, both with his goods and policy, to his great hurt and hindrance in this world help to the setting forth of the New Testament in English.[6]

Anne's own Tyndale New Testament survives. It is a presentation copy of the 1534 text, printed on vellum with full-colour woodcuts and gilt edges, and is now in the British Library.

Anne Boleyn used her position and influence to advance the careers of evangelically minded clergy. Indeed, many of the key evangelical leaders in post at the end of the reign owed something to Anne. So did up-and-coming clergy, notably Matthew Parker, who would become her daughter Elizabeth's first archbishop of Canterbury. Inevitably Anne was blamed for the break with Rome. She was also blamed for the deaths of traditionalists who opposed the king's new title, including John Fisher and Thomas More. Yet despite the hatred and vilification, Anne Boleyn was not a heretic; she was an evangelical. Her books taught her justification by faith but without the implication that moral living was irrelevant, which was what always alienated Henry VIII: "Faith which gives the true fear of God, is it that doth prepare us to keep the commandments well."[7] Nevertheless, Anne and what she represented was dangerous. No sign of concern about the role of the church, or the priest or the church's penitential machinery. No rejection of tradition, but tradition taken for granted and bypassed in search of the personal Jesus. And the focus of that Jesus was the eucharist. On transubstantiation, which Henry VIII increasingly saw as the test of sound belief, Anne was commitedly orthodox. Her last hours were spent praying before the sacrament.

Thomas Cromwell

As queen, Anne Boleyn was in a unique position, but she was not the only evangelical in government circles. The layman who dominated the 1530s was Thomas Cromwell. In 1529 he seems to have been conventionally religious, although highly critical of the clergy, but soon after he was clearly in the evangelical camp. As well as his brilliant handling of the Supplication against the Ordinaries and the legislation which followed, Cromwell directed a highly effective campaign to defend the king's new position.[8] He also took the first steps to associate evangelical reform with social and economic reform. Few of his schemes "for the common weal" reached fruition, but the work put in and the links with younger reformers, particularly at Cambridge, gave the evangelical gospel a social dimension. In January 1535 Henry appointed Cromwell as his vice-gerent [delegate] to exercise the supreme headship. The king's priorities meant that the first task was to recover for the crown what the king saw as the unjustified wealth of the church. Some 200 small monasteries were closed and their assets taken into royal hands.[9] That was openly opposed by Queen Anne, who agitated for the wealth to be invested in education, but Cromwell saved himself by a pre-emptive strike against her. It was a dirty business, but thanks to skilful manoeuvring he prevented the disgrace and death of such a powerful supporter from derailing the evangelical cause as traditionalists had hoped.

Doctrinal Change

The summer of 1536 saw fierce debates over Henry VIII's first doctrinal statement. The resulting *Ten Articles* was a compromise, but favouring reform. Only three sacraments (baptism, the eucharist, and penance) were mentioned (instead of the traditional seven) and justification by faith alone was affirmed. Giving honour to saints was approved, but

> *as for censing them and kneeling and offering unto them with other like worshippings, although the same hath entered [been motivated] by devotion and fallen [in]to custom, yet the people ought to be diligently taught that they in no wise do it.*

Praying to a saint was also permissible, but

> *so that it be done without any vain superstition, as to think that any saint is more merciful or will hear us sooner than Christ, or that any saint doth serve for one thing more than another, or is patron of the same.*[10]

Particularly significant was the treatment of purgatory in the final article. Purgatory was a red rag to a bull to evangelicals, implying, as it did, that to be saved men and women had to accumulate merit. Article 10 endorsed praying for the dead, but only as a matter of charity and long custom. It referred to "abuses under the name of purgatory" and declared that "the place where they [the dead] be, the name thereof, and kind of pains there, be to us uncertain by scripture, therefore this with all other things we remit to Almighty God... to whom is known their estate and condition".[11] To enforce the Articles Cromwell issued "injunctions" [orders] of a clearly reformist kind which also implemented a recent statute limiting saints' days.[12]

January 1537 saw Cromwell summon what was in effect the first national synod of the Church of England. This led to the next doctrinal formulary, *The Institution of a Christian Man*. Again a compromise, it restored the missing sacraments but with the gloss that they were of lesser authority. The real presence was affirmed without mentioning transubstantiation or the sacrifice of the mass. Published in the autumn, it was popularly known as *The Bishops' Book* because Henry had not had time to scrutinize it. By then moves were also in hand to suppress the greater monasteries. Their shrines and relics were pillaged, and famed images were publicly dishonoured and burned. In 1538 Cromwell took decisive action on an English Bible. Parishes were told that at mass, the Gospel and the Epistle must be read or "declared" from the pulpit in English. Cromwell secured Henry's support, and his second set of injunctions (October 1538) instructed parishes to provide English Bibles and "every person" to be encouraged "to read the same".[13] He invested £400 of his own money in a quality edition ordered from a top Paris press. The result was the *Great Bible*, with its famous title page, and a text which was only replaced in 1568.[14]

A Change of Climate

The publication of the *Great Bible* would be hugely significant in the longer term, but it actually marks the end of almost a decade of gradual but relatively confident evangelical advance. Thereafter progress became patchy and uncertain. When Henry read *The Bishops' Book* he put numerous amendments on the table. His redraft on purgatory effectively took the evangelical position, dropping the term itself and dismissing the purgation of the dead as "undiscussed and undetermined in the canon of the Bible".[15] Most amendments were, however, conservative, particularly on the role of good works in salvation. The king, moreover, was becoming concerned about the impact of change. Since the ending of Thomas More's campaign against heresy, ecclesiastical discipline had begun to break down, particularly in London. Justification by faith alone was openly preached. There were instances of iconoclasm, services in the vernacular, laymen preaching, clergy taking wives, and evidence of a lunatic fringe. None of this was extensive, but rumour flourished and the king began to fear that reform was opening the door to disorder. The events in Münster were fresh in the mind and a lesson of what followed when anabaptism and sacramentarian belief were allowed to take hold.[16]

In March 1535 a royal proclamation gave anabaptists and sacramentaries twelve days to leave the country, on pain of death. In June, some two dozen Flemings were convicted of heresy – more than half went to the stake and the rest were exiled. In the autumn of 1538 Henry learned that documents captured in Saxony suggested significant anabaptist progress in England. Cromwell immediately set up a heresy commission and the king issued a proclamation in November which ordered the arrest of known "Anabaptists and Sacramentaries", gave the rest ten days to leave the country, restricted discussion of the sacrament to the universities, and introduced greater censorship. The proclamation also sought to rein in unofficial reforming initiatives. Ceremonies or sacramentals "not yet abrogated by the king's highness's authority" were to continue in use as "signs to put us in remembrance of things of higher perfection" but with the warning "not to repose any trust of salvation in them".[17] Priests who had married were to be expelled from the church. And to publicize his commitment to transubstantiation, Henry (as we have seen) took the lead in the show trial of the sacramentary John Lambert.[18] Increasingly Cromwell found himself threatened by traditionalist bishops and nobles who found ammunition in the growth of sacramentarian belief in Calais, England's foreign base. Cromwell believed in the real presence, as did almost all England's senior evangelicals, but increasingly they faced the classic problem of the moderate reformer: how to keep extremist supporters in check.

When parliament met in April the king had the campaign against sacramentaries put on the statute book. The resulting *Act Abolishing Diversity in Opinions* provided draconian penalties for denying the miracle of the real presence, the efficacy of communion in one kind, the need for priestly celibacy, the binding nature of vows of chastity, the legitimacy of private masses, and the expediency and necessity of confession to a priest. In later Protestant legend, the so-called Six Articles became the notorious "whip with six strings", but the act was no traditionalist charter.[19] The clauses on celibacy, vows, and private masses were certainly a setback for reform and the article declaring that Christ's body was "present really" in the sacrament of the altar was less nuanced than Cranmer would have had it, but there was no use of the word "transubstantiation".[20] The act made no mention of purgatory, prayer to the saints and images, and said nothing on the key issue of justification by faith. Traditionalist bishops had wanted to say that confession was "necessary by the law of God" but that was blocked by Henry himself. Indeed it seems that the act was in part drafted to make England appear conservative in face of a Europe muttering about the possibility of a papally inspired invasion.

No persecution followed. Henry continued enthusiastic about the *Great Bible* – he instructed Cranmer to write a preface for the second impression and put Cromwell in charge of all the production of English Bibles for the next five years. Many of the Calais prisoners were released and when as the year ended the king agreed to marry a German noblewoman hostile to Charles V, everything seemed to be set fair. Yet when Anne, the sister of the duke of Cleves, arrived in January 1540 Henry took an instant dislike to her. He could not avoid going through with the marriage, but Cromwell somewhat unfairly got the blame. His enemies in Calais and London renewed their efforts, and religious controversy in London led to the arrest of prominent reformist preachers. Finally in June the traditionalists convinced Henry that Cromwell himself was a sacramentary. He was arrested, condemned as a traitor and a heretic, and executed on 28 July 1540. Two days later Robert Barnes and two other reformers were burned as heretics and three traditionalists executed as traitors.

Thomas Cranmer

The arrest of Thomas Cromwell pitched Thomas Cranmer into the role of the country's leading evangelical. A Cambridge academic and biblical humanist, he had become an evangelical after working for the king on the validity of papal claims and experiencing reform during an embassy to Germany in 1532 (where he broke his vows of celibacy and married the niece of a Lutheran pastor). On the death of the traditionalist Archbishop Warham, Cranmer had, out of the blue, been appointed to succeed at Canterbury. His first substantial act was to declare Henry's marriage with Katherine null and void. Ten days later, on 1 June, he crowned Anne Boleyn queen. Thanks to that loyal service Cranmer never lost Henry VIII's ultimate confidence, but during the 1530s he had been less influential than Cromwell. He threw his weight behind reform and reformers, but once Cromwell had begun work as vice-gerent, initiative passed out of the archbishop's hands. Now, deprived of both Anne and Cromwell, he was totally exposed.

Following Cromwell's execution and the burning of Barnes and his two colleagues, hundreds of Londoners were arrested. Was the Six Articles legislation to be implemented at last? No, Henry had decided that enough was enough. The accused Londoners were released and although the act remained on the statute book for a further six years, only some thirty people would suffer under it, plus three more who died in prison. Even so, Cranmer was now the prime target of traditionalists determined to roll back what they saw as the gains heresy had made under Cromwell. Henry, too, was becoming more difficult. Perhaps without Cromwell he was less willing to risk change. Perhaps, too, he was becoming more conservative with age. Nevertheless there were still reformist successes. In May 1541 a proclamation threatened to fine parishes which failed to purchase a Bible. In July further holy days were pruned and in September Henry VIII ordered the two archbishops to destroy every surviving "shrine, covering of shrine, table, monument of miracles or other pilgrimages".[21] In fact the most famous shrine in the country – of St Thomas Becket at Canterbury – had been destroyed all of three years earlier. Europe had gasped with horror, but Henry had been hugely delighted at having Henry II's "turbulent priest" ground into the dust.

Survival

Despite these gains, conservative resistance was building up within the church. Attacks on Cranmer's people had begun in December 1540 and by 1542 there were the first signs of an impending assault on Cranmer himself. The epicentre was Canterbury Cathedral, a hotbed of conservatives strongly supported by prominent lay figures in Kent. In April 1543 secret articles accusing the archbishop of heresy were submitted to the privy council and then to the king. The crisis atmosphere was fed by heresy accusations levelled at a number of men close to the royal court (three of whom were burned under the Six Articles act). Prominent individuals were prosecuted for eating meat during Lent and eight printers gaoled for producing unlawful books.

Cranmer, meanwhile, was facing the uncongenial task of accommodating Henry's criticisms of *The Bishops' Book*. On the king's insistence, "justification by faith alone" was dropped from the replacement *King's Book*; good works arising from faith were described as "meritorious towards the attaining of everlasting life".[22] A second major defeat was over Henry's determination to permit images in churches, provided they were not abused. Even so, there were some crumbs of comfort for reformers.

The book lists the seven orthodox sacraments and is wholly traditional on the mass and baptism, but again makes clear that only those two had been instituted by Christ. Purgatory continued being denigrated. In future the term itself was not to be used because of papal abuses, "and no more dispute or reason thereof".

> *Here is specially to be noted that it is not in the power of any man to limit and dispense how much, and in what space of time, or to what person particularly the said masses, exequies and suffrages do profit and prevail; therefore charity requires that whosoever causes any such… to be done should yet (though their intent be more for one than for another) cause them also to be done for the universal congregation of Christian people, quick [alive] and dead; for that power and knowledge… pertains only unto God, which alone knows the measures and times of his own judgement and mercies.*[23]

Effectively, praying for the departed was declared a lottery.

The King's Book was published on 29 May 1543. A fortnight earlier, Henry had assented to a statute markedly objectionable to evangelicals. *The Act for the Advancement of True Religion* asserted that while "the highest and most honest sort of men" profited from reading the Bible, "the lower sort" were being misled, so in future no one below the rank of yeoman was to read the Bible – even privately – and women only if of gentle or noble birth.[24] The act, too, had some effect. A Cotswold man wrote in a volume of English history: "I bought this book when the Testament was abrogated that shepherds might not read it. I pray God amend that blindness."[25] And all the while the secret accusations against Cranmer festered in the king's hands.

The summer of 1543 was, however, the lowest point for evangelicals. By September Henry's sense of obligation reasserted itself. As Cromwell had said to Cranmer, "You were born in a happy hour… for do or say what you will, the king will always well take it at your hand."[26] In a typically flamboyant gesture, Henry arrived by river at Cranmer's palace at Lambeth, summoned the archbishop and said, "Now I know who is the greatest heretic in Kent." He thereupon handed over the case papers and told Cranmer to investigate the accusations himself![27] In November, one final attempt saw conservative counsellors persuade Henry to have Cranmer examined, only for the king to change his mind within hours and brief Cranmer, so that the next day the council was left with egg on its face. What is not known is how much the return to favour owed to influence exerted by Katherine Parr, the evangelically minded widow Henry had taken as his sixth wife in July. But from then on, as with Anne Boleyn, the individual most personal with the king was now a reformer.

With Cranmer secure, cautious evangelical advance could begin again. In January 1544 parliament significantly weakened the Six Articles act by making accusations time-limited and transferring prosecutions from the church to a lay jury. In May, Cranmer's first vernacular church service was published and in June Henry ordered it to be used in every parish "in our native English tongue".[28] When at the end of September the king returned from invading France, he and his archbishop were soon discussing a possible further revision of the service books. In May 1545 came the final doctrinal statement of the reign, the *King's Primer*, which supplied an official translation of church liturgies for children and adults with no knowledge of Latin, and included eighty pages of prayers from various sources, including some specially composed by Cranmer. The following January saw the archbishop drafting, at Henry's request, regulations to suppress various traditional practices such as creeping to the cross on Good Friday. But Bishop Stephen Gardiner, who was negotiating for an alliance with Charles V, sent a warning from Brussels that his efforts would be hampered by further religious changes, whereupon Henry instructed Cranmer to "take patience herein and forbear, until we espy a more apt and convenient time for the purpose".[29] Despite this, the same month saw a vital evangelical victory when (with the queen's help) Henry was persuaded not to strip the universities of their assets and instead to set up Christ Church and Trinity as the wealthiest colleges at Oxford and Cambridge.

It is, however, important when listing evangelical advances after 1543 to remember the qualification "cautious". Increasingly a lack of support is detectable among some senior clerics who earlier had genuinely looked for religious revival. A handful had become bishops – including Edmund Bonner – but had then found themselves faced with the need to restrain enthusiastic reformers within royal guidelines. Bonner even had to threaten to remove the Bibles from St Paul's if they continued to cause disturbances. Men like Bonner were also worried that too much change was happening too fast. An even more serious concern was the continued growth of sacramentarian heresy. Of the lay folk arrested in London in the aborted heresy purge of 1540, 20 per cent were accused of offences against the mass.

It was against that background that the final religious crisis of Henry VIII's reign developed in April 1546. His increasing ill health turned thoughts to the eight-year-old Prince of Wales and the opportunities which would arise in a new reign, provided one picked the right side. The traditionalists led by Stephen Gardiner realized the importance of striking soon. Peace with France was in the offing, and would bring back to England the king's favourite soldiers, Edward Seymour, earl of Hertford and the prince's uncle, and John Dudley, Viscount Lisle, both cautious reformers. The conservatives secured a proclamation against erroneous books and a welcome for the first papal envoy to London since the break with Rome. Incautious reformist preaching gave them an opening. Arrests followed of both clerics and laity, and a number of sacramentaries went to the stake. They included Anne Askew, an outspoken reformist gentlewoman who, despite exceptionally severe (and illegal) torture, refused to incriminate the real targets, the ladies of the queen's household. Gardiner did persuade the king that the queen herself should be investigated for heresy, but she was warned by supporters at court and was able to make her peace with Henry. That was the final throw of the traditionalists. The papal envoy was left in limbo and when peace with France was celebrated in August, Henry and Cranmer discussed with the French envoys the possibility of undertaking further reform jointly with Francis I, possibly even a revised mass in the vernacular and an end to clerical celibacy. The archbishop was rarely at court after that – possibly working on such a liturgy – so he missed (or avoided) the political manoeuvres which led to Gardiner's disgrace and put reform-minded courtiers and politicians, led by the earl of Hertford, in a position to govern in the forthcoming minority. But when the dying king asked for Cranmer he came at once and held Henry's hand until he died.

17

BARE RUINED CHOIRS

The biggest material change effected by Henry VIII's reformation was the destruction of England's religious houses. The end of monasticism as an institution had less of an impact than might be expected. It did bring an end to pilgrimages and intercessory prayers and so struck another blow at purgatory, but the regular clergy were not the spiritual driving force they had been in earlier centuries (though there were signs of change to come). On the other hand, the physical destruction did, as we shall see, call for mental adjustments.[1] The dissolution of the monasteries also ripped out an integral part of the society and economy of the country. Monasteries held half of the church's assets, they were deeply rooted in local communities and entrenched nationally – more abbots and priors than bishops sat in the House of Lords, and together they gave it a clerical majority. The revolution in landownership which would eventually result from the dissolution is "second only to that which followed the Norman Conquest".[2] Nearly six centuries later, the physical scars are evident nationwide.

The dissolution is explained by Henry's unshakable conviction that the church had become as wealthy as it was at the crown's expense, and his determination to have something done about it. However, it is unlikely that he began with the intention of wiping monasticism off the map. The 1536 legislation which earmarked the smaller, less viable monasteries for closure included a provision for the king to spare any houses he wished, and perhaps half of those scheduled were reprieved.[3] The monks from the dissolved houses were either given pensions or, like the nuns, were moved to larger houses. Stories of roaming hordes of homeless religious are a myth. So too tales of the hundreds of abbey servants thrown out of work – the need for farm labourers did not stop when estates passed to the crown. In fact, demolishing the buildings and selling off the stone and the moveables of a nearby monastery could provide a short-term boost to the local economy. There was also a good deal of looting, often by the local poor, while the nobility and gentry competed fiercely to lease or buy monastic property. Remarkably, only two or possibly three cases are known where the local community set out to prevent a house being dissolved.

Armed Protest

There is, however, a possible exception to this general picture of a change easily absorbed. On 2 October 1536 unrest broke out in parts of Lincolnshire which spread a week later to engulf the whole of England north of the Humber. These were areas where the smaller monasteries may have been particularly significant socially and economically. Lincolnshire had thirty-seven small abbeys and lost thirty-four, whereas Suffolk, a county with much the same area but twice the wealth, had only fourteen, of which it lost ten. Over the whole of the north, almost half of all the houses went down. Thus in 1536 we have the dissolution of monasteries and in 1536 a massive popular protest. Were they cause and effect? Tempting though that may seem, the "Lincolnshire Rising" and "The Pilgrimage of Grace", as they are known, are far too complex for that simple explanation. The region was very diverse. The Lincolnshire episode was earlier and distinct. The Pilgrimage itself was an aggregation of perhaps nine risings, concurrent but with big local differences. What is more, with the Pilgrims in particular numbering possibly 30,000, we know little of what the rank and file felt, only the lists of grievances they endorsed. Those, however, were developed progressively over three months by the more articulate and informed leaders, who certainly added complaints of their own.

Scholars have argued and continue to argue about the risings. Three things, however, are clear. First, despite the significant involvement of many gentry and some nobles, the thrust came from the lower clergy, yeomen, and craftsmen, commoners, but people who counted for something in their communities. Second, despite the raising of local problems, the overriding consensus was that things were seriously wrong with "the commonwealth". Third, what glued the protest together was the conviction that a prime example of what was wrong was the crown's religious policy. The protesters marched behind banners from their churches and the badge of the northerners was the five wounds of Christ. In all, the Lincolnshire Rising and the Pilgrimage of Grace amounted to a massive northern demonstration of no confidence in Henry's policies, a protest which was focused on fear for the faith. "Protest" not "rebellion", for although some of the rank and file muttered about marching on London, the leadership had no wish to challenge the king in person. Henry would have had no hope of resisting an armed force of this size, but the policy which won the day was a "Pilgrimage of Grace"; an assembly to seek grace from the king for his suffering subjects, backed up by a show of muscle he could not ignore.

The risings began on Sunday 1 October 1536 in the parish church of Louth, a market town twenty-five miles north-east of the county town of Lincoln. As the congregation prepared to process behind its three silver crosses, Thomas Foster, a singing-man [chorister], called out, "Masters, step forth and let us follow the crosses this day: God knows whether we shall ever follow them again."[4] He was responding to a rumour that the crown was about to confiscate the plate and treasures of parish churches, just as it was doing with the lesser monasteries – perhaps even amalgamating parishes. By nightfall an armed posse of townsfolk had taken charge of the keys to the church treasury and set up a 24-hour guard. There were rumours too of more government exploitation on the way. Christenings, marriages, and burials were to be taxed, and also farm animals. After all, at that very moment, commissioners were busy levying a subsidy, a tax for war which was now being demanded in peacetime! The priests added concerns of their own, again with justification. On 20 September an enquiry had begun into their fitness for office, raising fears that the less educated would lose their benefices. What was more, the clergy were facing increasing tax demands which threatened to become penal. There was also the recently issued *The Ten Articles* and Cromwell's injunctions, which questioned parish religion and especially praying for the dead, a major item in the income of poor priests.

The Lincolnshire protesters were clear that the blame for all this lay on the king's low-born advisers such as Thomas Cromwell and on Cranmer and the other heretical bishops. Their litany of grievance was taken over and elaborated by the Pilgrims from Yorkshire and the rest of the north. They gave greater prominence to complaints about the dissolution of the monasteries and a number of the abbeys were restored, but that may have reflected the priority of certain leaders, not the rank and file. In any case the final protest again went beyond particular complaints to a full-blown condemnation of interference and misgovernment from London. The regime was avaricious, sacrilegious, and dominated by evil ministers. The nation's proper forum of king, lords, and commons in parliament had been ignored or manipulated and the complaints of the clergy in convocation treated as hot air. It is very striking that the Pilgrims assembled their own quasi-parliament of lords and commons at Pontefract alongside a meeting of the northern clergy, and one of their main demands was the rapid calling of a national parliament to sit at York.

The fate of the Pilgrims need not concern us. Suffice it to say that they were deceived by Henry VIII, who strung out discussions until he was able to launch his revenge. What is our concern is that Henry was able to do this only because the rest of the country did not join the Pilgrims. There were southerners, both aristocrats and commoners, who shared the concerns of the north. But despite this, conservative nobles not only rallied to the king but were able to recruit men to fight for him. Faced with a choice between loyalty to the church and loyalty to the crown, the south chose the king and was ready to repress by force men whose deep anxieties many shared. Thanks to that, Henry VIII was able to continue as head of the church without let or hindrance. And that, after all, was how he saw kingship. Anointed by God, he believed he had the responsibility to rule and unique wisdom to do so. He told the Lincolnshire protesters that they were "bound by all laws to obey and serve [your prince] with both your lives, lands and goods, and for no worldly cause to withstand [him]".[5] And to the great of the land he declared: "Surely we will not be bound of a necessity to be served with lords. But we will be served with such men what degree so ever as we shall appoint to the same."[6] Yet whatever his bluster, the reality was that Henry VIII could only determine religion as he did because the majority of his subjects did not care enough to stop him.

An End to Monasticism
Although the initial moves against the smaller religious houses had been driven by financial considerations, the Pilgrimage of Grace transformed

Henry VIII's attitude towards monasticism itself. From then on he was fixedly hostile to "monkery". *The King's Book* insisted on the importance of good works, but was quite specific that:

> *by good works we mean not the superstitious works of men's own invention, which be not commanded by God, nor approved by his word, in which kind of works many Christian men, and especially of them that were lately called religious, (as monks, friars, nuns, and such other,) have in times past put their great trust and confidence.*[7]

After some months of uncertainty, from the end of 1537, government began to put pressure on religious houses to surrender voluntarily, both those which had been reprieved in 1536 and the large abbeys which had then been described as houses where "thanks be to God, religion is right well kept and observed".[8] Waltham Abbey, the last to surrender, went down in April 1540. With no houses left to move to, the religious were pensioned off. Over time, many of the monks secured appointment to a parish living. Nuns came off badly – both financially and because they were not allowed to marry; at least one group continued to live communally. The four orders of friars were also suppressed along with the Order of St John of Jerusalem, while hospitals followed in 1545. All that was salvaged from the wreck were six abbeys which were refounded as cathedrals.

18

CHANGE IN THE PARISHES

The response of Lincolnshire and the north to religious reform was mass protest. That was not the case further south. There the number and the variety of the parishes make it particularly difficult to generalize about the way the changes of Henry VIII's reign played out. Identifying the elements in royal policy which did impinge on the grass roots is relatively simple. What is difficult is assessing how those changes were received and what they led to.

New Policies

Given the limited doctrinal knowledge the church expected of ordinary people, *The Ten Articles* and its sequels must have passed most by.[1] What they would have noticed were changes in the liturgies they were accustomed to. The earliest came in the spring of 1534 when the order came to omit the pope's name when bidding the bedes. Instead, the priest was to begin by naming Henry and Queen Anne, with the king being prayed for as "Our sovereign lord King Henry VIII, being immediately next under God the only and supreme head of this Catholic church of England".[2] The same order instructed the priest to preach "in the presence of his greatest audience" condemning papal power, emphasizing the rightness of the annulment of the marriage to Katherine, and telling the story of the pope's "ambition, vainglory and too much mundanity [worldliness]". The recommended ending was:

Wherefore, good people, I exhort you to stick to the truth and our prince
according to our bounden duties and despise these naughty doings of this
bishop of Rome, and charitably pray that he and all others, abusers of
Christ's word and works, may have grace to amend.[3]

At the same time, every Englishman was required to swear an oath
recognizing the right of the children of Henry's second marriage to succeed
to the crown, while the clergy had to take oaths repudiating papal authority.
Everything suggests that the huge effort of organization which this required
was surprisingly successful. The clergy were also ordered to erase the name
of the pope from service books and even theological treatises.

Cromwell's 1536 injunctions built on this by ordering parish clergy to
preach in defence of the royal supremacy every Sunday for an initial three
months and then twice a quarter. Sermons were to uphold the Ten Articles,
and explain carefully which were "necessary to be believed for salvation"
and which were simply for "the decent and politic order of the church".[4]
Priests were also to implement the recent *Act for the Abrogation of Certain*
Holydays. This ordered that, with half a dozen exceptions, no festivals
were in future to be observed if they fell during the four law terms or in
harvest time; that is, between 1 July and 29 September. England's retreat
from public holidays had begun. Another injunction required parents
and employers to teach their children and servants the Creed, the Ten
Commandments, and the Lord's Prayer "in their mother tongue".[5] Parish
priests were to monitor this and conduct recitations from the pulpit, along
with exhortations about the need for hard work and learning a trade.
Parsons were also to stop offerings being made to statues, discourage
pilgrimages, and instead urge that the money saved from both be given to
the poor. Finally, the wealthiest clerics were to fund one or more students
at a university, others who were comfortably off were to give 2½ per cent
of their yearly income to the poor of their parish, while all were liable to
contribute up to 20 per cent towards specified property repairs.

In 1538 the pace of change in the parish quickened. In January,
Cromwell led a campaign against statues and objects linked to cults,
and this encouraged some spontaneous acts of iconoclasm. During the
year came the instructions that at mass the Epistle and Gospel should
be "declared" from the pulpit in English. The prohibition on eating meat

during Lent was relaxed until further notice to permit the consumption of white meat in addition to fish. October brought the vice-gerent's second set of injunctions.[6] As well as providing an English Bible accessible in church for anyone to read, priests were to warn parishioners who had not learned the Creed and Lord's Prayer in English to do so within twelve months or risk being barred from the Easter communion. They were to preach, repudiating any previous teaching they had given on "pilgrimages, feigned relics or images or any such superstitions". Images which were the focus of worship were to be removed, and lights were only to be burned on the rood loft, the altar, and beside the Easter sepulchre. The proclamation which the king issued the next month marginally relaxed the prohibition to permit candles at Candlemas, but adhered to the teaching of the Ten Articles that "the laudible customs rites and ceremonies" of the church were only reminders "of the spiritual things they do signify".[7] Two months later this was reinforced by the instruction to priests to explain to the congregation, each time they performed such a ceremony, that it was only a symbol. It conveyed no apotropaic power – holy water was a reminder of baptism, lights at Candlemas pointed to "Christ the spiritual light", ashes on Ash Wednesday spoke of penance and mortality, etc., etc.

Cromwell's execution put an end to the post of vice-gerent, but in 1541 the parishes found the church calendar adjusted again, with three abrogated feasts restored and others downgraded. The same year saw the king ordering the destruction of all surviving shrines.[8] Even in the more conservative climate of 1542 and 1543, proclamations confirmed the continued relaxation of the food restrictions during Lent. February 1543 saw all parish clergy being ordered to read a chapter of the Bible each week to their congregations. In May 1544 came the English litany, an occasional processional act of penance which Cranmer took largely from the established Latin version after reducing to three the original fifty-eight invocations to saints.[9] A plainsong setting was published a month later, as well as the order to bring the litany into parish use.[10] The following year the role of the English litany was extended to Sundays and major festivals. Also in 1545 came the *King's Primer*, which every local "schoolmaster and bringer up of young beginners in learning" was to use exclusively.[11] Finally, from February 1546, any church with a chantry was visited by royal commissioners, preparatory to that endowment following the wealth of the monasteries into the king's pocket.

Measuring the Response

The obvious place to find information on parish reactions to these royal orders is the accounts kept by churchwardens during their year of office. Unfortunately these survive for only 2 per cent of parishes, overwhelmingly from southern England. What is more, all that an account tells us is what a parish did or did not spend money on. This can show how promptly or otherwise churchwardens responded to instructions from the crown, but little more. Such accounts as do survive suggest that government orders were generally obeyed (with varying degrees of alacrity), even in areas which might be expected to be reluctant. St George's Morebath, an otherwise traditionalist parish on the edge of Exmoor, bought a *Great Bible* promptly and also a New Testament in English and Latin.[12] However, other parishes only purchased a Great Bible when the fine of £2 a month was introduced in 1541. Not only was that severe, but half of it would go to anyone who grassed on the parish. At Morebath, a further copy of the *Great Bible* was purchased in 1542, this time with corners of brass and with a chain to prevent removal. Two years later the parish dutifully acquired a copy of the English litany.

Trying to go behind parish accounts to decide how parishioners themselves felt is full of problems. The records which do survive from local magistrates, bishops, and the crown provide many examples of religious grumbling and accusations. But a dossier of individual cases is no more than a hint of widespread feeling – that is, if such a feeling existed, given England's significant diversities. A disproportionate number of reported complaints were by or about the clergy. Some of that, no doubt, was because education made them aware of the issues, but the issues also threatened their professionalism. Turkeys cannot be expected to welcome Christmas. Where a priest is found speaking out, it does not follow that he carried his parishioners with him – or, indeed, that they understood his complaint. Moreover, in most cases we do not know the background. Some disputes were clearly continuations of existing frictions and rivalries which had nothing to do with reform. The quarrels between Salisbury traditionalists and their reformist bishop – they accused him of heresy – reflect a history of jurisdictional disputes between the city and successive diocesans.

The change with probably the biggest local impact on parish life was the reduction in holy days. This downgraded not only two dozen major festivals, but also feast dates which were important in regional or local business calendars. The reduction also challenged popular celebrations. Robert Parkyn, the conservative priest of Adwick-le-Street near Doncaster, was particularly incensed that

> *children should [not] be decked nor go about upon St. Nicholas', St.*
> *Katherine's, St. Clement's, St. Edmund's eves or days, but that all such*
> *childish fashions (as they named it) to cease. Thus in King Henry's days*
> *began Holy Church in England to be in great ruin as appeared daily.*[13]

Services could still be held on these holy days, but attendance was voluntary and work was to go on as usual. Within the churches, the striking material change was the removal of the lights which had been kept burning day and night before images of the saints, and an end to the burning of candles on special occasions. Even so, once again royal commands appear to have been generally obeyed. At Morebath the removal of all prohibited lights was complete before the arrival of the actual order – probably following local pressure from Exeter. Instructions to remove jewels and ornaments from statues were similarly complied with. At Long Melford the coats and girdles adorning the statue of the Virgin and all the jewels, gold, and silver had gone by 1541.

19

CONFLICTING NARRATIVES

Given difficulties with the evidence, it is not surprising that historians tell two conflicting stories about the early Reformation in England. The first focuses on the hostility to religious change, which can be found in numerous parts of the country; the other focuses on an emerging body of vigorous and confident reformers.

Hostility to Reform

There is little doubt that a majority of the early Tudor clergy was hostile to reform and had been so from the start. In 1534, the year of the final break with Rome, Thomas Cromwell's protégé, William Marshall, published a primer critical of praying to saints and omitting all prayers for the dead. Market response forced him to issue a corrected edition with the somewhat lame excuse that he had not omitted the material because he thought that "our blessed lady and [the] holy saints might in no wise be prayed unto, but rather because I was not ignorant of... the vain superstitious manner... used in worshipping them".[1] Some conservative feeling undoubtedly reflected self-interest and unwillingness to change, but by no means all. The burning of early reformers such as Bilney was conducted by the lay authorities, but that was only after a process of accusation and condemnation by clergy who were offended and ready to strike back.[2] There is little doubt either that Henry's moves against the pope were disliked by many clergy. Some were prepared to protest immediately, notably the Observant Friars of Greenwich, who challenged Henry to his face. The final acceptance of his headship was never put to the lower house of Convocation because it would have been rejected, and a number of dioceses did protest subsequently. The clergy who met at Pontefract in the course of the Pilgrimage of Grace insisted that the pope was "the head of the church and vicar of Christ and so ought to be taken".[3] They were protected by numbers but some individuals were even willing to risk the horrific penalties introduced in 1535 and 1536 for denying the royal supremacy. A preacher last heard of in gaol had told a Thanet congregation that the pope had "not lost an inch of his authority, I warrant you".[4] The monks of the London Charterhouse, one of the early products of the Christocentric revival, attempted to witness by silence, but for refusing to swear to the supremacy, seven members were brutally executed and nine died in prison of deliberate neglect.

A more cautious approach was to use the secrecy of the confessional to undermine royal claims – a tactic employed, so Cromwell was told, by one of the survivors from Greenwich, the highly respected John Forrest, and by other priests too. Although churchwardens generally did what they were told, clergy might hope to escape with the minimum; for example, erasing the name of the pope from the service books with only the thinnest of lines or a pasted (and removable) label. Sermons would attack evangelical ideas and robustly defend tradition: "They say they have brought in the light into the world; no, no, they have brought in damnable darkness and endless damnation."[5] Some priests discouraged their parishioners from reading the Bible. One said this was like "to a dog that gnaweth a marrow bone and never cometh to the pith".[6] Laity too can be found objecting to Bible reading; others disliked alterations in bidding the bedes. The proclamation relaxing the rules for fasting in Lent also attracted complaints. The vicar of Ticehurst in Sussex rebuked his parishioners:

> *Ye will not fast Lent, ye will eat white meat, yea, and it were not for shame, ye would eat a piece of bacon instead of a red herring. I daresay there be a hundred thousand worse people now than there were this time twelvemonth within England.*[7]

Laymen too were offended at this evidence of royal backsliding.

The principal resistance was to the rubbishing of popular religion. That is hardly surprising when statues, some only recently installed and others honoured for generations, lost their candles and their finery in a couple of years. It was the same with sacramentals. The official teaching might insist that these were only symbols, but ingrained belief was not to be uprooted overnight. The situation was not made easier by government pronouncements being at the same time progressive (which was Cromwell's emphasis) and cautious (reflecting the king's concern for unity and order). Thus the proclamation of November 1538 listed sacramentals among the "laudible ceremonies heretofore used in the Church of England" which were to be continued, but at the same time warned that the requirement would last

> *until such time as his majesty doth change or abrogate any of them, as his highness upon reasonable considerations and respects… both may and intendeth to do.*[8]

Likewise with the 1538 injunctions. These only ordered the removal of "feigned" images which were the focus of superstition, but who was to decide? Much depended on the stance of influential local gentry and on the diocesan bishop. Reformers would take one view; conservatives would exploit every loophole possible. Arguments could become decidedly unseemly, whether confrontation between traditionalist clergy and reformed parishioners or vice versa, with statues being thrown out by one party and brought back by the other.

In the case of the abrogated holy days, Henry's concern not to go too fast provided a perfect opportunity for a parson to drag his heels. Holy days might no longer be days of obligation, but services were permitted, which made it very easy to celebrate with all the traditional pomp and more. Lay folk voted with their feet. Around Exeter in 1539, craftsmen, husbandmen, and labourers still stopped work at noon on saints' days, and fishermen declined to put to sea. On the feast day of St Eligius, the patron saint of farriers (1 December), getting your horse shod could prove difficult.[9] Human inertia also worked against reform. Churchwardens had to take royal commissioners seriously, but visitors sent by the archdeacon or the bishop would appear only occasionally. So if both the parishioners and the priest liked the old ways and nobody complained, any church official who did come could be told "all well" [*omnia bene*] and things could carry on much as before.

One way conservative priests could respond to confused lay folk was to assure them that change could not last. Christ's church had always triumphed over heresy. Others took refuge in the belief that Henry's break with Rome was not heresy but schism. According to Stephen Gardiner "all sorts of people are agreed upon this point with most steadfast consent, learned [educated] and unlearned, both men and women: that no manner of person born and brought up in England has aught to do with Rome".[10] Yet for a conservative like Gardiner to adopt that position was fatal. How, for example, could transubstantiation be defended when it had been promulgated not by the supreme head of the Church in England but by a council called by the pope in 1215 which met at his Lateran Palace in Rome? Thomas More and John Fisher had been well aware that schism and heresy were two sides of the same coin. Henry VIII's cousin, Cardinal Pole, told him in 1536 that "the deed you perpetrated… manifestly declares that you had in mind the overthrow of the foundations of the church itself".[11] But for refusing the king his title, More, Fisher, and the Charterhouse fathers had died on the scaffold. Even Pole, abroad and out of Henry's immediate reach, had to watch his back. Understandably, most conservatives preferred to accept the supremacy and its changes, and endure.

Growing Reform

The alternative to a narrative emphasizing a widespread dislike of religious change is a demonstration of the growing clamour of reformers challenging tradition. Assessing numbers is complicated by the difficulty we have seen in distinguishing the new impetus to reform from the existing Lollard challenge to the church.[12] But what is clear is that after the break with Rome the religious landscape of England ceases to be uniform. It is no longer a case of isolated groups of critics – Lollards, evangelical sympathizers at court and in London, and dissident academics in Oxford and Cambridge. The overall number of those committed to change had not yet reached a majority, but thanks to the noise they made, the nation knew that the authority of the English church was no longer to be taken for granted. "By the 1540s all observers agreed that religious discord had become endemic."[13]

Some whole parishes embraced reform. In others, support for tradition sank to a tipping point. At Pluckley in Kent in 1543, half refused holy bread.[14] During the 1540s illegal conventicles were discovered in a number of places, including Gloucestershire, Salisbury, Canterbury, and London, and these were only the ones the authorities detected. The reformist underground thrived on anonymity, but a contemporary estimate of one reformer in three may have been correct for some places. Research on the situation in London has established that there were some fifty evangelical clergy working in the city during the latter years of Henry VIII.[15] Occasional expressions of reformed ideas even appear in otherwise conservative areas such as Yorkshire.[16] There was no conservative/evangelical iron curtain and people did travel. Even within the broad divisions of north/west and south/east, there was considerable local variation. For example, there is little evidence of reforming opinion in West Sussex, which was dominated by a conservative bishop and conservative aristocrats and where commercial traffic was in decline. At Rye in East Sussex, an economically active port with European connections, reforming opinion was growing and doing so in spite of William Inold, the parish priest, a staunch traditionalist and covert papist. He openly defied the 1536 injunctions and enjoyed the support of many of the town council and seventy-five of the "most substantial commons" (as they called themselves). Opposing them were nearly as many councillors and a total of at least twenty men who allegedly held reforming opinions – some radical.[17] The two MPs that the town sent to the 1539 parliament were both reformers, as again in 1545. There was a similar reformist grouping in Plymouth, including three merchants who served as mayor in the late 1530s, two of whom also sat as MPs for the town.

We get an idea of the nature of reformed opinion from the material which was collected for Kent with the intention of blackening Cranmer in 1543. The most frequent conservative complaint was over iconoclasm by clergy, a charge levelled at laity as well. This image-breaking very probably reflected previous encouragement from Cranmer's diocesan agents. There was considerable dissatisfaction too over continuing ceremonies and praying for the dead. On the mass, the clergy expressed cautious disquiet, while the laity were more venturesome. Conventicles in Kent and elsewhere were typically groups of ten or so who met regularly to talk, share questions and ideas, and to discuss the Bible or any heretical texts they had. In some cases a member was able to lead; indeed, effectively to teach. Clandestine preaching could also be arranged and in some parishes, especially in London, parish priests would sanction evangelical sermons, confident they would be well attended. A good deal of networking also went on, and not simply in the immediate locality. Reformist clergy were helped financially and if trouble arose there would be support to raise bail or other costs. "Urban radicals, sacramentarian clergy, reformers in rural areas, reformers in the book trade – despite the real differences between them – all these were linked by layers of patronage and friendship."[18]

What had turned Christians who had grown up within the medieval church into reformers? For those whose religion had been pretty routine, the evangelical message could produce dramatic change. In 1539 Sir Nicholas Carew claimed that he had been brought to faith by reading the Bible for the first time when in the Tower of London awaiting trial and execution.[19] However, in all probability most reformers had been part of the country's ongoing Christocentric revival. "Early evangelicals were late medieval Christians."[20] Reform offered them the deeper experience of Christ which they had sought – an experience which revived Catholicism would bring to others a generation later.[21] Evangelicals, of course, did not see it that way. With the zeal of the newly enlightened, they needed to distance themselves from the past. Thomas Becon deplored "how we ran from post to pillar, from stock to stone, from idol to idol, from place to place, to seek remission of our sins", but at the time, that had been what a devout Christian had to do in order to be assured of salvation.[22] When Hugh Latimer was brought under the influence of Thomas Bilney, he abandoned his staunch defence of tradition and became the apostle of reform, but in so doing he was exchanging one significant spiritual commitment for another.

Seeing reform as growing out of earlier Christian aspirations makes it easier to understand how people came to welcome and embrace the evangelical message. From its beginning, Christianity has taught the need for conversion. It was not a sixteenth-century innovation, particularly conversion experienced as a conviction of past failure ["sin"] and a reorientation to a life-changing following of Christ. In *The Imitation of Christ*, Thomas à Kempis wrote that "a man converting himself to God is a new man".[23] The difference for sixteenth-century English reformers was twofold. First, the word of God was now available to speak to them directly and personally. Second, they had discovered that the "new man" was justified – made right with God – by faith, not by moral effort. Taken together, the resulting emotional pressure could trigger a classic Protestant conversion experience. "The old church was immensely strong and that strength could only have been overcome by the explosive power of a new idea."[24] We have already seen Thomas Bilney rescued from despair over his sins by reading in St Paul's first letter to Timothy: "It is a true saying and worthy of all men to be embraced that Christ Jesus came into the world to save sinners, of whom I am the chief and principal."[25]

We must, nevertheless, not assume that reform spread by a rolling wave of sudden dramatic conversions. Conversion is the reorientating of life to a personal commitment to God, and that does not always begin in a Bilney-like – or Luther-like – awareness of the need for forgiveness nor end in a Damascus road enlightenment. There is no evidence of Cranmer going through such a cathartic spiritual crisis. Of course, reformers frequently do describe their spiritual experience in terms of a dramatic journey from the stygian darkness of sin through repentance into the blazing light of acceptance by God, but in doing so they may easily be conforming to the scenario expected in a conversion narrative. In his twenties, Calvin's journey to faith took several years, but two decades later he had repackaged it as the "sudden conversion" of a devout papist.[26] For anyone who already believes that Christ can save him from his sins, conversion can be more a matter of understanding and affirmation, akin to the final piece of a jigsaw puzzle dropping into place. That does not imply that it was any less fundamental or without emotion. Quiet appropriation could go along with quiet joy.

The principal vector which spread awareness of reform was preaching. In the 1520s, following his conversion, Hugh Latimer was more than once suspected of preaching heresy, particularly in advocating the Bible in English. By 1530 he was one of the country's most effective and most contentious preachers. After Anne Boleyn had presented him to a Wiltshire parish, he travelled widely in the West Country, taking advantage of his university licence to preach anywhere without the approval of the local bishop. When he was made bishop of Worcester he sent his chaplains and other reformist clergy out to continue the work. All in all, a whole genealogy of converts can be traced back to Latimer. Cromwell too licensed and protected evangelical clergy, as did Cranmer and other sympathetic bishops, even when, to cool the temperature, the crown had ostensibly prohibited sermons on sensitive topics. Also, a significant number of former friars turned to reform, men who were already experienced in parish preaching, including some of the best educated of the nation's clergy.[27] In Essex, local clergy seem also to have joined together to evangelize, and almost certainly elsewhere too.

The most powerful element in the reformed message was undoubtedly the proclamation of the Bible in English. In the oxygen of the Scriptures, the flame of revival became incandescent. The Bible gave preachers new authority. They were not repeating church dogma; they were expounding truth directly from the divinely inspired book in front of them, "the word of God" which anyone could access for himself if he could read or have someone read to him. The story of Carew finding faith by discovering the Bible is not unique. Writing from the Inns of Court soon after the 1534 New Testament appeared, Robert, the heir to the Plumpton family, sent a copy to his mother in Yorkshire telling her to read Tyndale's prologue, where

> *you shall see marvellous things hid in it. And as for the understanding of it, doubt not, for God will give knowledge to whom he will give knowledge of the Scriptures, as soon to a shepherd as to a priest, if he ask knowledge of God faithfully.*[28]

Reading the Bible should have been easily accommodated in parish worship, alongside prayers which literate individuals read quietly during mass to those around them.[29] Bible readers, however, did not always use the required "low voice", while in some parishes enthusiasts found the reader challenged – one suspects shouted down – by conservatives reciting traditional invocations.

Preaching too engendered controversy. In 1533, the Lenten and Eastertide sermons which the mayor and clergy of Bristol invited Latimer to deliver offended many by denigrating the part good works played in salvation and repudiating the role of the Virgin Mary. He attacked the papacy, non-preaching bishops, and the friars, pilgrimages, images, and the worship of saints, while increasingly his target was purgatory – which made him highly critical of monasteries which existed to pray for the dead. Conservative clergy responded in kind and Bristol was in turmoil until Cromwell had Latimer's principal adversary arrested. The audiences which other reformist preachers drew polarized opinion similarly.

Anxiety that reform would degenerate into dangerous controversy was never far from Henry VIII's mind. In 1536 *The Ten Articles* were, he said, issued to bring about "outward quietness".[30] In December 1545 his last speech to parliament included an impassioned plea to end religious dissention.[31] First preaching:

> *I see and hear daily that you of the clergy preach one against another, teach one contrary to another, inveigh one against another without charity or discretion. Some be too stiff in their old Mumpsimus, others be too busy and curious in their new Sumpsimus. Thus all men almost be in variety and discord and few or none preach truly and sincerely the word of God according as they ought to do...*[32]

Then Henry turned to MPs and lay peers:

> *You rail on bishops, speak slanderously of priests, and rebuke and taunt preachers, both contrary to good order and Christian fraternity. If you know surely that a bishop or preacher erreth or teacheth perverse doctrine, come and declare it... to us... and be not judges yourselves of your own phantastical opinions and vain expositions, for in such high causes ye may err.*

The permission to read the Bible was also being abused:

> *it is licensed you so to do, only to inform your own conscience and to instruct your children and family and not to make scripture a railing and a taunting stock [resource], against priests and preachers (as many light persons do). I am very sorry to know and hear how unreverently that most precious jewel, the word of God is disputed, rhymed, sung, and jangled in every alehouse and tavern, contrary to the true meaning and doctrine of the same.*

The Centre Ground

The problem in reconciling these two narratives is that each focuses on an extreme and pays no attention to the middle. A majority of parishes provide no grist for either interpretation because royal instructions were apparently obeyed without trouble. No doubt if more sources had survived, additional examples of complaint and controversy would be forthcoming, but hardly enough to disturb the conclusion that compliance was pretty general. Yet how could that be? The answer is that, over the country, individuals with local standing were willing to use their influence and serve on commissions and enquiries to enforce the will of the crown.[33] Furthermore, their decisions had broadly to be accepted by the communities concerned. That was not a matter of democratic opinion; in peasant communities, the pecking order is strong.[34] In other words, both the implementation of change and the acceptance of change only came about with lay support, leadership, and acquiescence.

Some of this support no doubt came from committed reformers or from loyalists in the government patronage loop. In unhappy parishes, critics of the priest might welcome royal policy as vindicating their position. Changes were also less offensive because they came piecemeal. There were few big crises. Moreover, developments came in the king's name, and a person lukewarm or even hostile might nevertheless feel that to defy the king's authority was disloyal, while a reformer could be similarly constrained when Henry swung back towards tradition. The result was disunity, controversy, and confusion, not resistance. Another factor explaining quiescence is fear. Failing to report offenders was "misprision of treason", punishable by life imprisonment and the loss of all possessions. As the accountant John Gostwick (c.1493–1545) warned his son: "if your friend should open to you felony or treason... in any wise utter it [report it to the authorities] as soon as possible for the longer you keep it the worse it is for you".[35]

We must also recognize that in the same way that the traditional church could be attractive for other than religious reasons, so could reform.[36] Conservatives claimed that reformers were preaching "carnal liberty", telling men that they were forgiven and so encouraging them to ignore sin. Reformers did indeed preach liberty, but it was liberty from the erroneous ceremonies of the past and their constricting disciplines. That left cash in the pocket. Reformers were being optimistic in calling for the savings on pilgrimages and the veneration of saints to be put in the poor box. Similarly, lower investment on souls previously assumed to be in purgatory freed up capital. Permission to eat white meat made Lent more bearable. A priest did not have to be a committed reformer to welcome the questioning of clerical celibacy; some 15 per cent would marry when under Edward VI this became possible.[37] And the effect of all this went deeper than particular changes. The old ways had united communities. That ended when individuals began to opt out, so why cling to the past? Indeed in the longer term, reform, with its emphasis on personal faith, would destroy the oneness of the English church and the English people.[38]

This fragmentation of consensus was massively encouraged by the way royal policies undermined the sacred – what is called "desacralizing". The mass was surrounded by holiness and mystery – that is why the laity were kept at a distance. Introducing English into the liturgy threatened that mystery. Conservatives who joined in the destruction of the monasteries – feeling "If others are benefiting, why not me?" – risked being coarsened by what they did. Likewise iconoclasm. Images were sacred, so watching them being defiled necessarily questioned respect for hallowed things. Certainly, many must have been bewildered when attacking images – which had been a hanging offence at the start of the decade – was being selectively encouraged in and after 1536. Nor would Henry's final word on the subject in *The King's Book* have helped the confusion – images could rightly be knelt to and reverenced but "such things be not or ought not to be done to the image itself but to God and in his honour".[39] Cromwell and the reformers clearly believed that the public repudiation of images would detach the crowds from the cult of saints. In May 1538 a gruesome demonstration before 10,000 Londoners saw Friar Forrest roasted over a fire made from the statue of St Derfel, a saint credited with the power of saving souls from hell, whose North Wales shrine was said to have attracted several hundred pilgrims a day. However, what such demonstrations may have encouraged was not disbelief but cynicism. Early in 1538 a ceremony at St Paul's exposed the rood from the Cistercian monastery at Bloxley near Maidstone as a fake. It had supposedly responded to prayers by turning its eyes and moving its lower lip and was claimed to perform miracles, but Bishop Hilsey showed it was largely made of cloth and paper and was worked by pulleys and wires. However, townspeople at least were perfectly familiar with similar devices in mystery plays and the like, and pilgrims had for some years been unimpressed by Bloxley. Perhaps Tudor men and women were not as universally gullible and naïve as both traditionalists and reformers assumed.

A study of the south-west – where the data is most substantial – suggests that the removal of lights and other expressions of devotion was often followed by a decline in the devotion itself. At Morebath the priest and the parish seem simply to have adjusted to change. Annual collections to pay for lights on special occasions quickly withered away, but assets that had funded candles before statues were reapplied to lights which were permitted and to general church expenses, thus funding improvements in the fabric. Elsewhere redirection seems not always to have been the case. Parish guilds often withered when the reason to support an image was removed. What had the biggest impact was the doubt cast on purgatory. Fraternities – many of them poor men's burial clubs – had flourished in the first years of Henry's reign but went into decline in the 1530s and many of the smaller ones seem to have disappeared.[40] Prayers, masses, and obits continued to be offered for the recently deceased, but the long-term fate of the soul after death was now a matter of individual conviction; it was not the collective faith of the community. A profound consequence of this privatization was the weakening of a parish's sense of identity, the age-old continuity of prayer and intercession which hitherto had bound the living and the dead. Now it was just the living who mattered – prayers were only of value "in this world and in the time of passing out" of it.[41]

In the changed climate, assets to provide for continuing soul masses were increasingly embezzled. Support for works of mercy likewise. Chantries offer evidence of a similar retreat. They had always been vulnerable to predation by the family of the founder – different generations have different priorities. But the monastic dissolutions encouraged rumours of other confiscations to follow, and from 1536 chantries began to disappear more rapidly. Some were converted to charitable uses, but others were simply annexed by private individuals. No thought seems to have been given to depriving the souls suffering in purgatory of the intercessions they had paid for. And by no means all had been long dead. The pains of purgatory which John Fisher and Thomas More had painted so graphically clearly cut no ice with the sons of John Trotte.[42] They suppressed the almshouse at Cullompton in Devon which their father had established for the good of his soul only twenty years before.[43] That people who had been brought up to believe it was a Christian duty to assist parents on the painful path to heaven should refuse to do so any longer, argues a profound mental revolution. The fate of the country's collegiate churches points in the same direction. These provided teams ["colleges"] of priests to serve as a community of intercession. More than a quarter of these premier parochial foundations were dissolved between 1540 and 1545. The town of Warwick executed a particularly neat manoeuvre. It surrendered its college of St Mary to the crown and bought back the assets (in passing, getting the grant of a school and a town charter), but the change put an end to the intercessory prayers of thirteen clergy. No more either was heard of Warwick's thirty-nine sets of relics, which had included the oil that caused the fires of Pentecost, along with St George's ivory horn and St Brendan's frying pan.[44]

What this adds up to is that although Henry VIII's reign saw the late medieval religious revival split disastrously between right and left, the truly momentous consequence of his policies was destabilizing much of the significant middle. We need to envisage a spectrum – at either end convinced conservatives and convinced evangelicals – and between them a gradation of opinion from acceptance of the status quo through bewilderment to significant doubt about it. Alternatively, we can see a cadre of committed reformers surrounded by "a penumbra of sympathisers and opportunists", though no doubt conservatives would more readily have thought in terms of a plague spot.[45] The density of this penumbra was undoubtedly greatest in areas of the strongest evangelical penetration – the more populous and economically prominent south and east, particularly among skilled craftsmen and tradesmen. London was to the fore – commentators all noticed that – and then Kent, Essex and Suffolk. Elsewhere there was the Thames Valley and over to the Severn, which we have noted in early reform and before that in Lollardy. There was, too, the attraction to the young – reform was modern and exciting – while continuing foreign influence through the ports added the element of the exotic. Committed evangelicals might still be in the minority, but history is made by committed minorities and their sympathizers. When

Robert Parkyn wrote that "in King Henry's days began Holy Church in England to be in great ruin as appeared daily", he was thinking of it as a great engine of worship and grace, and in that respect he was correct.[46] But far more important and more subtle was the progressive impact on Christian belief and discipleship.

20

HENRY VIII: LEGACY

When Henry VIII died he left a country which was reformed. This was his proudest achievement. A painting on the wall of his palace of Whitehall boasted that he

> *drives the unworthy from the altars and brings in men of integrity. The*
> *presumption of popes has yielded to unerring virtue and with Henry VIII*
> *bearing the sceptre in his hand, religion has been restored and with him*
> *on the throne the truths of God have begun to be held in due reverence.*[1]

Yet the reform he boasted of was his own idiosyncratic notion of what reform should be. Instead of belonging to one visible Catholic (i.e. universal) church answerable to Rome, the English now knew that the Catholic church was a mystical union of free and equal national churches subject to God via their individual rulers. And Henry was the model for those rulers. The frontispiece of the Great Bible pictures God saying to him: "I have found a man after my own heart who does all my will."[2] Yet the exercise of that divine will had brought revolution to the English church. Religion was now "by law established". Bishops had ceased to be "by divine appointment" and had become civil servants. The vocation of monks, nuns, and friars had been denigrated as "superstitious observances" and the institutions of religious life destroyed. Saints' days had been devalued and so too had pilgrimages and relics. The discipline of Lent had been relaxed. Churches had been stripped of sacred objects. The rich ceremonial of parish religion had been reduced to what the state tolerated. The Bible in English now offered an alternative authority to the hierarchy and tradition of the church. Opinions which twenty years earlier would have invited a charge of heresy were freely canvassed. This was not orthodoxy, nor was it evangelical reform. Neither was it the middle way between the corruptions of Rome and the errors of reform as some historians have claimed. It was the inconsistent Christianity of one dominant individual.

The most marked example of Henry's unorthodoxy is the attack on purgatory and praying for the dead. This progressed through successive doctrinal statements precisely because of the king's support and personal input. As early as 1535 William Marshall could publish with impunity: "There is nothing in the *Dirige* [the Office of the Dead] taken out of scripture that makes any more mention of the souls departed than does the tale of Robin Hood"; in the 1545 *Primer* which Henry claimed as his own, those who "sleep in Christ" are destined for "the country of peace and rest".[3] At the end of the year, parliament approved a bill to suppress all chantries and transfer the assets to the crown, although citing financial rather than theological reasons. Henry VIII's position is evident in the will he revised a month before his death. This expressed the conviction that

> *every Christian creature... dying in steadfast and perfect faith, [and] endeavouring... to execute in his life time such good deeds... as scripture commands... is ordained by Christ's passion to be saved and to attain eternal life, of which number we verily trust by his grace to be one.*

He did also "instantly require and desire the Blessed Virgin Mary His Mother with all the holy Company of Heaven continually to pray for us and with us" but limited that to "whilst we live in this World and in the time of passing out of the same that we may the sooner attain everlasting life after our departure out of this transitory life which we do both hope and claim by Christ's passion and word". A note of insecurity does, perhaps, creep in with the later provision of £666 in alms for the poor to "pray heartily unto God for the remission of our offences and the wealth of our soul" and £600 per annum to the Dean and Chapter of Windsor for two priests to say mass for him in perpetuity and provide for thirteen "poor knights".[4] But this was nothing in comparison with his father's will with its call for 10,000 masses immediately, 2,600 more as soon as possible, £2,000 distributed in alms, obits all over the country, additional works of charity which cost well over

£40,000, a silver-gilt pyx worth £4 to every parish in the country without one, and a shower of gold and silver plate, images, relics, and vestments for his favourite churches.[5] And this was in addition to provision he had made in his lifetime, which included a chantry for three priests at Westminster.

What is particularly noticeable is that Henry VIII's final years did not see the expulsion of the reformist supporters Cromwell had introduced into the royal court, and especially into the king's privy chamber. That was the private suite in which Henry lived most of his life, appearing outside only for exercise or on ceremonial occasions. Servants in the suite were the closest the king had to companions, and evangelicals there could, without forcing their opinions on the king, give quiet support to the reformist cause. Katherine Parr, his reformist queen, is said to have hosted dinners where the king and others discussed theology – the topic of the day on the social round – with Henry not always victorious. Henry could even turn a blind eye if his close attendants stepped out of line, as George Blage, a gentleman of the privy chamber, did in 1546. Despite being condemned to being burned at the stake as a sacramentary, the king pardoned him and welcomed him back.

Prince Edward was the child of Henry's old age – born when the king was already forty-six. Immense care was taken with the boy's upbringing and training for kingship, but the men Henry chose to tutor his son were reformers. When in January 1547 the boy ascended the throne, he did so as a convinced evangelical and nothing known about him gives any hint that he had ever been taught the truth of transubstantiation. No doubt his tutors had been moderate and circumspect, but omitting to teach something can be as effective as attacking it. In choosing such men, Henry, who must have been aware of their stance, was probably influenced by the priority he placed on defending the royal supremacy. Tutors who were religiously more conservative could not be trusted to keep the pope at bay. That same fear also explains why the regency council Henry set up to rule on his son's behalf was weighted with the reformist courtiers and politicians who, as we have seen, had emerged victorious in 1546 from the failure of conservative attempts to turn back the clock.[6] The principal figures were Cranmer and Edward Seymour, earl of Hertford, who became duke of Somerset, and John Dudley, Lord Lisle, who was promoted earl of Warwick. By these final decisions Henry VIII died leaving England with an evangelical heir and a substantially evangelical entourage.

21

EDWARD VI: REFORM UNLEASHED

Henry VIII left England with a church settlement which was distinctive and highly personal. It was also unviable once his dominating personality was removed. Yet leaving the country in the hands of a substantially evangelical leadership meant that – whether he had intended it or not – he had put in power men who knew where they were going and would build on what he had achieved. They moved with a caution which at times can seem like uncertainty, but from the outset their intention was "to destroy one church and build another".[1] The caution was very justified. Although we have seen that reform had growing support, important nobles were hostile, others lukewarm. Few of the bishops – key figures in the church – were convinced evangelicals and some were or had become vigorous and effective opponents, notably Stephen Gardiner (Winchester) and Edmund Bonner (London). The new leaders had also to watch the international situation. England was at war with Scotland, which was receiving support from the French, who were not reconciled to losing Boulogne (recently captured by Henry VIII). Mary, Edward's half-sister and the next in line to the English throne, was a staunch traditionalist, and her cousin and mentor Charles V, the equally orthodox Holy Roman emperor, had bases less than fifty miles away across the Channel and was on the point of defeating the Protestant princes of Germany.

Softly Softly

The new regime allowed Henry VIII to be buried with traditional pomp, but the reformed beliefs of Edward VI and his advisers were evident in Cranmer's address at the coronation five days later. Edward, he said, was called to emulate the youthful biblical king Josiah and purge his kingdom of idolatry, papal tyranny, and images.[2] Despite this, for the first few months care was taken not to alarm conservative opinion – even to the point of leaving in gaol prisoners accused of breaking the Six Articles which was still the law of the land. The new regime had also to settle in, with Edward Seymour, duke of Somerset, needing to cement his position as Protector of the Realm. Then in June 1547 came publication of the *Book of Homilies* for reading in lieu of sermons, and this unambiguously taught justification by faith. A visitation was launched, ostensibly a reworking of Henry's 1538 enquiry, but the visitors (nearly all reformers) were given discretion and turned the exercise into an attack on tradition. Processions and rosaries were forbidden, lights before the rood were to be removed, often along with the roods themselves. Henry's injunctions had ordered the removal of images that were objects of worship, but many visitors now took the view that all images were necessarily being abused and so must go. Gardiner and Bonner objected and were imprisoned.

The two bishops would have been hugely more than affronted if they had been aware of another rejection which was in the offing. Cranmer and his evangelical colleagues had finally accepted that they had been wrong to teach that Christ was "materially" present in the bread and wine of the eucharist. A belief that had been the cardinal principle of the late king's faith and which they had enforced to the point of burning people as heretics was false. The eucharist involved no material change. Transubstantiation taught by the papacy and its followers was a delusion and even Luther's compromise position was wrong. As Zwingli and the reformers in Switzerland and the Rhineland had been claiming for the previous twenty years, the presence of Christ was spiritual. There is no precise date for this revolution in opinion – doubts had been growing for some time. The martyred William Tyndale had held the radical view but the martyred Robert Barnes went to the stake convinced of the truth of the "real presence". We know that Cranmer finally became persuaded of his previous error after discussions with his chaplain Nicholas Ridley, the future bishop and martyr, and the most probable date for this is thought to be the end of 1546. But thanks to the need to move softly following Henry's death, the change was handled with caution.

The first surreptitious move was taken in November 1547 when Edward VI's first parliament met. It abolished the heresy laws, including the Six Articles. It also passed an *Act against such as shall speak irreverently against the sacrament*. This was ostensibly directed against radicals, but a final clause provided that the laity should be given communion in both kinds (i.e. both bread and wine) since "that was more agreeable to the first institution of Christ and to the usage of the apostles and the primitive church".[3] This measure with its clauses facing both ways successfully split conservative opponents in the House of Lords, although they did succeed in blocking a bill abolishing compulsory clerical celibacy – not that this prevented clerics jumping the gun. A separate measure to revive the Henry VIII statute abolishing chantries did run into difficulties in the Commons, but not because this bill now claimed that chantries maintained "vain opinions of purgatory and masses satisfactory".[4] The objection was to losing the funds which chantries provided for community projects such as the maintenance of bridges and roads. In order to get the bill passed, the crown was forced to buy off London and a number of urban centres. Further reform came in January 1548 when the bishops were instructed to forbid candles at Candlemas, ashes on Ash Wednesday, palms on Palm Sunday, and creeping to the cross on Good Friday.

The movement for reform was not only concerned with changes in liturgy and ritual. Much to the fore in sermons and in print was the concern for the common weal which had characterized the evangelical gospel since the days of Thomas Cromwell.[5] In London in January 1548 Hugh Latimer broke into a sermon on the responsibility of the clergy to attack rich citizens for lack of pity. "In London their brother shall die in the streets for cold, he shall lie sick at the door… and perish there for hunger. Was there ever more unmercifulness?"[6] This linking of religious reform and concern for society was very evident among a number of middle ranking officials. One of them, John Hales, wrote in a letter to the Protector in July 1548:

Surely God's word is that precious balm that must increase comfort, and cherish that godly charity between man and man, which is the sinews that

tie and hold together the members of every Christian commonwealth and
maketh one of us to be glad of another.[7]

And it was not only argument. A number of the Protector's policies were influenced, most notably the enquiry he launched in June 1548 into conditions in agriculture. Hales, who led the Midland commissioners, had no doubt of its moral purpose:

> *to remove the self love that is in many men, to take away the inordinate*
> *desire of riches wherewith many be encumbered, to expel and quench*
> *the insatiable thirst of ungodly greediness… and to increase love and*
> *godly charity among us, to make us know and remember that we are all,*
> *poor and rich, noble and ignoble, gentleman and husbandmen and all*
> *others… but [only] members of one body mystical of our Saviour Christ*
> *and of the body of the realm.*[8]

Implementing the legislation about communion in both kinds gave the opportunity to make a further evangelical advance. An "Order of Communion" in English was inserted in the Latin mass, something which was certainly not envisaged in the act. In the autumn of 1548 important churches ceased to display the sacrament on the altar for people to adore. Sermons and literature followed. Eventually in December 1548, in a four-day debate on the eucharist in the House of Lords, Cranmer publicly avowed his change of heart. This overturning of the understanding of the sacrament was momentous and definitive. It destroyed the last vestige of agreement among reformers of all shades in England that the Christian church needed to change, even though they might differ on how. Henceforward denial of the real presence, so recently the defining mark of the Lollard and the sacramentary, would become the fault-line between what we can now call English Protestants and English Roman Catholics.[9]

This new understanding was immediately embodied in a parliamentary bill to enact "*The Book of Common Prayer and Administration of the Sacraments and other Rites and Ceremonies of the Church, after the Use [custom] of the Church of England*".[10] This, the first of what would be two Edwardian Prayer Books, was still cautious, very much an initial document and Cranmer left enough rough edges to accommodate moderate conservatives.

Thus he described the eucharist as "The supper of the Lord and the holy communion, commonly called the mass", while the catechism avoided all discussion of the sacraments.[11] The eucharistic liturgy gave thanks for the virtues exhibited by the saints "and chiefly… the most glorious and blessed Virgin Mary" and commended to God's mercy the faithful departed who "rest in the sleep of peace".[12] Bishop Gardiner said that although he would not have made the book as it was, he was prepared to use it. But despite the caution, the text does by its silences express Cranmer's conviction that there was no physical presence of Christ in the eucharist and brought England in line with the *Consensus Tigurinus* between Bullinger and Calvin.[13] The service still separated the consecration by the priest from the communion of the people, but elevation of the sacrament was expressly forbidden: no more "gazing at that thing which the priest held up in his hands".[14] Many of the details of the mass such as the holy loaf were dropped (families which had provided it were now to pay for the communion bread and wine) and a note explained that only ceremonies which "edified" had been retained.[15] A new calendar listed only New Testament saints plus the feast of All Saints. The "hours" of the medieval church were reduced to matins and evensong [morning and evening prayer], which became simplified congregational services with prayers in English and enhanced Bible reading. "Every man and woman" was instructed to attend their parish church (with penalties for absence or misbehaviour) and also to communicate once a year.[16] A Lectionary, too, was introduced, which took the clergy through the whole of the Old Testament in a year and the New Testament three times. There were also changes to the rites of baptism, while before being confirmed, a child had to be able to repeat the catechism. Revised provisions for the ordination of clergy removed all reference to them "offering sacrifice for the living and the dead".[17] Refusing to use the book was made a criminal offence and so too was compelling a priest to use a different liturgy. All this significantly reduced the potential for "voluntary religion". The price of reform was tighter regulation.[18]

Reform Becomes Confident

The first Prayer Book went into use at Whitsun 1549, and the following December orders were given to destroy all Latin service books from the old regime. That year also saw statutory approval for clergy to marry. During 1550, evangelicals replaced key conservatives on the bench of bishops and in other important church posts, and, by the end of the year, orders were given to remove stone altars – where the sacrifice of the mass took place – and replace them with communion tables. In 1551 work began on the revision of canon law and by the end of the year the text of the second Edwardian Prayer Book was ready to be put to parliament.

Where the first Prayer Book had been cautious, the second was confident and unambiguous.[19] The eucharist was now described as "the Lord's Supper" or "Holy communion" – no longer "the mass".[20] To emphasize that it was a communal meal, the communion table was to be brought down into the chancel or into the nave of the church so that communicants could gather round it. The priest was no longer to face east with his back to the congregation, but stand on the north side of the table so that all could see what he did. No more secrecy. Only those taking communion were to attend (as in 1549) but a minimum of three had now to be present, a number made more realistic (it was hoped) by an order that every parishioner had to communicate three times a year. The liturgy was changed and reordered to prevent traditionalists reinterpreting it. There was no longer a separate stage where the bread and wine were consecrated. Instead there was a prayer that communicants by receiving "bread and wine... in remembrance" of Christ's death should partake of "his most blessed body and blood".[21] If that did not make clear enough that Christ's presence was spiritual, there were fundamental changes in what was said to the person taking communion. In the medieval ritual, the priest had prayed (in Latin), "May the body and blood of our Lord Jesus Christ preserve my body and spirit for eternal life."[22] In the 1549 order the priest said to the communicant: "The body of our Lord Jesus Christ which was given for thee, preserve thy body and soul to eternal life", and a similar wording with the wine.[23] Now, in the 1552 Prayer Book the words were: "Take and eat this in remembrance that Christ died for thee and feed on him in thine heart by faith with thanksgiving"; the wine likewise.[24] In 1552 good quality bread was specified instead of unleavened wafers "to take away the superstition which any person has or might have in the bread and wine" and instead of the tradition of putting the bread directly into the mouth, it was specifically to be put into the hands of the recipients.[25] Elsewhere in the book there were other changes. At matins and evensong the laity were brought in further e.g. by joining the priest to say the Creed. Sacramentals were omitted in the rites of marriage and extreme unction. The mention in the 1549 Book that part of the burial service could take place in the church was dropped, and the service itself offered no prayers for the dead. The reason, as the traditionalist Robert Parkyn remembered bitterly, was "because their souls were immediately in bliss and joy after the departing from the bodies and therefore they needed no prayer".[26]

Reform Frustrated

The Act of Uniformity, which put the second Edwardian Prayer Book into law, received the royal assent in April 1552, but before it could come into force on 1 November, the act and the course of the Reformation generally ran into heavy political weather. The duke of Somerset had been ousted from power in the autumn of 1549 by the council, led by John Dudley, earl of Warwick, but with Cranmer's approval and with no break on the progress of reform. But in October 1551 Dudley decided that he could no longer tolerate Somerset's attempts to regain power. He took the title of duke of Northumberland and days later had his predecessor arrested and subsequently executed. Cranmer opposed killing the duke, but there was more than that to the gulf which began to emerge between the evangelical clergy and their increasingly estranged aristocratic allies. The root of it was money. The lay counsellors wanted to strip the church of even more of its assets, principally because of the desperate state of royal finance, but also with some eye to their own advantage. The clergy were concerned about the future funding of the church and, of course, for themselves, but were particularly anxious that confiscated chantry assets were being secularized when the situation in the common weal called for the relief of widespread suffering being caused by inflation and a series of epidemics.

Northumberland responded by turning to reformers more radical than Cranmer, bringing in the Scotsman John Knox to "be a whetstone to quicken and sharp the Bishop of Canterbury, whereof he hath need"; in other words, to force Cranmer to accept more radical reform and so justify seizing even more church assets.[27] At court in September, Knox preached a sermon fiercely attacking the new Prayer Book for continuing the custom of kneeling at communion. This smacked of traditionalist adoration of the host and contradicted the principle that "all worshipping… invented by the brain of man in the service of God, without his express commandment is idolatry".[28] The council was half persuaded and held up printing of the new book. A furious Cranmer hit back. Knox's principle was precisely what those dangerous anabaptists taught, and, in any case, the council could not alter a text approved by parliament. Printing was resumed and a contrite council added a postscript to the book which spelled out Cranmer's position. Known as the "black" rubric [instruction] because the other rubrics were in red, it declared that kneeling was a gesture of humility which avoided disorder and did in no way imply any adoration of the bread and wine. These remained "in their very natural substances", and "the natural body and blood of our Saviour Christ are in heaven and not here".[29]

At the end of 1552 the evangelical clergy finally lost patience with the leading politicians and nobles over the social crisis. Especially in London and at court the pulpits rang with denunciations of their "covetousness" – pursuing personal advantage rather than social responsibility. This massive campaign touched Northumberland on the raw – he believed in a church which was subservient to the state and that the clergy were sitting pretty on "so great possessions to maintain their idle lives".[30] When parliament met in March 1553 he had a furious altercation with Cranmer in the House of Lords. The recent preaching campaign was "scandalous behaviour, tending to foster disorders and sedition", in particular

certain agitators [who] had dwelt recently on the incorporation of church property and lands and on the dividing up of bishoprics contemplated by the king, proclaiming that those who sought to diminish and restrict the rightful perquisites of the church were heretics, breaking God's law.

The church was forgetting its proper place. "Let [the bishops] forbear calling into question in their sermons the acts of the prince and his ministers, else they should suffer."[31] And Northumberland backed his fury with action. When Cranmer introduced legislation to reform church law – the result of years of work – the duke sabotaged it, partly out of pique and partly because it would have given the church precisely the independence he objected to.

Despite this breakdown in relations, reform continued to make some progress. In January 1553 measures were put in hand to strip churches of everything of value. This struck a further blow at tradition, although the principal motive behind the confiscations was again the crown's financial plight. In March an impeccably evangelical primer was published. In May a new catechism followed. Even more important, attached to the catechism was the long awaited statement of Church of England doctrine. Thanks to the lengthy gestation, the number of sections had varied over time, but were now finalized as the *Forty-Two Articles*. In Elizabeth's reign they would be revised again and become the *Thirty-Nine Articles*. They purported to have been agreed by "bishops and other learned men" but were actually issued on royal authority alone.[32]

By May 1553, however, the future of royal authority was beginning to look shaky. Earlier in the spring Edward VI, hitherto a healthy fifteen-year-old, had begun to show signs of the tuberculosis which would kill him. He had been experimenting with schemes to ensure that his successor would be male – the old fear of a queen regnant – but at the end of the month his doctors reported that he could not last beyond the autumn. Henry VIII had insisted that Edward's half-sisters, Mary and Elizabeth, could not inherit the crown as they were illegitimate in the sight of God and the law, but had nevertheless claimed the right to nominate them as next in line. Edward therefore decided to imitate his father and nominate his own successors. There was no suitable Tudor male available, so he chose his cousin Jane Grey to succeed immediately and thereafter her sons. Everything seemed safely in hand when the boy died on 8 July. However, Mary avoided arrest, mobilized resistance, and, despite Jane representing herself as resisting a foreign papal threat and the duke of Northumberland leading a strong force to arrest Mary, the Grey government collapsed on 19 July. The core of Mary's supporters had been Catholic sympathizers but she carefully avoided appealing to traditionalists publicly and promised to leave religion alone until parliament met. Nevertheless in July 1553 evangelical advance in England effectively hit a brick wall.

22

EDWARD VI: REFORM ON THE GROUND

The changes required of England's parishes during the reign of Edward VI were aimed at replacing a visual Christianity – belief understood through images – with belief conveyed through words. In place of a faith which could be expressed through externals (actions and objects), right faith had to be internalized through experience of the Bible. It was the message of the late medieval Christocentric religious renewal, refined for the age of print and presented to one and all. But was the attempt successful?

Compliance

As with responses in the reign of Henry VIII, parish conformity characterized the reign of his son. There was some dragging of feet and a very few instances of non-compliance, but the overwhelming picture is of obedience. The statues were removed, and many of the niches they had stood in were filled and plastered. Altars were demolished – the eucharist was now celebrated at a table in the chancel or the nave. Sacred pictures on the wall were covered with lime-wash and in some churches replaced by verses of Scripture. In the windows, the likenesses of saints were obscured or replaced with plain glass. The crucifix and the figures of the Virgin and St John on the rood screens were removed and replaced by the royal coat of arms. In some churches the screen itself was dismantled. In 1549 and 1550 came the call to hand in service books that had been required for the mass and other liturgies.[1] In 1553 a start was made on the confiscation of chalices and other liturgical items in gold and silver, along with jewels, robes, base metals, and embroidered hangings, leaving only a chalice and paten and the minimum set of linen vestments required by the 1552 Prayer Book.

General obedience was, of course, not the same as general consent. A number of parishes did undoubtedly greet these changes with enthusiasm – which says a good deal for the quiet advance which reform had made in Henry VIII's last years. Almost immediately there were reports of statues and roods being destroyed. In 1548 Yatton in Somerset took the trouble to get a translation of the mass into English. The available data shows that in eleven counties, a fifth of parishes for which churchwardens' accounts survive had removed their altars before the step was officially required. Where registers do not survive, for example in Norwich, other evidence confirms removal had taken place.[2] Initiative is similarly evident with the 1549 Prayer Book. Before the king had signed the uniformity legislation, "[St] Paul's choir, with divers parishes in London and other places in England, began the use after the said book… and put down private masses".[3] That was three months before the act would come into force. All this shows that we are wrong to see religious change exclusively as a matter of royal dictat. Parishes had their own dynamic.[4] Indeed, "it is impossible to conceive of parish religion without the selfless or self-interested co-operation of thousands of men and women throughout the realm".[5]

Parish dynamic is equally seen in the parishes (probably the larger number) which were reluctant to conform. One after another, they turned whatever they could into cash to avoid the predatory clutches of the authorities. Cost was the excuse to hand. Making the changes called for was not cheap – accounts suggest that several weeks' work might be required – and on top there was the need to purchase the new items the parish had to have – service books and a strong chest to serve as a poor box. We cannot, therefore, equate selling Catholic treasures with having reformist opinions. There are instances where that seems to be the case, but parishes had always sold assets to fund special expenditure and, in any case, most only disposed of items surplus to requirements. Where conservatism is clearly evident is where items were removed and hidden or were sold (and so came off the church inventory), with the covert understanding that they would be preserved and restored if or – as was hoped – when the old ways returned. One development which could possibly be a consequence of

Henry VIII's assaults on the sacred was an increase in thefts from churches. That was not a new problem, but it seems to have reached a crescendo in the 1540s and early 1550s. The one area where we can be sure change had bitten deep is once again respect for the dead. Funeral brasses which called for prayers were torn out in their hundreds and disposed of as scrap. Even at Long Melford, where items certainly were preserved in hope of a return to Catholic ways, the brasses sold weighed three hundredweight [152 kg].[6]

Open Opposition

All this meant that by the time Edward VI died, the English worshipped in ways and in churches very different from what they had been accustomed to. That in such a short space of time the beliefs of the majority had changed correspondingly is hard to credit. Continued affection for the old ways seems certain in cases where people conspired to protect Catholic artefacts, although some may have been motivated as much by sentiment and tradition as belief. Even today that can be a gut reaction when changes are proposed to a church building. But whatever the reason for it, dislike of royal policy was common. Many seem to have voted with their feet. The evangelical bishops reported significant absenteeism from parish services and a growing readiness to shop around for churches where the Prayer Book was presented in as traditional a way as possible. In an attempt to deal with this, the 1552 *Act of Uniformity* identified the "great number of people in divers parts of this realm" who "wilfully and damnably before Almighty God abstain and refuse to come to their parish churches and other places where common prayer, administration of the sacraments and preaching the Word of God is used upon the Sunday and other holy days".[7] In future, from 1 November 1552, everyone without good excuse was to attend regularly for the whole service or face the church courts. Also, for a lay person to attend a different form of service was made a crime dealt with by jury trial, with six months' imprisonment for a first conviction (without the possibility of bail), then one year, and finally life for a third offence.

The response of the local bishop certainly counted for a good deal in determining the attitude of a diocese, and at no time in the reign were evangelical bishops in a majority. Until ousted in 1549, Bonner was a major hindrance to reform in the diocese of London (which included Middlesex and Essex). Similar obstruction occurred at Winchester, where Gardiner even appears to have tolerated a group of nuns who insisted on wearing their habits in public. He was sent to the Tower in 1548. In the spring of 1549 opposition in the south-west of the country moved beyond grumbling and non-cooperation to open violence.[8] The year before, Helston in the west of Cornwall had seen an unsavoury government agent murdered while trying to enforce the destruction of religious images, but early in June 1549 the arrival of the new Prayer Book triggered mass protest at Bodmin. Then on Whit Sunday, trouble flared up in Devon when the parish priest of Sampford Courtenay celebrated the communion according to the new rite and the following day was persuaded to say mass in the old fashion. Other villages joined in. A Devon contingent met with the Cornish protesters at Crediton and together they moved to besiege Exeter. In all, numbers may have approached 10,000. They had a catalogue of complaints – taxation, inflation, and the behaviour of landlords – but, as with the Pilgrimage of Grace, religion welded the protests together. Something of this was down to the prominence of priests in drawing up the final complaints, but the detailed demands do also seem to reflect the person in the pew: "we will not receive the new service because it is like a Christmas game"; bring back services in Latin, the sacrament hanging over the altar, bidding the bedes, holy bread and holy water every Sunday, images, and all the "old ceremonies used heretofore by our mother the holy church"; ban the English Bible and restore two abbeys in every county.[9] Attempts at pacification by the local authorities and the privy council in London came to nothing, and an army had to be sent to suppress the rebels. Peasant casualties in a series of hard fights and skirmishes and in subsequent executions are said to have reached 4,000.

The summer of 1549 also saw massive protests outside the south-west. These were driven by similar social and economic grievances but without the religious colouring. In only two areas was religion a majority issue. The first was in a small region of East Yorkshire, where an attempt to revive the Pilgrimage of Grace was dealt with locally. The other instance was in part of Oxfordshire and there troops were required. However, the particular Oxfordshire grievance was not with the Prayer Book but with local fat cats who had profited from the suppression of the chantries and fear that the property of the parish churches was about to disappear down the insatiable throat of government indebtedness – as much of it would four years later.

Reform Supported

Elsewhere the widespread unrest in the summer of 1549 took a very distinctive form: sit-down protest, not armed force.[10] Many thousands gathered in camps at strategic points, particularly in the counties of the south and east – indeed, enough of them for the summer to become known as "the camping time". From there they presented their economic and social grievances and in marked contrast to the demands of the western "Prayer Book Rebellion", they appealed to Protector Somerset in the language of commonwealth and evangelical reform. This was no negotiating ploy, and it shows how the appeal of reform was broader than mere doctrine. What is even more striking, Somerset replied in like tone, as he wrote to the Essex protesters, "We be glad to perceive by the allegation [citing] of sundry texts of scripture that you do acknowledge the Gospel [for] which you say you greatly hunger."[11] Clearly he believed that far from being religiously conservative, the camps of the east and south and the Thames Valley were best reached by appealing to reform, both religious and social. That he was right was demonstrated at the camp outside Norwich. Its reformist agenda included replacing beneficed clergy who could not preach, insisting that parsons reside in their parishes, that tithes be commuted, and that wealthy clerics provide a school for the parish. At a number of camps, prominent evangelicals were invited to preach. Norwich employed a local cleric to say morning and evening prayer daily from the newly arrived Prayer Book and on at least one occasion the cathedral choristers sang the *Te Deum* in English. Unlike the rest of the camps, which were dispersed by mediation, mishandling at Norwich led to violence and a bloodbath.

England Fragmented

That in the west conservative uprisings occurred and in the east there was large-scale support for reform is not an indication that by 1549 the country was geographically divided over religion. Traditionalists can be found in the east and reformers in the west. However, the contrasts between these large-scale protests and between the responses of individual parishes enable us to identify, for the first time in England, opposite religious alignments at the grass roots. The same is evident at higher levels. On the one hand were the reformers, still probably in a minority, but significant and powerfully placed. Nearly one-third of MPs would oppose abolition of Edward VI's religious settlement. On the other hand stood conservative opinion, on the defensive but increasingly clear-eyed. Bishops such as Gardiner, who had defended Henry VIII's supremacy, were now convinced that the only guarantee for traditional doctrine was a return to Rome.

However, once again, we must be careful not to assume that everyone held one fixed opinion or the other. Parish clergy enthusiastic for reform might be relatively few in number, but that is hardly surprising. From the mid 1530s, the number of ordinations had declined so that a majority of existing priests belonged to a previous generation and had been in orders before reformation issues were even thought of. Even so, how many of these possible traditionalists raised their voices and how many enthused their flock? The evidence of priests defying the law suggests that some at least were responding to lay pressure. Moreover, there was one change which many priests did welcome – permission to marry.[12] Not that they necessarily took "till death us do part" literally. When church law changed under Mary I, most married clerics seem to have ditched their wives in order to be re-employed. Equally, when Elizabeth brought in a new church settlement, perhaps 90 per cent of priests conformed and kept their jobs. This culture of obedience to authority had been in place in the English church for more than a century, probably a reaction to the challenge of Lollardy, and the emphasis on conformity became greater with the arrival on the scene of orders from the new supreme head. A similar concern for self-protection is evident among laity holding public positions. The fear in most town councils was of stepping out of line. It is also the case that there were those who adhered to neither reform nor tradition. Indeed, a new term begins to be heard to describe them: "neuter". Early in Elizabeth's reign it was calculated that a third of local magistrates were indifferent.[13] Whatever their reasons, the silent in-betweens must not be forgotten.

The Example of London

London was a microcosm of all this.[14] Within days of Henry VIII's death one city church, St Martin Ironmonger Lane, had jumped the gun, dismantled its rood, removed the images of saints, inscribed Scripture texts on newly whitewashed walls, and set up the royal arms. London preachers attacked the observance of Lent, and the unsettling injunctions of June 1547 soon followed.[15] Not only did these result, as elsewhere, in a massive sale of church treasures, a number of parishes enthusiastically followed the example of St Martin Ironmonger Lane. July saw St Botolph's Aldgate purchasing six books of the Psalms in English "to have the service of the Church there upon them sung, to the end that the people should understand to please God better".[16] In September, in conformity with the injunctions, St Paul's Cathedral began to sing the litany in English, and during mass to have the Gospel and the Epistle read in the vernacular. By then images of the saints were disappearing in church after church along with much stained glass and wall paintings, which were covered up with Bible verses. The privy council got cold feet, fearing for law and order, but instructions to replace images which had been removed unofficially had limited success. In November 1547 the great rood of St Paul's was demolished and all the statues there removed. St Matthew Friday Street (near the Mansion House) appears to have adopted the 1549 Prayer Book as soon as it was introduced into the Commons in the previous December. By the time an order was given in May 1550 to replace the stone altars in the city churches with wooden tables, one in three of the London parishes for which we have data had already done so. Frequent attacks on the mass were launched in sermons and in tracts and scurrilous pamphlets. Individual young people agitated, some as young as thirteen. The strength which reform in London had attained by the end of Edward's reign is evidenced in the reluctance of some parishes to abandon the Prayer Book services. Two months after the Catholic Mary succeeded, the imperial ambassador reported that "in most of the churches the services" were still being "sung and consecration is made after the fashion of the new [i.e. Protestant] religion".[17] As late as January 1554, thirty London parishes were under suspicion for not having services in Latin. Reform in London had, it seems, been well on the way to achieving critical mass.

This, however, was only one strand of opinion. Opposition to change had been evident in London from the moment of Henry VIII's death. Some conservatives had been so fearful of what the new reformist leaders would do that they quickly decamped abroad, taking holy relics with them. Other Londoners stayed and fought, led by their bishop. Bonner's initial attempt to resist the injunctions earned him a spell in prison and that experience kept him quiet for some months.[18] However, early in 1549, with the new Prayer Book in the offing, the bishop began to allow private masses and then turned a blind eye when "the Apostles' Mass" and "Our Lady Mary's Mass" were resurrected as Prayer Book services designated "the Apostles' Communion" and "Our Lady Mary's Communion". From July, Bonner was ordered to confine celebrations of the eucharist at the cathedral to the high altar, and to stop people attending secret masses in the chapels of foreign ambassadors. Then, when ordered to publicize his submission by preaching at St Paul's, Bonner's sermon unequivocally asserted the physical presence of the body of Christ in the sacrament. He pressed the mayor and aldermen to boycott reformed services and fought back against Cranmer and commissioners sent to investigate his conduct. He was sent to the Marshalsea prison and a month after the sermon was deposed. From his cell, the former bishop soon got in touch with the exiles and the propaganda they were beginning to produce. His resistance, too, undoubtedly heartened conservatives among both prominent Londoners and clergy who continued to ape the old services as far as they dared. Unsurprisingly fights broke out over changes to the churches.

Challenges to the reforming regime also came from the other end of the religious spectrum. With the heresy laws now abolished, radical opinions could flourish. Often labelled "anabaptist", these could go far beyond the relative orthodoxy of the Schleitheim group.[19] Some denied the Trinity or were heterodox on the humanity of Christ, but the biggest threat came from "antinomian" ideas. These taught that human experience fell into two parts – an inner life where it was impossible for the redeemed Christian to sin, and an "outer man" of the flesh where the "bodily necessities of all earthly things" were permitted, including drunkenness and fornication.[20] Censorship had to be restored and measures taken to combat such radical belief – hence the extra provisions in the *Forty-Two Articles*.[21] Reformers with less extreme positions also created problems. London had a sizeable population of immigrants and by 1549 there were unofficial "stranger" churches (later formalized) for those who wished to worship in their own languages and traditions. Those traditions inevitably embodied the more advanced views of Swiss, Rhineland, and French reformers, so that the "stranger" churches constituted a standing rebuke to the slower and more cautious approach to change in England. What is more, Cranmer wanted to make the country into the hub of Reformation Europe and deliberately attracted a number of high-profile leaders of reform abroad, including Martin Bucer and Peter Martyr. These Continental big-wigs themselves kept up a barrage of comment on change – or the lack of change – in England, although they did veil their remarks in decent academic Latin. Former British exiles added further to the mix. John Hooper had to be given a taste of prison before he would agree to wear the required vestments when being consecrated bishop of Gloucester. John Knox we have already noted attempting to undermine the privy council's confidence in Cranmer.[22]

Despite this, mainstream reform continued. Late in 1547 Nicholas Ridley had been appointed to the diocese of Rochester and began removing altars from its churches. In April 1550 he replaced Bonner at London and by the end of the year the city's altars too had gone. He put in hand a visitation of the diocese which condemned the whole gamut of traditional belief and practice, including purgatory, images, relics, rosaries, and sacramentals. He personally quizzed parsons, curates, and lay representatives from each parish, as well as interrogating clergy individually and insisting on conformity. Ridley and his supporters also moved beyond criticizing social evils to working with the City fathers to do something about them.[23] In 1546, the lord mayor had prised out of royal hands St Bartholomew's – one of London's surviving medieval hospitals – and the following year Barts began taking in the sick poor. Its focus, however, was too narrow for the huge problem of London poverty and it was badly overloaded with surplus priests and officers. Ridley raised the matter when preaching to the king and with royal support he and the City petitioned to be given the surplus royal palace of Bridewell as stage one in a comprehensive plan for relief. As the bishop wrote to William Cecil, the second secretary of state:

> I must be suitor unto you in our good Master Christ's cause, I beseech you to be good to him. The matter is, Sir, alas he has lain too long [in the open] without lodging in the streets of London, both hungry, naked and cold.

Energized by the City and the bishop, Londoners had already come forward:

willing to refresh him, and to give him both meat, drink, clothing and firing, but alas, Sir, they lack lodging for him.[24]

The petition was successful and ultimately the City secured three specialized hospitals in addition to St Bartholomew's – Christ's (children), St Thomas's (the infirm), and Bethlem ["Bedlam"] (the insane); Bridewell was secured as a workhouse for the unemployed and idle.

In all, over £50,000 was raised for the hospitals during Edward's reign by citizens of all complexions, but it was easier to unite over social needs than to achieve religious unity. One conservative observer noted that there was "such division through London that some kept holy day and some none".[25] During the crisis of July 1549, William Paget (then secretary of state) pointed out that:

The use of the old religion is forbidden by law and the use of the new is not yet printed: printed in the stomachs of eleven or twelve parts of the realm, what countenance soever men make outwardly to please them in whom they see power rests.[26]

All this became evident when Jane Grey was proclaimed queen on the death of Edward VI in early July 1553. Only one Londoner protested; the rest were silent, stunned because they had expected Henry VIII's daughter Mary. Ten days later Mary was proclaimed instead and London collapsed in a riot of drunken celebration. Much was undoubtedly down to relief that both further rule by the hated duke of Northumberland and the alternative of civil war had been avoided, but the new queen took it as a welcome for her staunchly conservative Christianity. Two years earlier she had paraded through London with 130 mounted servants, each displaying a forbidden rosary and, when she made her royal entry to the city, plenty of houses were decorated with sacred statues and banners. The French ambassador, however, thought otherwise: "All these things have happened more because of the great hatred felt towards the duke [of Northumberland] who wished to keep everyone in fear, than for love of the queen, despite the united show of a desire to honour and obey her."[27] The duke's desperate struggles to repair the royal finances had indeed made him hugely unpopular. Mary was also unwise to overlook what she owed to evangelical reformers. Bishop

Hooper was the most prominent – he sent her horses and himself rode round the Gloucester diocese promoting her title. The military support of the East Anglian peasants was crucial to her success and they petitioned Mary to maintain the use of the liturgy and Bible in English.[28] In London, when ten days after the queen's arrival Bonner's chaplain preached a sermon vindicating the former bishop, a riot broke out and only the intervention of John Bradford, a Protestant preacher (but no supporter of Jane Grey), enabled the chaplain to escape. The queen's councillors were so shocked that they threatened to cancel the City's charter if the mayor and aldermen allowed another such "seditious tumult".[29]

Edward VI's reforms had been implemented gradually over seven years and five months. Despite his father's groundwork, that was too short a period to root new beliefs in the "stomach" – we would say "heart" – of the majority of the nation, even perhaps many of those who lived in the populous and economically active south and east, and not least the people of London. But beyond any doubt, the developments between 1547 and 1553 had given identity to a significant reformed community within English Christianity, and had so changed the physical assets of the nation's church and churches that anyone attempting to turn back the clock would face a monumental task.

23

ANTICIPATING THE COUNCIL

The policies of Henry VIII and Edward VI smashed the old church, but the young king had died before the new could be given solid foundations. For the next five years and eight months Edward's sister Mary set out to put Humpty Dumpty together again. Or did she? No chapter in the story of the English Reformation is so disputed. There is the Protestant saga derived from John Foxe's *Book of Martyrs*, which tells of a queen who allowed her bishops to attempt the ethnic cleansing of Protestants – hence "Bloody Mary". Then there is the naïve Mary, a woman who did attempt to put Humpty together again because she had not recognized how fractured things had become during the course of her lifetime. When England needed converting, Mary fed it "sterile legalism".[1] The third possibility is Mary the unlucky – facing a task which was arguably impossible but for which, in any case, she had neither the necessary resources nor the personal good fortune of long life and a child to succeed her. And lastly we have the positive Mary, a queen who backed men of ability committed to effective programmes of renewal akin to those developed by the Council of Trent, programmes which would have succeeded had she lived.

As Mary made her triumphal journey in July 1553 to London and government, no one had any doubt that she would reject her brother's recent religious policies. Within weeks Gardiner, Bonner, and the other deposed bishops were reinstated. The new queen, however, had far more in mind than reversing Edward's reformation – nothing less than returning England to the papal obedience her father had rejected in 1533. She was, nevertheless, cautious and, when parliament assembled in November, promoted changes which only reinstated religion as it had been when Henry died. Achieving reunion with Rome would, in any case, prove more difficult than initially it had appeared because of the issue of the monastic lands which the crown had confiscated and sold off. In any case, Mary's priority was to find a husband. The heir presumptive to the throne was the reformist Elizabeth, daughter of the hated Anne Boleyn (whose bright eyes Mary blamed for it all). Only the birth of a child of her own could ensure that restoring the Roman church would be permanent, and Mary was already thirty-seven.

Mary's parents had begun to separate when she was twelve and throughout the trauma of her teenage years (which we would describe today as parental abuse) and during the battle to resist her brother's reformation, Mary had come to see the Habsburgs – her mother's family – as her great support. It is not surprising, therefore, that she was lured into marrying her second cousin Philip, the son of the head of the family, Charles V, whom we last met struggling with Luther and the German reformers.[2] The possibility of a foreigner becoming king of England by marriage was anathema to most of Mary's subjects, and in January Sir Thomas Wyatt launched a rebellion in Kent which came close to toppling Mary. The ostensible target was the intended marriage to Philip – better known to us as Philip II of Spain – but the leaders of the plot were almost all Protestants, and under interrogation their religious intention did occasionally show. Once Mary was safe, the wedding with Philip went ahead, even though the terms of the marriage ensured that he would have only a restricted authority.

The queen, of course, was still head of the church and despite her intention to return to Rome, she used her supremacy to replace seven Edwardian bishops and fill a number of other vacancies. The injunctions she issued in March 1554 banned the language of headship but used its powers to command action against clergy who had married, as well as ordering the removal of heretics and reinstating processions, holy days, and "laudable" ceremonies.[3] That all looked backward, but there was one hint of reform: an order that each bishop should provide homilies "for the good instruction and teaching of all people".[4] Further progress depended on reunion with Rome. The obvious papal legate to handle this was Mary's distant cousin, the long exiled Cardinal Reginald Pole.[5] He was also selected to become the archbishop of Canterbury, though that had to wait because Cranmer had been appointed with papal approval and so could not be removed until the pope's authority was restored. The issue of the former church lands had also to be resolved. The pope accepted that in law these were lost, but Pole held out as long as he could, and never ceased to argue that a good Catholic would make voluntary restitution. Eventually by November 1554 matters were settled and in a three-day ceremony, parliament petitioned for England to be absolved from schism and received back into the Roman church. All anti-papal statutes passed in and after 1529 were repealed, the royal supremacy was annulled and *De heretico comburendo* reinstated. In February the first Protestant was burned at the stake, but it was not until December that Cranmer was degraded and the process could begin to appoint Pole to Canterbury.

Revival Once More

Reginald Pole, as we have seen, had long been committed to Christian renewal but always preserving the unity of the church.[6] He had, despite some regret, reconciled himself to the early anti-Protestant decrees of the Council of Trent, but he had not abandoned his vision of reform. England would now be his opportunity. Very generally, older scholars have dismissed Pole as otherworldly and ineffective. James Mackie wrote that "though his ideals were noble, his methods [were] ineffective and his judgement was bad".[7] More recent scholars have been less sure, arguing that Pole's work in England shows him to have been the apostle of reform.

Under Pole's leadership, traditionalists reclaimed the mantle of religious revival after twenty years and more when it had been the possession of the evangelicals. The emphasis was now on the restoration of the sacrifice of the mass as a return to the historic faith of the English people. "Believe as your fathers believed."[8] Henry VIII was presented as wholly orthodox. The continuity of the commitment of the English and their rulers to the Catholic Church was thus unbroken, except for the aberrant clique which had captured the boy Edward. Hence Mary could talk of her father's "pious memory" and exploit the identification he had established between loyalty to the crown and loyalty to religion as laid down by the crown. As little as possible had, of course, to be made of the break with Rome, and Henry's idiosyncratic reforms were airbrushed out entirely.[9]

It would, however, be wrong to conclude that the advocates of revival were satisfied simply with restoring the pre-Reformation mass. As we shall discover, that was the way many, possibly most, English people saw it, but not the new leaders of the church in England. While capitalizing on this existing love of tradition, the writings and principal sermons of Pole and his allies envisaged what was very close to a post-Tridentine Catholicism. Bishop Thomas Watson's 1558 homily on the sacraments declared that the mass "is not given to repair the ruin and decays of this temporal life which like a vapour continues but a [little] while, but to repair the decay of our spiritual life in Christ", a far cry from teaching that devoutly hearing mass would protect against illness, blindness, and sudden death for the rest of the day.[10] Instead of the mechanics of transubstantiation, writers concentrated on the miracle of the real presence and bypassed scholastic reasoning about substance and accidence. The devout way to recognize Christ in the host was not by reason but by faith. Frequent communion was recommended, which anticipated the Tridentine emphasis on the sacramental, as did building a purpose-built "tabernacle" for the reserved elements, in place of a moveable pyx, and having a light always burning before it. Protestant criticisms were taken seriously. There was a new stress on the authority of the Bible, with a strong claim that Catholic belief in the real presence of Christ in the eucharist was no more than the literal acceptance of Scripture: "He said not 'This is a sign or figure of my body... a figure of my blood'. But most plainly he said, 'This is my body, this is my blood'."[11] There was emphasis on interior faith and spiritual transformation, with much recourse to St Augustine and the idea that salvation was God's free gift by grace. Nor are these the only indications of attention to Protestant criticisms. The place of individual moral merit in salvation was played down. To attend mass was to declare "that we put our singular and only trust of grace and salvation in Christ our Lord, for the merits of his death and passion, and not for the worthiness of any good works that we have done or can do".[12] And it was explained that the reason the mass assisted salvation was because it was identical with Christ's sacrifice on the cross; Protestants were wrong to say that priests in the mass were trying to sacrifice Christ for a second time. Even more radical, for a worshipper to adore the material host was idolatry:

"Let him not fix his thought upon the visible whiteness or roundness of the bread... but let him intend to honour the body and blood of Christ."[13] In all this concern for renewed personal spirituality there was one governing assumption – the authority of the Roman church. That was axiomatic for all those who wrote to promote Mary's restoration. The church guaranteed truth. In Watson's words:

> *salvation cannot be attained without knowledge and confession of*
> *God's truth revealed to his church and by her to every member of her*
> *and child of God, whose sentence and determination is sure and certain*
> *as proceeding from the pillar of truth and the Spirit of God by whom*
> *we be taught and assured in God's own word [of the truth about the*
> *body and blood].*[14]

The church alone "was the locus of salvation" with a "divine monopoly on right belief".[15]

Reform in Action

Immediately after the reconciliation with Rome, the cardinal summoned a legatine synod (December 1555 to February 1556) and put to it the reform programme he had thought out during his time in Italy. The Trent decrees which would have the greatest long-term importance would be those intended to raise the standards of the priesthood, especially education and behaviour. Guided by Pole, the synod decided that seminaries should be established in every diocese to train priests for ordination, and by 1558 four were in existence. Special attention was also given to Oxford and Cambridge – weeding out "heretics", and providing a sound training for clerical "high fliers". Other decisions aimed at providing regular parish sermons, but given the immediate shortage of preachers, specific preaching teams were also sent out. The two issues they were to concentrate on were specified as the papacy and the sacraments. It was agreed to issue a new translation of the New Testament, a catechism, and homilies for poorly qualified priests to give in place of sermons. By the time Mary died, only the homilies on the sacraments had been published, but since Bonner had anticipated the need for homilies in the diocese of London, Pole was happy to use the bishop's own *Profitable and Necessarye Doctrine with Certayne Homelyes adoined* (1555). Pole, too, had plans to revive the moribund English College in Rome, so rebuilding the personal links between this country and the papacy which had effectively atrophied under Wolsey and the young Henry VIII. He also paid attention to administration – setting up an office to provide in England the permissions and the like which for the last twenty years had been handled by Cranmer and would now otherwise have had to go to Rome.

Concern for renewal is also evident in steps taken to replace the primers which Edward VI had confiscated. On Mary's accession, printers in England and France had rushed to supply the traditional Sarum text, in English as well as Latin, while carefully avoiding "the wonder-world of charm, pardon and promise in the old primers"; that had "gone for ever".[16] In 1555 a semi-official text was published which went through eleven editions. What made it distinctive was extra devotional material and prayers (some from Protestant sources) specially intended to foster personal spirituality. Thus one is headed "a fruitful meditation not to be said with the mouth lightly but to be cried with the heart and mind oft and mightily" and ends "good Lord Jesus" that "I may fix my sight in nothing but only in thee".[17]

Effectiveness

England was, thus, a proving ground for Catholic renewal which would be promoted by the Council of Trent, indeed anticipating some measures which would not be formally adopted until the Council's final session (1559–63). Pole's approach and energy certainly refute Mackie's verdict "ineffective". But what of "judgement bad"? Pole's recipe for action was undoubtedly realistic and relevant to his Italian experience and to established Catholic churches and parishes on the Continent which were in need of renewal. Yet was that the situation in England in the mid-sixteenth century? Reconciling the lapsed and re-establishing Catholic norms was a laudable aim, but what if there were no norms to re-establish? The Marian church fixed on the death of Henry VIII as the date at which the English church had gone into schism, but in canon law the age of maturity was fourteen. So it could be asked whether, when the link between England and Rome was re-established in December 1555, there were any lapsed Catholics in the country under the age of twenty-three. So what would being "absolved from schism" have meant to them, especially given the ambitious plan to reconcile parishioners individually before Easter 1556? That large age group, too, would have only childish memories of the colour and ceremony of earlier church life; the lights had been out for seventeen years. They hardly knew anything but communion in both kinds and were used to the liturgy in English – for several years, all of it. In 1556 a petition from Norfolk would specifically ask for the restoration of English, alleging that a laity unlearned in Latin could not repeat the Lord's Prayer, the Creed, and the Ten Commandments.[18]

On occasion Pole himself seemed to be of two minds about renewal or restoration. We have seen how earlier episcopal opposition to the Bible in English had backfired, and Pole was careful to stress the benefit of reading the Scriptures.[19] But he also held to the principle which had been dominant in England before 1538 that unsupervised Scripture reading by lay folk was dangerous. Hence it was not a contradiction when most of the *Great Bibles* were removed into church cupboards.

> *[The desire to cleave to the Scripture] of itself being good, yet not taking the right way to the accomplishing of the same makes many to fall into heresies, thinking no better nor speedier way [exists] to come to the knowledge of God and his law than by reading of books, wherein they be sore deceived. And yet so be it be done in his place, and with right order and circumstance it helpeth much.[20]*

"As you take the book of [from] your mother's hand [i.e. the church] so also take the interpretation of the same of your mother... and not of yourself."[21] God gives light only to those who follow the teaching of Christ. In Pole's mind, England's real need was to be guided, not to question.

> *The observation of ceremonies, for obedience sake, will give more light than all the reading of the scripture can do, [however competent the reader is] to understand what he reads, [if that goes] with the contempt of ceremonies. But... they are most apt to receive light, that are more obedient to follow ceremonies than to read.[22]*

The cardinal, indeed, believed the rejection of ceremonies had been the start of the slippery slope.

*Heretics make this the first point of their schemes and heresies, to destroy
the unity of the church by contempt or change of ceremonies, which
seems at the beginning nothing. As it seemed nothing here amongst you to
take away holy water, holy bread, candles, ashes and palm; but what it
came to, you saw and all felt it.*[23]

Edmund Bonner was at one with the cardinal on sacramentals. The most
detailed of the injunctions he issued for the diocese of London in 1555
concerned "the true meaning of the ceremonies of the Church", which
he listed in detail and with appropriate explanations.[24] What parishioners
made of Pole and Bonner we cannot know. For fifteen years it had been
dinned into them, first that sacramentals were whatever the king approved
for the time being, and latterly that they were positively harmful. There is
a deal of difference between restoring meaning to existing ceremonies and
reintroducing them.

Where there was clearly no momentum was to restore monastic life
to the English church. Historically, the austerity and piety of monks and
nuns was supposed to display ideal spirituality to the laity, and, despite
lower standards nationally, a few strict houses had stood out – notably
the Carthusians martyred by Henry VIII. But under Mary only seven of
England's original 800 communities could be reassembled, all around
London, and only the queen came forward as a benefactor. In all, the
reformed communities totalled (with some reinforcement from abroad)
perhaps 100 individuals, and this at a time when 1,000 or more former
religious were enjoying a pension or had been re-employed. "While twenty
years of religious turmoil and secularization had not extinguished the
sense of vocation in a few individuals... the appearance of anything like a
widespread desire for the monastic life as a vocation would never be seen in
England until thirty years later."[25]

Practical Difficulties

The biggest practical obstacle which stood in the way of Pole's plans to
revive Catholic Christianity in England was the condition of the clergy. This
was a traditional starting point for reform, as Colet had emphasized.[26] It
was also commonly accepted that low clerical standards had been a major
contributor to the church's recent disasters. An educated, impressive, and

respected clergy would be the key to Catholic revival in Europe. Yet the clergy which Pole had returned to England to lead was in anything but high public esteem; indeed, it was experiencing "a conspicuous diminution of the status and prestige the priesthood had enjoyed before the Reformation and of the perceived importance of priests in the lives, and deaths, of English Christians".[27] Impressive, a vicar such as William Horne of St Petrock's in Exeter certainly was not; he had sworn that he would be torn apart by wild horses rather than say mass again, but was later found robing for mass and saying "it is no remedy, man, it is no remedy".[28] Moreover, in 1555 parishioners might understandably be suspicious of the authority of men who not so long before had taught that purgatory existed, then that it did not exist, and now would be making a further U-turn, especially as for years they had been told that the whole purgatory business was a confidence trick to put money in priestly pockets. Moving disgraced formerly married priests to new benefices after doing public penance in front of their congregations can hardly have improved respect either, still less where their new parishes were near to the old. The incidence of clergy marrying had varied. In the north of the country it was only a small percentage. In the diocese of London it was perhaps one in three. At Sandwich in Kent, the deprivations left parishioners with no priests at all. Yet where else could Pole go than to the existing priesthood? All that was possible was to do what he could do with the material to hand and hope for a better standard in future recruits.

Bonner led the way. In 1554 he had initiated a massive enquiry into the state of his diocese including sixty-four separate questions for his clergy. He did much of the interrogation himself and his enquiry became a pattern used elsewhere in Europe.[29] He followed this up in the following year with what was the most complete attempt to promote the Pole agenda for renewal. Clergy were to study the *Profitable and Necessarye Doctrine* and expound it from the pulpit, chapter by chapter. They must explain ceremonies in detail. They were to set an example in church and outside, and keep the chancels of their churches and their houses in good repair. Cardinal Pole's own 1556 instructions to the clergy of the province of Canterbury also began with the renewal agenda for priests.[30] Those who were qualified should preach regularly. The rest should read extracts from Bonner's *Necessary Doctrine* until the homilies became available. Clergy must study the Bible and report their progress annually and also teach young parishioners if requested.

Those who could only read to their congregations from Bonner's book had to pay out of their own pockets to bring in one preacher every quarter. They were to conduct services as impressively as possible and to dress and behave accordingly. In ministering to the dying they must encourage the making of a will in good time and urge bequests for the poor and the church.

The quality of the priesthood was not the only obstacle to the cardinal's plans and hopes for reform. Another was money, or rather the lack of it. The former monastic estates were lost to the church, but more immediate were problems in the parishes. Many of these did not pay enough to attract a graduate incumbent of the calibre Pole wanted. In others, the low income forced priests to take on more than one parish ["pluralism"] or to absent themselves in order to live. A minority, by contrast, were lavishly provided for. The cardinal, however, could do little to correct pluralism, absenteeism, poor education, and poverty. His hands were tied because lay patrons, not bishops, had the right to present to most churches. Furthermore, perhaps 40 per cent of England's parishes had been "impropriated benefices". These were parishes where a monastery had been given the rectory and its income, and to perform the services had put in a paid, or rather a poorly paid, vicar. These impropriations had been sold off along with the monastic land so that the erstwhile monastic income now went to lay rectors, and the vicars remained no better off than before.

Pole also faced major problems in dealing with the church assets which he reasonably might hope to recover. Mary was anxious to divest the crown of all its ill-gotten gains but she could not unscramble the past, and existing financial relationships between the church and the crown were anything but clear. It was often impossible even to be sure what church goods had been confiscated and by whom and where they were (or the proceeds of those which had been sold). An even bigger problem followed on the return to the church of "first fruits" [premiums on entry to a benefice], which Henry VIII had annexed – and his annual 10 per cent tax on clerical incomes ["the tenth"]. Not only had the bishops themselves to try to collect sums due, the quid pro quo for returning first fruits and tenths to the church had been taking over the crown's obligation to pay the pensions of former monks, nuns and friars. These were in a totally confused state. It took until February 1556 to draw up a supposedly authoritative list, but that merely exposed instances of fraud and further anomalies. Auditing episcopal accounts did not begin until February 1557 and very little was ever achieved of Pole's plan to use surpluses in the revenues of some dioceses to subsidise impoverished livings.

Renewal Established?

Pole's freedom to promote Catholic renewal in England came to a sudden end in April 1557. Pope Paul IV – his long-term enemy Caraffa – was locked in conflict with Mary's husband, Philip II, and had old scores to settle with Pole.[31] The appointment as legate was revoked and he was recalled to Rome. Mary refused to let the cardinal go, and the former legate was left to limp on, using as best he could his authority as archbishop of Canterbury. Effectively he had been in a position to promote renewal for only twenty-nine months. Nor had Pole been able to devote all that time to church affairs; Mary continually called on him as her major counsellor. We would, however, be wrong to judge Pole's efforts at renewal as total failure. Crucially he nurtured Catholic revival in key areas of England's society. First there was the higher clergy. Many important posts in universities, cathedrals, and elsewhere were vacant following the dismissal or departure of Protestant incumbents. These were replaced with men Pole felt were sound. Reordering the bishops was even more crucial but took longer. Almost half of those in post in 1553 were willing to conform – yet again – but it took several years before Pole's episcopal colleagues were of the quality he needed, even though Mary had consulted him about vacancies before he arrived in England. A majority of previous bishops had been trained in law and the most important of them had been heavily involved in government; many had not resided in their dioceses and had performed their episcopal duties by delegation. In contrast, most of Pole's new candidates had been trained as theologians. Such evidence as survives suggests they did reside in the diocese (as the synod had specified) and were "diligent in visitation and in the conduct of ordinations, with much emphasis on discipline and good order".[32] Pole's efforts achieved far less with the lower clergy, but events in the next reign show that, even so, many of them would be willing to embrace exile and worse in order to remain loyal to Catholic renewal. The other area where renewal took root was in and around Mary's court. During her brother's reign, she had made her household the focus of tradition. It had provided the infrastructure for her challenge for the throne and when she was successful it became the core of her privy chamber. Robert Rochester, the controller of the royal household, was the brother of a Cistercian martyr. The return of orthodoxy had also heartened devout Catholics generally, particularly among the gentry, as well as endorsing the conservatism of magnates such as the earl of Derby, who had been out in the cold during Edward's reign. The achievement fell far short of national spiritual renewal, but "the theological and intellectual stiffening which Pole managed to give the church" did inspire a core of Roman Catholic loyalists, a core which endures into modern times.[33]

24

CATHOLIC PRIORITIES

At the end of August 1553 Jane Grey had a visitor. Since the collapse of her government, she had been confined to the Tower of London and was avid for news. "'I pray you, have they mass in London?' 'Yea, forsooth, in some places.'" Jane was not surprised: "'It may be so.'"[1] Strictly speaking the mass was still illegal, but on 18 August a proclamation had been issued allowing services in Latin, as in 1546, and this had given traditionalists the green light. Responses varied.

In the beginning of September there were very few parish churches in Yorkshire [where] mass was [not] said or sung in Latin on the 1ˢᵗ Sunday of the month or at [the next at the latest].[2]

On the other hand, the qualification "in some places" was correct. In London "the old service in the Latin tongue" begun "not by commandment but of the people's devotion" was only found in St Paul's and "in 4 or 5 other parishes". This less than majority response could be because Protestant feeling was much stronger in the city than in the north.[3] Alternatively, Edward's commissioners had been very thorough in London and had only just finished stripping the churches of their valuables in the latest episode in what was now over five years of pretty continuous change. But when, after the repeal of the Edwardian legislation in November, orders arrived to refurnish and re-equip all churches for "the old service", parishes seem to have complied generally, as they had with earlier royal injunctions ordering the opposite.

Parish Catholicism: The Recipe

We have very little data for Mary's churches – accounts survive for only a small number of the country's parishes – but nothing indicates resistance. One parish expressed clear approval when it sold the table "which served in the church for the communion in the wicked time of schism". Subsequently it would drag its feet when Elizabeth came to order otherwise.[4] That comment, however, is exceptional; what church accounts uniformly reveal is poverty. Returning the stripped buildings and plain services of Edward's church to what they had been was hugely expensive. In the very few cases where it was possible, confiscated goods not yet handed over to the crown, or which the crown could identify, were recovered. Parishioners returned the items they had hidden, others gave money to fund purchases, or were persuaded to restore items they had bought or commandeered. Parishes would also go to some lengths to pursue their former possessions. However, plenty of current owners simply dug their toes in and refused, and as the list of what parishes were instructed to provide was huge, so was the cost. But the orders from the top were uncompromising. Churches had to be restored to what they had been.

The visitation of the diocese of London in 1554 called for a holy water stoup and sprinkler at the church door, half a dozen liturgical manuals, a cope and vestments for three clergy at High Mass, surplices, a chalice, a paten, a pax, cruets, a processional crucifix, cloths and altar trappings, a censer, an incense boat, a sacring bell, a pyx, candlesticks, and so the requirements go on. In 1555 roods were added, along with the rood beam itself – a major construction capable of bearing a person's weight – and images at least five feet high. In 1556, a statue of the church's patron saint was called for. When London churchwardens eventually jibbed at the cost, Bonner was at his most bullying. Three years later Archdeacon Nicholas Harpsfield conducted a visitation of Pole's own diocese and he focused on the same issues which Bonner had in 1554. He found forty-five churches with no holy water stoup, fifty-three with no candles burning before the rood, sixty with no cross on the altar, and forty-three with no candle beside it. There were churches without a paten, without a chalice, without a pyx, without a pax. Many did not display the reserved sacrament. Others had no hangings for the altar or no complete set of mass vestments. And the archdeacon was now insisting that churches should have a second (side) altar and at least six lights for the rood. Most of these defects were quickly remedied, but it does seem that at least a number of Kent parishes had been ready to make do and not spend until they had to.

This evidence of activity on the ground in both London and Canterbury shows that whatever Pole's ambitions for spiritual revival, "Mary's policy was to restore, not to innovate".[5] That is also true of the teaching the Marian church provided. In the summer of 1555 Bonner published *Homelies Set Forth by... Edmund Bishop of London*, "to be read within his diocese of London, of all parsons, vicars and curates unto their parishioners upon Sundays and holydays".[6] There were thirteen of these mini-sermons. They do include a significant amount of quotation from Scripture as well as from the early Fathers, but denigrate anyone who reads the Bible unsupervised. "Though they be never so diligent in reading of scripture yet shall they never truly understand scripture but run continually farther and farther into error and ignorance."[7] The emphasis in the homilies is on correct belief. There is little to encourage prayer or the spiritual life, other than occasional sentences and two pages on the sufferings of Christ; Thomas à Kempis might never have existed. The theme of one homily is the real presence of Christ in the eucharist, but another offers a lengthy traditional defence of transubstantiation, and a third tackles a dozen arguments against both. The homily which poses the crucial question as to "how the redemption in Christ is apply-able to man" answers that what is required is to believe rightly and to live rightly, which

> *no man is able otherwise to know but only by the catholic church which catholic church our Saviour Christ has appointed to be the only school... to learn such truth... for the attaining of everlasting life. This catholic church and no other company, has the true understanding of scripture & the knowledge of all things necessary to salvation.*[8]

Thereafter the homily digresses into a defence of church authority. All Christian people "are required to make a solemn vow at their baptism to believe the catholic church. And he that does so is in an assured trade [course] of salvation if in his conversation [way of life] he follows the same".[9] Such an assurance would hardly be likely to have satisfied Thomas Bilney's troubled search for redemption "apply-able" to him. But it exemplified

Bonner's absolute conviction of "the centrality of the church in every aspect of Christian life".[10] Two more of the homilies are specifically devoted to the authority of the church. Another deals with "the primacy or supreme power of the highest governor of the militant church", i.e. the pope, and for good measure Bonner added "another homily of the Primacy". Thus on only five of the thirteen Sundays in a quarter would a congregation hear of anything other than the sacrament of the altar and church authority.[11]

Pole might promote the use of Bonner's book but it is a long way from the cardinal's *spirituali* days and the confident faith of the *Beneficio di Christo* (already available in English in manuscript):

> *This only faith and trust that we have in the merits of Christ makes men true Christians, strong, rejoicing, merry, in love with God, ready to do good works, possessors of the kingdom of God and his dearly beloved children in whom truly and certainly the Holy Ghost dwells.*[12]

Yet to be fair to both Bonner and Pole, the *Homelies Set Forth* were adhering to the teaching priorities specified by the 1555 synod, and when in 1558 the *[W]holesome and Catholic doctrine concerning the seven Sacraments* was at last published, those homilies did show significantly more concern for lay spirituality.[13] They were shorter than Bonner's, more sensitive and accessible, and they ranged more widely. Bishop Thomas Watson, the author of the collection, gave by far the most attention to penance – one and a half times more than the eucharist – and presented what was essentially a blueprint for spiritual discipline. As well as advice on the confessional, he covered issues of Christian living such as temptation, despair, presuming on God's mercy, and "confession to a man's neighbour whom he has offended".[14] The sermons on marriage anticipate the marriage preparation classes of later centuries, putting "the aid and comfort of man... in their common life together" before the "multiplication of mankind".[15] Unfortunately for Pole's reputation, the set appeared only three months before his final illness, so his memorial is restoring Catholic practice in the parishes, not spiritual renewal on any wide scale.

Along with the limited emphasis of his homilies, Bonner's 1555 injunctions called for church discipline to be reinstated. Holy days and days of fasting were to be observed. Worshippers were to attend only their particular parish church and be confessed only by the incumbent – no indulging in preferences. Except for illness, attendance was mandatory from the age of fourteen. No one, especially the young, was to escape to a tavern during service time or to go sporting on the evening before and so not keep a vigil preparatory to hearing mass. In church they were to behave properly and go to kiss the pax "in procession"; that is, according to social status.[16] A liturgy was provided for "a decent uniform fashion... in bidding of the bedes" which appears to have excluded local variation.[17] The 1555–56 catechism which Bonner published for the instruction of children was exclusively comprised of liturgical material for rote learning, including the responses altar boys needed to know to reply to the celebrant at mass.[18]

Pole's 1556 instructions to the twenty-two dioceses in his province were similarly focused on restoring proper religious behaviour among the laity rather than spiritual revival – although he would probably have claimed that eventually one would lead to the other. Names were to be returned of anyone failing to confess and take communion at Easter. Parishioners were to attend services regularly, behave properly, and occupy the time at mass with "beads or books for prayer", and they were to reverence the host and sacramentals.[19] Choirs were to be re-formed, taverns shut at service time, tithes paid, fasting observed, and either husband or wife had to turn out for a parish procession in mid-week as well as on Sunday. Churchwardens were to put their churches to rights and attend on their bishop for instructions. This same emphasis on restoration is evident in the 1557 visitation of Pole's own diocese of Canterbury. There is no mention of the homilies or the Bible or preaching; what the laity were to receive was instruction in the Creed and the Ten Commandments. A principal concern is lay heresy, in particular any denial of "the real and substantial presence of Christ" in the sacrament of the altar.[20] Next on the list is despising the other sacraments, rites, and ceremonies and refusing confession. Absence from church follows, along with improper behaviour in services. Other behaviour to be checked included avoiding confession and the sacrament at Easter, failing to fast, attending illegal preachings, lectures, or readings in matters of religion, working on Sundays and holy days, and deciding the opening hours of taverns.

Parish Catholicism: Practice

In asking how this Marian recipe was received by parishioners, we have to be very cautious. It is relatively easy to document the recovery of church apparatus and the syllabus of teaching; far harder to tell how this was received. Most of the sparse evidence which has survived consists of official assessments, with all the limitations that implies. Harpsfield's visitation of Kent tells us how an archdeacon saw the situation, but was this how parishioners viewed it and what did they not tell him? And we need to remember that, as always, such evidence as can be discovered at the popular level comes from the committed of one camp or the other. Nothing will tell us about mere conformism or disengagement.

All this said, it seems probable that the Marian restoration was generally welcomed. True, not by everyone – and not only because of the cost. The reintroduction of the mass in 1553 was greeted with dumb insolence in the Cambridgeshire parish of Orwell. Conservative parishioners reported that their priest laughed, and with the comment "'we must go to this gear'… used himself unreverently".[21] When the host was elevated, his supporters leaned back in the pew, ostentatiously. One London employer banned his apprentices and servants from singing in the parish choir. Other Londoners explained, tongue in cheek, that they dare not take the mandatory Easter communion because they were not in the required state of charity with their neighbours. More generally, however, the return to the old ways seems to have been rapid. A Protestant who had abandoned his studies at Oxford for the safety of Strasbourg recalled how on Mary's accession "the papists" there "dug out as it were from their graves, their vestments, chalices and portasses [breviaries] and began mass with all speed".[22] In Yorkshire, Robert Parkyn rejoiced "that holy bread and holy water was given, altars was re-edified, pictures or images set up… [and] all the English service of late used was voluntarily laid away and the Latin taken up again", a virtual echo of the demand in the 1549 Western Rising for "holy bread and holy water [to be] made every Sunday, palms and ashes at the times accustomed, images to be set up again in every church and all other ancient old ceremonies used heretofore by our mother the Holy Church".[23] Not that we can necessarily assume that this welcome reflects an informed understanding of Catholic doctrine. As Margaret Spufford has written:

If the mass ... in one fashion or other communicates the relationship
of God to man, then interference even with the details of the forms of
expression of this relationship is bound to cause concern amongst the
faithful, which often they cannot account for.[24]

In other words, people could have welcomed the return of the old ways because of the simple conviction that this put things back as they ought to be. The irony, of course, is that since ceremonies which had previously united communities had been officially denigrated, reviving them was divisive.

The most striking evidence of rapid acquiescence comes from the gazetted Protestant parish of All Hallows Bread Street in the city of London. Its rector, Lawrence Saunders, would be the second of the martyrs to die.[25] Six months before the execution, Saunders's predecessor, Thomas Sampson, sent an open letter "to the true professors of Christ's Gospel" in the parish, bitterly criticizing them for succumbing. Particularly revealing is his accusation that "you have drawn and pulled upon your heads those abominations... before that by laws they had been thrust unto you".[26] In other words, this parish, despite its evangelical pedigree, had restored the mass before the legislation of November 1553 had come into force.[27] A more general indication of popular support was the return of processions. Some of these were secular, led by the queen or called to celebrate military victories, but we know of some sixty religious processions in London.[28] Bishop Bonner called many of them – in July 1556 he even increased processions to three times a week, plus Sundays and holy days, with again every family in the parish represented. Individual churches began processing again on the name day of their patron saint, most notably the "goodly procession at Paul's with 50 copes of gold, with [the hymn] *salve festa dies* ['Hail thou festival day']", revived in January 1554 to celebrate the patron saint of the cathedral.[29] Parishes also processed for Corpus Christi. City professional groups such as the sextons or the parish clerks had their own processions. Those of the London livery companies could run into hundreds:

The 13th May [1554] was the Fishmongers and St Peter's in Cornhill
procession, with a goodly choir of clerks singing [salve festa dies], and a
4 score of priests [i.e. eighty] wearing copes of gold, and so following my

*Lord Mayor and all the aldermen in scarlet; and then the company of
Fishmongers in their livery, and they and their officers bearing white rods
in their hands, and so to [St] Paul's and there they did oblation [offered
at the high altar] after the old fashion.*[30]

And such demonstrations were not confined to London. The most
remarkable, perhaps, was the procession of prominent Canterbury citizens
which Nicholas Harpsfield led in the summer of 1559 to protest against
Elizabeth's reversal of Mary's Catholicism.

The part of Mary's (or Pole's) restoration programme which had least
success was reviving belief in purgatory and prayers for the dead. As we
have seen, for seventeen years before Mary's accession, the very existence
of purgatory had been under attack by the crown and by church leaders.[31]
Although prayers continued being said around the time of death and the
funeral, confidence in the longer term value of prayers for the departed
had been profoundly undermined. Wills and testaments of the sort
left by Thomas Kebell had become rare, and under Mary there was no
significant recovery.[32] Except, that is, for the queen herself. Her tragic
(and dishonoured) last will left nearly £4,000 in cash and £1,266 in landed
endowment to provide prayers in perpetuity for herself, her husband, and her
ancestors.[33] Nor did fraternities and their core intercessory function make
a comeback. Of the hundreds that had been dissolved at the same time as
the chantries, barely a handful reappeared, although the opportunity these
had provided for significant lay involvement in religious life might make
one expect that they would.[34] In London, only one was re-established: the
fraternity of "the name of Jesus in the Shrouds [i.e. crypt] of St Paul's",
and that was not until July 1556, following pressure from a group of prominent
Catholics and significant encouragement from the queen. Perhaps previous
royal raids on church assets had made people cautious about investing. On
the other hand, there was no parallel hesitation over restoring the mass,
and that contrast suggests that the campaign of Mary's father and brother
against purgatory and prayers for the dead had been largely effective. We
have also to recognize that another result of their actions was "the narrower
devotional range of Marian Catholicism".[35] Few churches seem to have
been able to finance more than one altar, and chantry income was no longer
available to fund the pre-Reformation complement of priests, even if they

had been available. In most places only the parish mass was provided each day, in sharp contrast to the richness of the old religious provision.

In all this we have to remember that Mary reigned for only five years and four months. What would have happened if she had lived longer, we cannot know. Robert Parkyn wrote of Mary "preserving and maintaining holy church", and perhaps preservation and maintenance was an essential precondition for revival, a revival which in the event remained stillborn.[36]

25

PROTESTANT DISSIDENTS

The most obvious example of Mary's church focusing on the past is its handling of heresy. A small number of the most prominent Protestants were confronted in set-piece debates intended to discredit their teaching publicly, but virtually all other suspects were asked the black-and-white question Lollards had faced ever since the start of the previous century: "Do you believe in the miracle of the mass?"

Government Policy

Mary, Pole, and his colleagues started from a conviction that fundamentally the English people were loyal Catholics led astray by heterodox clerics and self-seeking politicians. Get rid of them, and normal devotion would return. On that assessment, the government's initial policy made good sense. It was impossible to discipline all the aristocrats and gentry committed to the Edwardian regime, so the duke of Northumberland was made a scapegoat and a warning, while others were heavily fined. The foreign reformers Cranmer had imported were quietly allowed to depart, along with the leaders of the strangers' churches in London. Their congregations were more reluctant to leave, drawn as they were from immigrants settled in London for economic reasons (10 per cent of the population). Little indeed could be done about any who had taken out naturalization, but pressure was put on the rest, and from February 1554 the crown ceased to be concerned about them. Initially, it was also relaxed about English lay folk and clergy moving abroad, eventually a total of perhaps 1,000. It was even unwilling to exert itself to prevent quite prominent churchmen from leaving the country. The Protestant dramatist and polemicist Bishop Bale was detained twice and on each occasion was released to continue his journey to the Low Countries. At the same time, an ongoing campaign was begun to get Protestant leaders to conform. There were quick successes. The duke of Northumberland led the way in a very public disavowal of reform on the day before he was executed. Thomas Harding abandoned his Protestantism in a matter of weeks, much to the horror of Lady Jane Grey – he had been a chaplain to her family. He would go on to become the principal English apologist for reunion with Rome.[1] Over the next two years, other Protestants who had been prominent in Edwardian Norwich conformed, although some fled abroad later.

The Martyrs

It was, however, not given to all reformers to recant or escape. Some prominent clerics such as Bishop Ridley had been immediately imprisoned for their part in the 1553 crisis; others, such as Thomas Cranmer, refused to flee. He was arrested in September when he challenged the queen's initial religious moves. Other prominent Protestant clergy were detained on charges of sedition and in the spring of 1554 Mary ordered further arrests. At that stage, imprisonment was the only option available in law, but once the heresy statutes had been revived in January 1555, these Protestant leaders became the priority target. John Rogers, the former lecturer in divinity at St Paul's who had rescued Tyndale's manuscripts and been largely responsible for the *Great Bible*, was burned on 4 February, the first of the forty-three who would die at Smithfield, London's slaughterhouse area. Laurence Saunders, rector of All Hallows Bread Street suffered in Coventry four days later. On 9 February, Rowland Taylor, Cranmer's right-hand man, died at Hadleigh in Essex where he had been rector. On the same day Bishop Hooper was, on Mary's specific order, burned at Gloucester "for the example and terror of such as he has there seduced and mis-taught, and because he has done most harm there".[2] He was followed at the end of the month by Robert Ferrar, bishop of St David's.

The queen and the senior Catholic clergy expected Protestants to be cowed into conformity by the horrific deaths of such prominent leaders. Four months after the first executions, Dr John Story, possibly the most aggressive of Catholic persecutors, asserted that, in London, "the sharpness of the sword and other corrections, hath begun to bring forth what the word in stony hearts could not do, so that by discreet severity we have good hope of universal unity in religion".[3] He was wrong. How wrong was demonstrated as over forty-six months at least 229 men, 55 women, and 1 baby were burned to death, while some 30 individuals are known to have perished in prison.[4] The most prominent were undoubtedly twenty-six clergymen, who included notable scholars, as well as five bishops – Hooper and Ferrar, Ridley and Latimer five months later at Oxford, and finally Cranmer in March 1556. The majority of lay victims appear to have been craftsmen; only a handful ranked as gentlemen. This was partly because some of those with status and income decided to take refuge abroad, but more because it was risky to disturb the existing social order by sending the prominent and the wealthy to the stake. Bonner's officers complained that juries "do most commonly indict the simple, ignorant and wretched heretics, and do let the arch-heretics go, which is one great cause that moves the rude multitude to murmur".[5] The self-styled "hot gospeller" Edward Underhill was one of the royal guards and noted there was "no better place to shift in the Easter time [i.e. avoid communion] than in Queen Mary's Court, serving in the room [post] I did".[6] Whistle-blowing was a definite "no-no" in some places, as a servant from Dedham Heath, near Colchester, discovered in 1555. His reward for reporting that his employer was harbouring heretics was to be put in stocks "to teach him to speak good of his master".[7]

The initial policy was to maximize impact by burning individuals in various locations, but from 1556 the condemned were executed in groups of three or more at a few selected sites. Thus in June 1556 at Stratford in Essex [now east London] thirteen died in the one fire. Although (with the exception of the far northern counties) most English shires saw at least one execution for heresy during Mary's reign, nearly 80 per cent took place in the south-east: 61 in Kent, 38 in East Anglia, 27 in East Sussex, and 113 in the diocese of London (principally in the city and in Essex). This reflected the distribution of Protestant beliefs but also the fact that the persecution was driven by the queen and the privy council at Whitehall, and Archbishop

Pole at Lambeth; contrary to Foxe, Pole was fully involved, although rarely at first hand. The heaviest responsibility fell on Bonner as bishop of London and he was continually being urged to condemn more heretics and condemn them faster. Not that Bonner disapproved of burning as a last resort, but in some cases he spent considerable time and effort in persuading those accused to think again. There are instances where he (and other bishops) would accept a fudged confession rather than a death, particularly if they were swamped by numbers. According to Dr John Story, Lord Rich sent Bonner eighty-two suspects from Essex in four batches, and most of those must have escaped the stake.[8] To a bishop, success in a prosecution was securing a recantation, not sending the accused to the fire.

Bishops were not the only people the crown and the legate leaned on. Area commissions were established to search out heretics. Local JPs were told to get involved and to recruit secret informers at parish level. Many prosecutions, perhaps most, resulted from pressure by a committed Catholic. Some were clerics, in particular orthodox priests, who were sent into reformist parishes to turn the clock back. Others were senior clergy, such as Nicholas Harpsfield, archdeacon of Canterbury and close associate of the family of Sir Thomas More (whose biography he wrote). As Bonner's vicar-general he tried about 400 Londoners in forty months from November 1554, determined to cow dissidents with swingeing fines and penances. On his 1557 visitation of Kent as Pole's deputy he doubled as a heresy commissioner and was as meticulous in ferreting out religious deviants as in enforcing Catholic churchmanship. It can hardly be an accident that twenty-four burnings took place in the Canterbury diocese that year.[9] Some laymen too were obsessed with stamping out heresy wherever they could find it, and acted as "promoters" on their own initiative – even ordinary individuals such as "Robin Papist"; that is, the London printer Robert Caly.[10] The many executions in Essex reflect the efforts of four magistrates in particular: Richard Lord Rich, Thomas Lord Darcy, Judge Anthony Browne, and Edmund Tyrrell. All but Tyrrell were turncoats, prominent supporters of the disgraced Edwardian regime who needed to demonstrate their new allegiance. When in June 1555 Anthony Browne asked Thomas Watts from Billericay, Essex, "where didst thou first learn this religion", the answer was: "Even of you, Sir, you taught it me, and none more than you. For in King Edward's days in open session… you then said the mass was abominable and all their trumpery besides."[11]

The Use of Force

Today, burning a human being alive because of what he or she believes is repellent. Despite the time lag, accounts of burnings in the mid-sixteenth century can still make the reader sick to the stomach. Yet did contemporaries feel the revulsion we do? Burning had for 150 years been the recognized penalty for heresy.[12] The criminal law of the day was rough, ready, and brutal; executions were common. In order to deter, they were conducted in public – and could turn into a spectacle. When Christopher Wade was burned as a heretic at Dartford in Kent in the summer of 1555, local growers arrived "with horse loads of cherries and sold them" to the crowd.[13] Is it only anachronistic sensitivity which sees the Marian martyrs as significant – a sentiment encouraged over the years by the expert propaganda of John Foxe?[14]

Thomas Cranmer and other reformers recognized both the crime of heresy and its punishment. This makes them vulnerable to a charge of approving the burning of heretics provided they were not *their* heretics. The jibe is, however, only partially justified. Evangelicals had indeed precipitated the prosecution of John Lambert, but possibly on more than the denial of the real presence.[15] When, under Edward VI, Cranmer and the evangelicals were in control, *De heretico comburendo* and related statutes were repealed. The reign did see two burnings sanctioned at common law, but the accused (as possibly Lambert) had blatantly impugned the Apostles' Creed, Christianity's foundation statement. This suggests that for reformers the threshold at which heresy merited death was considerably higher than for Mary and her bishops. A number of Marian martyrs held unorthodox opinions and Cranmer had been concerned that such ideas circulated in his diocese, but burnings had not followed.

What stands out in the Marian persecution is its intensity. In population terms, the number of deaths was equivalent to 6,000 today. Moreover, the impact was accentuated by the concentration of the burnings in the southeast. Until Mary's persecution, executions for heresy had been uncommon in England. Despite the 1401 statute, most Lollards escaped by recanting. In the early sixteenth century there were deaths, but still comparatively few. Between 1540 and 1546, even the notorious Six Articles act took only thirty-three lives.[16] As we shall see, fluctuations in the incidence of executions make annual totals very artificial, but in the first full year of

Mary's persecution (February 1555 to January 1556) there were eighty-seven burnings.[17] The maximum in any year of the Six Articles was twelve.[18] In the first half of 1558 the incidence of deaths fell for reasons which are disputed, but one could be that the country was in the grip of an epidemic so deadly that the population (which had been rising steadily) actually declined.[19] Even so, burnings were back to normal in the autumn.[20] The persecution was also exceptional by European standards. In the Habsburg Low Countries persecution was notorious, but during the Marian years executions amounted to only some four deaths a month, and that in a larger population where heresy was endemic.[21] In Paris, the notorious Chambre Ardente was executing only one or two heretics a year.[22] As Eamon Duffy writes, "It is simply untrue to suggest that by the standards of the day, the Marian persecution was not very severe".[23]

Persecution: Results

How effective was this severity? It is a recurrent myth that in the long run persecution never succeeds. In early seventeenth-century Japan, a Christian community of 300,000 was wiped out, a process involving some 3,000 executions. The advisers who arrived in England with Mary's husband Philip II could point to the success of the Inquisition in Spain. Indeed, Philip's confessor was an expert on heresy and had written a manual on persecution.[24] Some scholars claim that until halted by Elizabeth, persecution in England was similarly on course for success. Their argument turns on the reduction in the number of executions in 1558. In the ten and a half months before Mary's death, only forty-three heretics were burned, as against eighty-seven in the full year February 1555 to January 1556, eighty-three in 1556–57, and seventy-one in 1557–58.[25] This they see as evidence that Protestant resistance was down to a final hard core and that only the change of monarch saved it.[26] But such a conclusion is statistically untenable, given the idiosyncratic data. The incidence of executions fluctuates wildly. In some months there were none; in June 1556 there were twenty-one; while June 1557 hit twenty-eight. This inconsistency means that the data will not support conclusions based on arbitrary annual totals. Everything depends on the period chosen. The most intense twelve months was, in fact, July 1555 to June 1556, when 40 per cent of all the Marian burnings took place.[27]

What determined much of the fluctuation was the incidence of local "pogroms" – when a "promoter" had a burst of success or a particular bishop a blitz, or possibly when an enthusiastic persecutor such as Nicholas Harpsfield arrived or the gaols were cleared. For example, almost half the national total of executions in 1557 is accounted for by two purges only, one in January in Kent and one in Kent and Sussex in June.[28] The pattern of executions tells us nothing about the supply of victims; what it reflects is the initiative of the persecutors. As for the drop to eighteen executions in the first six months of 1558, this could have been a response not only to the epidemic of sickness, but to government preoccupation with the loss of Calais, the withdrawal of Pole's legatine authority, and the queen's false pregnancy.[29] There had, on the other hand, been similar "slack" periods earlier. But whatever the reason, from July onwards executions were back to normal – twenty-five burnings against thirty in the equivalent period of 1557 and twenty-one in 1556. Statistics simply do not support the conclusion that "the numbers of those refusing to conform was itself diminishing".[30]

Efforts made in 1558 to sustain the momentum of the attack tell the same story. Clearly the authorities did not think that eradication was yet succeeding. And there are signs of desperation. In contrast to his earlier confidence, in June 1558 Dr John Story advocated an end to burnings in London, "for I saw well that it would not prevail and therefore we sent them into odd corners into the country".[31] He was right. The Protestant hotbed of London produced ten martyrs in the whole of 1557 but sixteen between January and November 1558, including those who, as Story says, were burned in "odd corners".[32] The London promoter who arrested Juliana Living threatened: "you shall be ordered well enough. You care not for burning, by God's blood there must be some other way found for you." She replied, "What will you find any worse way than you have found?" This elicited the response:

> Well, you hope and you hope but your hope shall be a slope. For though the Queen fail, she that you hope for [Elizabeth] shall never come in. For there is my lord's Cardinal's grace and many more between her and it.[33]

There is, of course, no way of knowing what would have happened had Mary lived and the persecution been kept up for longer. It is conceivable that it would have driven Protestantism deep underground.[34] Nevertheless, it is clear that by the time the queen died, persecution had yet to succeed.

A further widespread assumption is that persecution is always counter-productive. Tyndale described the gospel as "a light that must be fed with the blood of faith", a conviction going back to the second century.[35] The Marian executions could certainly draw large crowds, but the evidence as to popular reaction is mixed. Some victims were greeted with abuse – John Denley, burned at Uxbridge (Middlesex) in August 1555, had a faggot of brushwood thrown in his face to stop him singing. With others the reverse was true. At the burning of John Rogers "some of the onlookers wept, others prayed to God to give him strength, perseverance and patience to beat the pain and not to recant".[36] The Catholic apologist Miles Huggarde provides a first-hand description of later reactions:

> *[They say] it is mere tyranny thus to persecute the little flock and elect of*
> *God, crying by the way as they pass to death: "Be constant dear brethren,*
> *be constant in the faith, stick to it, it is not this temporal pain which*
> *you ought to regard, your breakfast is sharp, your supper shall be merry.*
> *Therefore the Lord strengthen you."*[37]

Some support was spontaneous. When William Hunter, a nineteen-year-old London apprentice was burned at Brentwood (Essex) in March 1555, he was assisted by his family, and passers-by prayed for him. At other executions, protest was clearly organized. And we must not discount simple humane feeling. When in September 1556 the sheriff's men arrived at Laxfield (in Suffolk) to burn John Noyes, his neighbours doused their fires and were only defeated when fire was successfully kindled from the embers in one house.

There are anecdotes suggesting that the Marian firmness persuaded some, but it is impossible to say whether this was widespread. Northumberland's recantation was little help to traditionalists. It was trumpeted across Catholic Europe, which saw triumph in a repentant head of state, but was little noised in England where he was generally dismissed as a shifty operator who could never be trusted anyway.[38] In July 1555 there was a major coup when Sir John Cheke was captured in Flanders and, when faced with being burned, had recanted. He had been very active among exiles publishing anti-Catholic material for England. It was quite the opposite with Thomas Cranmer. Months of relentless pressure elicited a series of recantations, each more abject than the last, and according to church law that should have been enough. Mary, however, was determined to burn him and when the day came, Cranmer recovered his balance and integrity, repudiated his recantations, and affirmed all his old evangelical convictions. What should have been the "showing off of the Catholic Church's most important prize since 1553 – perhaps the most important re-conversion of the whole European Reformation" became a propaganda disaster.[39] The authorities were not as overconfident at other times. Executions were increasingly held early in the day to avoid large crowds, and by July 1558 Bonner was suggesting that burnings should take place in secret, partly because finding men to assist was becoming difficult. For failing to carry out burnings, sheriffs in a number of counties were investigated in 1557–58 and two, in Essex and Hampshire, were punished. There was particular concern for the impression martyrs might have on the young in London. Early in 1556 privy council orders were given to keep apprentices and servants at home during a burning and the City followed this up with instructions to the beadles in each ward to keep children and servants indoors before 11 a.m. At every execution a preacher was put up to insist that prisoners were being burned because of their evil life and their intransigent refusal of mercy. JPs and other authority figures were required to attend. London was also ordered to have enough force present "to see such as shall misuse themselves either by comforting, aiding or praising the offenders".[40] Indeed, security concerns may explain the move to group executions, even though that sacrificed the deterrent impact of burnings being spread as widely as possible. And there was another fear. The truth of Christianity has from the beginning been authenticated by "the noble army of martyrs". Might observers not conclude that martyrdom vindicated Protestantism? The day after Rowland Taylor was burned, his successor at Hadleigh preached that Taylor's fortitude was "a devilish thing, for to see an heretic constant and to die moves many minds".[41] Huggarde admitted that:

At the deaths you shall see more people in Smithfields flocking together
on a heap in one day than you shall see at a good sermon or exhortation

made by some learned man in a whole week, their glory is such upon
these glorious martyrs.[42]

Much of his book, indeed, is devoted to demonstrating that Protestant
martyrs were bogus. Some observers thought otherwise; they collected the
bones of victims to keep as relics.

Protestant Survival

The failure to bring English Protestants to heel despite nearly four years of
repression prompts the question, "Why?" Persecution had been intense. The
clue is in evidence that some prisoners had to be moved by night and others
under armed guard. The burnings were not succeeding because victims
enjoyed sufficient support, from convinced Protestants, fellow travellers,
and possibly neutrals. It was a classic instance of the counter-insurgency
axiom that extremists must be denied community backing. The south-west
was distant from royal urging and not heavily infected with Protestants,
but there were enough of them, both laity and clergy. Yet very clearly they
were tolerated. The only martyr was a particularly strident woman whom
her husband, children, and neighbours decided had to be dealt with. In
areas where burnings did take place, supporters seem to have been present
on most occasions. Though in a minority, they were not afraid to give
public and vocal support to the victim. When, in August 1556, twenty-three
reformers were arrested "at one clap", the privy council backed away for
fear of what might happen if they were burned together. Instead it had
them released with a bare minimum recantation; six of them continued to
offend and went to the stake a year later. Support was particularly evident
in London and reformist hot-spots such as Colchester in north-east Essex.
In London, imprisoned Protestants were maintained and supported by the
apprentices and the city's gospellers – Tudor gaols did not provide food,
clean clothing, and the like. Close confinement was rare (even in the Tower
of London), so access was relatively easy. Inmates met together to pray,
study the Bible, have regular services, preach, and receive visitors. They
were also able to keep up a lively correspondence and even write books.
Remarkably, given the peril they were all in, a fierce controversy was waged
between the majority who believed in predestination and a vocal minority

of "Free-willers". Outside, priests were jeered at by the young, there were mock processions, anti-Catholic practical jokes, and "naughty plays", while subversive handbills, ballads, and songs did the rounds.

This evidence of Protestant persistence poses a further question. Given that pressure exerted by the crown and Mary's senior churchmen apparently left the choice of death or exile, how did dissidents survive? The answers are varied. At least into 1556, Colchester continued a pattern of unofficial extra-parochial worship which had emerged under Edward VI to meet a shortage of incumbents – meetings every Sunday for Prayer Book services, "sometimes in one house, sometimes in another".[43] Elsewhere dissidents went underground. From time to time, the authorities uncovered conventicles meeting in "safe houses" or the open air and even on ships in the Thames. None of these, of course, could adhere to the 1552 book entirely. They had to create their own immediate structures and these readily fell into a congregational pattern of elected leaders. Some saw doing without bishops as a stopgap; others viewed it as a step to further reform, notably independent roving evangelists who worked under cover. Other reformers simply succeeded in lying low; the England of Queen Mary was not a super-efficient police state.[44] Parishes appear to have felt little responsibility for outsiders and visitors, which made moving elsewhere in the country a possibility. Underhill the "hot gospeller" did that several times. Enthusiasm for making arrests was patchy; Underhill even claimed that "there was no such place to shift [hide] in, in this realm, as London, notwithstanding their great espial and search".[45]

The great majority of Protestant sympathizers who remained in England did, however, neither lie low nor go underground. They conformed. They became "Nicodemites". Like their co-religionists in France, they convinced themselves that it was permissible to attend Catholic rituals and behave as required.[46] John Bradford, the future martyr, was scathing about them, people who "pretend outwardly popery, going to mass with the papists and tarrying with them personally at their antichristian and idolatrous service, but with their hearts (as they say) and with their spirits they serve the Lord".[47] To be fair, Bradford was only challenging believers to accept the sacrificial implications of the faith as he had. By contrast, exhortations to suffer rather than compromise had a decidedly hollow ring when coming from those safely out of Mary's reach. In fact, the exiles needed Nicodemites in England. Many had required help to get out of the country. Sympathizers sent news, collected money, managed estates, and remitted receipts. MPs friendly to the exiles blocked the efforts of Mary's government to cut off funding.

There was, moreover, the positive argument for Nicodemism we have already seen in France, notwithstanding Calvin's fulminations from his safe study in Geneva.[48] God would only allow evil to triumph temporarily, so why not endure? It was called "waiting for the day"; the wheel had turned before – it would turn again. Alternatively an evangelical parish priest might see compromise as the lesser of two evils, more responsible than abandoning his flock to a successor who might well be an ardent persecuting papist. Why not remain in post and be as lukewarm as possible towards the Catholic restoration? Some certainly did that and were in place to welcome the return of Protestantism under Elizabeth. Then there was the Lollard tradition. Evasion and if necessary recantation had preserved their flame of truth for over a century, and more than one reformer had already chosen that route through the minefield of Henry VIII's reformation.[49] Practical considerations blurred the issue too. Exile was not simple, especially for those with no rental income and who, as English speakers, would have difficulty in finding employment abroad; families had to be fed. Nor could responsibilities to partners, employees, and customers be jettisoned overnight – if ever.

Moreover, Nicodemism arguably held more danger for the Catholic restoration than open resistance. After the burning of William Hunter, Judge Anthony Browne challenged his brother Robert "to do as his brother had done". Despite his own evident convictions, Robert's reply was: "If I do as my brother has done, I shall have the same as he had."[50] Enforcing conformity by the threat of burning did not secure hearts and minds. This was most noticeable in reformers from the elite. Among them Nicodemism was pretty well universal. The principal example was the queen's half-sister Elizabeth. Initially reluctant to conform to the Catholic Church, she then did so, attending mass regularly and even going to confession. A number of those connected with Edward VI's government did the same, including Nicholas Bacon and William Cecil, both of them sons-in-law of the prominent exile, Sir Anthony Cooke. Bacon retained his government post nevertheless. William Cecil lost his but stayed on the edge of the court and politics and was from time to time employed by the crown. For some months he gave covert support to the reformist printer, John Day, and in December 1555 joined with other MPs to block the government bill to force exiles to return or lose their property, but he escaped with only a stern warning. Other prominent Nicodemites may have included Matthew Parker, Elizabeth's first archbishop of Canterbury, although as a former married priest and prominent reformed cleric, he had to "lurk secretly".[51] There were others such as the finance expert, Walter Mildmay, and Queen Katherine Parr's brother, the former marquis of Northampton, who had barely escaped being executed as a supporter of Jane Grey. Thus when Elizabeth succeeded Mary, there was already to hand a cadre of experienced ex-Edwardian reformers. To a very real degree, what ensured the future for English Protestantism was not the sacrifice of martyrs nor the high principles of exiles, but the compromises of Nicodemus.

26

CHANGE ONCE MORE

Mary I died early on Thursday 17 November 1558. Tradition has it that Elizabeth was walking in the park of Hatfield House later that morning when privy councillors arrived to greet her as queen. She received them beneath a great oak and knelt immediately to say, *"a Domino factum est et mirabile in oculis nostris"* ["this is the Lord's doing and it is marvellous in our eyes"].[1] It is a good story, and may contain a kernel of truth; Elizabeth knew everything there was to know about milking a situation. Yet the only thing correct in this picture of a young, naïve, and surprised princess is her age. Elizabeth was twenty-five, seventeen years younger than her sister. Mary had been sinking for a couple of months and more, and, although we know little of the detail, Elizabeth had been discreetly lining up her supporters and putting together the skeleton of a new administration. And high on its agenda would be what to do with Mary's church.

A Protestant Queen

There was never a possibility that Elizabeth would continue England's link with Rome. She was the physical embodiment of her father's defiance of papal authority. In Catholic eyes she was illegitimate; they believed that Katherine of Aragon's marriage had never been annulled. Nor could the new queen disappoint her Protestant supporters, particularly in London. They had greeted her accession with relief and rejoicing. In her coronation procession, she would be given a Bible and would ostentatiously kiss it, hold it up, and clasp it to her breast. Most important, Elizabeth was herself a convinced Protestant. Returning to her father's settlement would not be enough. As well as rejecting papal authority, Elizabeth did not accept transubstantiation, a defining conviction she had had to keep hidden for five years. That said, Elizabeth was always a restrained Protestant. She classed as *adiaphora* ["things neutral"] the issues reformers argued over so vehemently. All that mattered was to settle such questions in good order and stability. She had no interest in and no willingness to countenance Protestant in-fighting. She was also unaffected by developments in Protestant thinking which were taking place on the Continent. In religious terms, Elizabeth was, to tell the truth, somewhat old fashioned. Her first instinct was to use the 1549 Prayer Book in her private chapel, and she insisted on having a cross and candles on the holy table there.[2] Jewel even said that despite most of the roods having been removed, the queen

> *considered it not contrary to the word of God, nay rather for the*
> *advantage of the church that the image of Christ crucified, together with*
> *Mary and John should be placed, as heretofore, in some conspicuous part*
> *of the church, where they might more readily be seen by all the people.*[3]

And Elizabeth's conservatism extended to a vehement dislike of clergy wives.

A Hard-Won Reformation

The queen and her close advisers may have known where they wanted to go, but they were well aware they were walking into a minefield. England was at war with France – it had just lost Calais – and there was a French army in Scotland. Indeed Mary Stuart, the sixteen-year-old queen of Scots, was the French king's daughter-in-law and many thought she was the rightful queen of England. Elizabeth's one ally was Philip of Spain, her sister's erstwhile husband, and although peace negotiations were in progress, only by keeping in with Philip was there any hope of recovering or even securing a face-saving deal over Calais. The royal coffers were empty, which meant persuading parliament to grant taxes. Most menacing of all, there was religion. Any changes would have to go through parliament. Would there be protests? And if legislation was secured, would it be accepted in the country at large? How deeply had Mary's Catholicism taken root in England's parishes? The one bright omen was that Cardinal Pole had died the day after Mary and that, before parliament assembled in January, four more bishops would die.

Temperament reinforced by experience had made Elizabeth cautious, and in the early weeks of the reign she gave out confusing signals, possibly deliberately. Her accession proclamation forbade any changes, and mass continued being said. But action against heretics was stopped. Protestants were put up to preach and when Catholic bishops responded they were put under house arrest. Historians have argued again and again over these weeks, but two plans seem to have been under consideration: restore the supremacy plus minimum changes to keep reformers quiet or go for an overall Protestant settlement – a Prayer Book as well as the supremacy. By the end of December a decision had been taken to go for broke, probably because it appeared that the bishops would not again accept a royal supremacy, though they had all done so under Henry VIII. On Christmas Day in her private chapel Elizabeth ordered the priest not to elevate the host and when he refused she walked out. Two days later she sanctioned her chapel service for general use, including the 1545 litany, and ordered the Epistle and Gospel to be delivered in English. Clergy in post (who had all been approved by Mary) were ordered not to preach, and it was small comfort that reformist clergy whom Mary had expelled were also warned to keep away from their old parishes and to keep quiet. Attitudes among the surviving bishops hardened and considerable persuasion was needed to find one who would agree to crown the queen.

Parliament assembled on 25 January 1559, ten days after the coronation. At the start the queen made plain the way things were going when she dismissed the traditional escort by the monks of Westminster with the words, "Away with these torches, we see well enough."[4] The crown seems to have introduced bills to restore the supremacy and to return to Edward VI's 1552 Prayer Book and his provisions for ordaining bishops and clergy [the ordinal]. These drafts were amalgamated into a single bill which was readily passed by the Commons and sent to the Lords. There the ticking time-bomb left by Cardinal Pole exploded. His "Tridentine" bishops supported by the newly confident Catholic peers savaged the proposals. All that was left was an empty husk. Parliament was due to be dissolved before Easter, and faced with the opposition in the Upper House – an almost unique instance – the crown wavered, thrashing around to salvage whatever it could get.

But at the last minute it recovered its nerve. Parliament was only prorogued and a debate set up to discredit the opposition. The Catholic bishops stood up for themselves and two of them were imprisoned for disobedience. After Easter, separate bills were introduced. The first restored the royal supremacy. The surviving bishops were fiercely opposed – experience under Henry and Edward continued to convince them that the very survival of English Catholicism depended on the link with Rome. The bill nevertheless passed because the conservative lay peers were indifferent on the issue of papal supremacy: England had done without the pope for most of the last twenty-five years. The second bill reintroducing a Book of Common Prayer had a much rougher ride. The prospect of abandoning the mass mobilized all the conservative peers in the Lords, but eventually, after making some concessions and in the absence of the imprisoned bishops, the bill passed by a majority of three.[5]

The 1559 Prayer Book

One concession changed the queen's title from "supreme head" to "supreme governor". This was in deference to sensitivities over the New Testament dictum that a woman must not "usurp authority over a man", but it had no practical effect on the royal supremacy.[6] In contrast, the other concessions the crown made to secure the 1559 Prayer Book had consequences which would reverberate for centuries. The most significant were around the eucharist. This, as in the 1552 book, was described as "the Lord's Supper" or "Holy Communion", but the words of the 1549 book were incorporated in what was said to the person taking communion.[7] The result was:

the body of our Lord Jesus Christ which was given for thee, preserve thy body and soul into everlasting life [1549] and take and eat this in remembrance that Christ died for thee, and feed on him in thy heart by faith with thanksgiving [1552].

The blood of our Lord Jesus Christ which was shed for thee, preserve thy body and soul unto everlasting life [1549]. Drink this in remembrance that Christ's blood was shed for thee, and be thankful [1552].

The Edwardian explanation that kneeling at communion did not imply adoration of the sacrament was also dropped, and injunctions issued later in the year specified that congregations should kneel for prayers, continue to bow at each mention of the name of Jesus, and that at communion "for the more reverence to be given to these holy mysteries", wafers should be used rather than "common fine bread".[8]

Precisely why these changes were made is disputed. Later centuries claimed that the intention was to allow communion to be understood in either a Catholic or Protestant sense, but this is contradicted by the sweeping away of the whole of Mary's restored Catholicism. The Prayer Book exhortation to communicants clearly rules out transubstantiation, and it hardly seems likely that dropping the prayer to be delivered "from the bishop of Rome and all his detestable enormities" was a gesture towards the pope.[9] As for the communion wafers, they were specified not to have sacred symbols and to be larger and thicker than before. One possible explanation for what seem to be concessions to the past is that they might reassure people who were Lutheran-inclined and believed in the real presence (such as Richard Cheney, soon to be bishop of Gloucester) and possibly stand well with Lutheran princes in Germany, which England might need as allies. A further consideration could very well have been Elizabeth's determination to have a church which as few people as possible would reject.

A Hybrid Church

The decision to base the settlement on the 1552 Prayer Book plus concessions created a church which was unique. In doctrine it was undoubtedly Protestant. Instead of mass, the *Book of Common Prayer* required clergy and church to say morning and evening prayer daily.[10] The bread and wine is described as spiritual food. That communion is a meal is demonstrated by having the priest stand at a table, not at an altar, and by the requirement that others must eat and drink with him. The book takes for granted that there is no universal church authority: every country is entitled to "use such ceremonies as they shall think best".[11] The *Thirty-Eight Articles* of 1563 (later *Thirty-Nine*) states that justification is by faith only and condemns key Catholic beliefs, including transubstantiation, unwritten verities, and seven rather than two sacraments, along with practices such as the use of Latin, praying for the dead, and clerical celibacy.[12] All this was in step with "Reformed" understanding abroad – "Reformed" from this point referring to the axis established by the *Consensus Tigurinus*, embracing the Swiss churches and their associates in France, the Low Countries, Scotland, the Rhineland, Eastern Europe, and elsewhere.[13] This is often described as "Calvinist", but initially England had stronger links with Basle and Zurich than with Geneva and Calvin, who was as yet only on the brink of achieving his final international theological leadership.[14]

So the Church of England followed Reformed doctrine, but it was not in the least like Europe's other Reformed churches. The structure was traditional. Its clergy continued to be divided into bishops, priests, and deacons – just as the Roman Catholic Church was and the medieval church had been. In Reformed churches on the Continent all ministers were equal, and increasingly churches were governed through a hierarchy of committees: national synods at the top, then regional synods, next district committees called presbyteries, and finally in each church a meeting of elders. The Church of England also retained cathedrals and its old judicial structure of church courts. Most striking of all, the services laid down by the *Book of Common Prayer* were frankly old fashioned when compared with those in Reformed churches across the Channel. It still expected clergy to minister in surplices. Abroad, preachers wore black gowns to show they were ordinary Christians with academic credentials who had been ordained to perform a function. Elizabeth's church was, in other words, a hybrid.

This was certainly not what Protestants who had taken refuge in Europe from Mary's persecution were used to. They had left the England of Cranmer's second Prayer Book but had settled in Reformed churches in the Rhineland and Switzerland where Protestantism was far more advanced. A number of the exiles, led by John Knox, embraced this advance. Others, led by Richard Cox, felt it right to adhere to the Edwardian order overall, although they still felt free to make what they saw as minor improvements, such as not kneeling at communion and not wearing the surplice. The split became highly charged, indeed venomous, and ended in the "Knoxians" moving to Calvin and Geneva, while the "Coxians" (the main exile group) remained at Frankfurt. The result of this was that when the time came for exiles to return to England, they came not to restore the English Protestant church but to change it – some radically, some less so.

Stalemate

The exiles returned to a religious crisis. With so many of Mary's senior ecclesiastics refusing to accept Elizabeth's settlement, how was she to find leaders for the church? She had to hand Matthew Parker and a number of other reformers who had lain low under Mary, but they were not enough. Her only other recourse was to find leaders among the returning exiles. Many parish vacancies, too, had to be filled with men who had experienced reform abroad. From the start, therefore, many, both in the hierarchy and among the parish priests, took up their new posts convinced that the 1559 legislation was only an interim stage in reforming England's religion. A good start (as we shall see) seemed to have been made with the issue of injunctions later in 1559 and reform-minded clergy began to anticipate the next stage by making unofficial changes.[15] Sweeping further reforms were brought forward by the bishops at the 1562–63 Convocation. Then, to their dismay, the queen intervened to block change.[16] Worse than that, Elizabeth instructed Parker to put an end to what she thought was anarchy in her church.

What followed is called the "Vestiarian Controversy" because the major issue was the refusal of Protestant ministers to wear "vestments", distinctive clerical clothing and robes for services, which they felt identified them with Catholic priests and the mass. Some clergy were suspended and in 1566 Parker issued his *Advertisements*, a set of wide-ranging rules which included not only instructions on what the clergy were to wear in church and in the street, but also directions on how services were to be conducted. In the end only two or three London ministers persisted in their refusal to conform, but the affair did change attitudes. It exposed the bishops, especially former exiles, to the charge of being hypocrites, willing to impose what they did not believe in, just to cling on to office. Instead of Elizabeth's church offering an opportunity, in the eyes of reform-minded clergy it began to look like an obstacle.

Lay pressure for further reform also surfaced in Elizabeth's parliaments on a number of occasions. After all, statute had created the settlement and a number of MPs were sympathetic to change. A major attempt was made in 1566 with the support of Parker and his colleagues but the queen refused to give way to pressure to alter the Prayer Book. A number of her ministers, including William Cecil and Nicholas Bacon, were also to a greater or lesser degree in favour of change, but they, like the bishops, had ultimately to accept the queen's will. The personal beliefs of Henry VIII had determined the initial theology of the Church of England; his daughter willed its liturgy – and, unlike his theology, her liturgy lasted.

Whether in 1559 the queen recognized the implications of a settlement which married Protestant theology to Catholic structure is not clear, but the tension which that created surfaced again and again in her reign and has shaped the Church of England ever since. Why she remained so insistent on the letter of the 1559 settlement bewildered people at the time and raised suspicions about her Protestant zeal. There were, after all, the cross and the candles in her private chapel. Puzzlement has continued ever since. Part of the reason was her personal taste for praying rather than preaching, and she valued the choral music of Tallis and Byrd, even though they seem to have had Catholic sympathies. Also there was her intolerance of battles over what she saw as *adiaphora*. Another possibility is that she had been frightened by the conservative opposition in the Lords; some of those involved were powerful regional magnates. In the early years too there was the difficulty of telling how far change could go without upsetting people generally. But the most compelling motive is likely to have been the importance Elizabeth placed on the royal supremacy. Being "supreme governor" of the church was much more than a mere title. It meant that it was for the sovereign to make changes. Inevitably, therefore, agitation for further reform implied criticism, and the noisier the campaign, the more the note of disobedience. The head of the church was not to be pushed. Indeed, for Elizabeth to give way to agitating enthusiasts would be to admit that the supreme governor was not supreme. If she gave way once, where would it stop? The interesting but unresolvable speculation is whether she would have remained so immoveable if she had not from the very start been faced by zealots such as Knox, attempting to twist her arm.[17]

27

PARISH RESPONSES

On 24 June 1559 it became mandatory throughout England and Wales to use the *Book of Common Prayer*, and only the *Book of Common Prayer*. In the same month, a visitation was begun to apply the new religious settlement locally and enforce "injunctions given by the Queen's Majesty, as well to the clergy as to the laity of this realm".[1] These injunctions were based on those issued in 1547, but with some important additions. Priests were permitted to marry and were, as we have seen, to wear traditional costume and square caps to distinguish them from laymen, and provide fortnightly religious instruction for the young. The Marian concern for discipline during service time, in church and outside, was to be enhanced by bishops overseeing the appointment of "three or four discreet men" in each parish to police attendance.[2] The licensing of books was tightened still further – something which all governments had wrestled with since the 1530s. The changes necessary to comply with the *Book of Common Prayer* were called for, notably removing the altar in an orderly fashion. The table to be used in future for communion was to be kept where the altar had stood until needed down in the chancel. The Edwardian requirement for every church to have a "comely and honest pulpit set in a convenient place for the preaching of God's word" was renewed.[3] All Catholic images, decorations, and furnishings were to go, and the most energetic visitors interpreted that requirement as strictly as their predecessors had done in Edward's reign.

Positive Response

The evidence of implementation is once again random and spasmodic, but it seems that within a reasonable time "English prayer books were bought almost everywhere", although sometimes after official prompting.[4] This is not surprising since after *The Act of Uniformity* a priest found using any other liturgy risked six months in prison plus forfeiting a year's income. In London the visitors arrived in the July, and over 24, 25, and 26 August huge bonfires were made of "all the roods and Marys and Johns, and many other of the church goods, both copes, crosses, censers, altar-cloths, rood cloths, banners, books and banner staves, wainscot with much other gear".[5] In fact, the following year the queen had to rein back iconoclasm since it was beginning to involve family monuments. Thanks to the enthusiasm of the visitors, altars, roods, and a great deal else had disappeared in many churches within a couple of years. Within a decade, "a relatively rapid and complete destructive reformation" had been achieved.[6]

For Protestants who had endured through Mary's reign, Elizabeth's accession was the green light. Reformist clergy threw off their Nicodemism; some who had been ousted by the previous regime sought to reclaim their old parishes.[7] Parishes with a sizeable number of reformers began, as they saw it, to put things right. Protestants were especially active in London. Elizabeth's order for the Epistle and Gospel to be read in English was implemented by the lord mayor and aldermen within forty-eight hours of receipt, "which commandment was that day observed in most parish churches of the city".[8] The prohibition on images was anticipated as early as 9 January 1559 with the defacing of a famous London statue. In Colchester, reformers brought the first prosecution for non-attendance at church in April 1559, which shows that they must already have introduced Protestant services. Many city parishes too did not wait until 24 June for the Prayer Book to become law. The act was signed by Elizabeth on Monday 8 May. The following Sunday "the service began in English in divers parishes in London after the last book of service of Common Prayer used in the time of King Edward the VI".[9] Protestants had evidently been as adept as Catholics at keeping their service books out of sight. The Protestants in Rye had the altars down by the spring, the choir levelled by October, and weekly communion operative in December. The rood loft was removed in September 1561 and in the next two months the church walls were decorated with Bible verses. Some reformist parishes took a permissive attitude towards the *Book of Common Prayer*. Services were conducted at choice from the chancel, the pulpit, or the nave. The liturgy was not strictly adhered to. Clergy administered communion to recipients kneeling, sitting, or standing as they thought fit. Some did use the font for baptisms, others a basin. Clergy abandoned professional costume, dressed as laymen, and conducted services in black "preaching" gowns instead of the official surplice.

Such Protestant innovations did, as we have seen, draw the queen's wrath.[10] However, more insidious than a looming discipline problem was a shortage of priests. In Colchester, the resignation of the last Marian cleric in September 1559 left all twelve of the town's benefices vacant. As well as such departures for conscience, the church had lost priests in the frightening epidemics of Mary's last years, perhaps disproportionately so, given their duty to administer the last rites to the dying. In the diocese of Ely 20 per cent of posts were vacant, in Suffolk 33 per cent. Overall, perhaps 10 per cent of parishes had no priest. That situation made it impossible to consider weeding out any but the most intransigent of the existing clergy, even though all had been ordained as "massing priests".[11] Some, indeed, had been in post during all the Reformation changes and would continue for decades more. How much of the reformed message could they be relied on to deliver, indeed of any consistent message? As for the vacancies, returning exiles could not fill them all. Initially the bishops felt obliged to accept as many ordination candidates as they could find, but they soon recognized that, in Archbishop Parker's words, it did no good to admit into "the ministry sundry artificers and others not traded and brought up in learning". They were "very offensive to the people" and "do [a] great deal more hurt than good, the gospel there sustaining slander".[12] Appointing lay readers was another device considered and largely abandoned. All that could be done was to tolerate an increase in pluralism which came to affect over a quarter or perhaps a third of the country's livings. The problem was still more acute when it came to preachers. Protestants were, as we have seen, convinced that the sermon was the God-ordained method to bring about Christian commitment, but there was simply not enough of them.[13] In London almost half of the ministers could preach, but in the diocese of Peterborough only one in eighteen.[14]

Reluctance

Against the instances of parishes which welcomed Elizabeth's church, there is much more evidence of the opposite. Parish after parish acquiesced with reluctance. Statistics are rare but do survive for much of Lincolnshire, an isolated county which Henry VIII had described as "one of the most brute and beastly of the whole realm, and of least experience".[15] In the first couple of years three-quarters of its roods were removed but only a fifth of parishes had by then complied on altars and images.[16] With less obvious items such as vestments and the vessels required for mass, the pace could, it seems, be even slower. Often nothing was done until royal visitors arrived or a local Protestant notable decided to intervene. In Lincolnshire, 153 parishes claimed to have removed all trappings of Catholic worship, but that was not until 1566 and after a specially intensive enquiry.[17]

One reason for delaying compliance with the Elizabethan injunctions was very possibly déjà vu or even despair. Ever since Cromwell's initial injunctions in 1536, royal edict had followed royal edict, and some people must have felt, "Here we go again." Delay, therefore, was plain common sense. The re-equipping Mary had demanded had only recently been completed after much effort and at considerable expense. The material burned in London in August 1559 was said to have "cost above £2,000 renewing again in Queen Mary's time".[18] What if Elizabeth did not last? What if she married? A Catholic husband might turn the settlement upside down. Caution, indeed, could well explain why some parishes appear readier to remove the statues on the rood loft than the loft itself. Carved figures could be relatively easily replaced but lofts were large and often beautiful structures, capable, for example, of supporting a choir singing on festival days. They represented a major parish investment, not to be destroyed lightly. Indeed, in some cases when demolition became unavoidable it was done carefully and the timbers stored – just in case. In October 1561 Elizabeth gave specific instructions to cut lofts down to the rood beam, which was to be kept as "a comely partition" between the chancel and the nave, and have a crest on it, normally the royal arms. Most southern and Midland parishes seem to have complied, but in the archbishopric of York many lofts were still in place ten years later.[19] An example of even more caution is the parish of St Catherine's Ludham – a bus ride from Norwich. Under Edward VI the parishioners had dutifully destroyed the rood and rood loft, but under Mary could only afford to replace it by a crucifixion painted on boards (in the eyes of Pole's bishops, very much a second best). On Elizabeth's accession they substituted a canvas painted with the royal arms but were very careful to retain and hide the crucifixion. It survives to this day; they were not to be caught out again.

Opposition

In a good many cases it is clear that foot-dragging went beyond resenting yet more injunctions and was a deliberate attempt to protect and preserve Catholic ways. In 1559 the churchwardens of Yatton in Somerset petitioned for their images of Mary and John to be exempted. Morepath in Devon refused to destroy the altar and provided a communion table by the simple procedure of putting a board on top and that only in 1561. Once again sacred objects were concealed. In some churches, later centuries have discovered images of saints hidden in walls or under the floor.[20] That was so at Long Melford and there too Roger Martin kept a reredos "in my house decayed, and the same I hope my heirs will repair and restore again one day".[21] To tackle concealment, visitors increasingly demanded detailed lists of the items a parish had once owned and what had become of them – paying particular attention to those now in private hands (as the injunctions required). Even so, in plenty of places Catholic items continued to defy successive inspections over several years. As late as April 1567 nine parishioners of Aysgarth in the North Riding of Yorkshire were forced to do public penance for keeping "hid certain idols and images un-defaced and likewise certain old papistical books in the Latin tongue".[22]

As we have seen, only a minority of parishes and clergy had been reached by Pole's renewal programme, so most of this resistance must be explained by conservatism, a preference for the comfort of tradition. The welcome for Mary's restoration of the mass was principally a welcome for the known and valued, a return to the good old ways.[23] It restored the rituals proper to life events, "actions to be performed in a particular way on particular occasions".[24] The parish clerk of Ripon continued producing communion wafers on which, in direct violation of the injunctions, he impressed sacred pictures.[25] Communicants continued to cross themselves as they had always done and some insisted on taking the wafer in their mouths rather than their hands. Swear words remained solidly traditional. Funeral rites were particularly resilient – candles round the coffin, bells tolling, and prayers for the dead on the eve of All Souls; crosses continued being placed on graves. In the words of the notable Reformation scholar A.G. Dickens:

> *The survival of medieval customs, the retention of proscribed relics of the old religion, the complete lack of enthusiasm for reformed doctrine and practices, a general conservatism and a reluctance to obey the Elizabethan injunctions, these were widespread.*[26]

He was writing about Yorkshire, but the assessment applies nationwide.

The Threat to Catholic Survival

Catholics were inspired to conduct this rearguard defence of their sacred objects by the assurance that "a day would come". It was, however, quite another problem when it came to living as a Catholic in the meanwhile. The first to suffer were the clergy. The Elizabethan legislation required all clerics, lay office-holders, and those "suing livery" [inheriting large estates] to take an oath, declaring:

> *in my conscience that the Queen's Highness is the only Supreme Governor of this realm... as well in all spiritual or ecclesiastical things or causes as temporal, and that no foreign... prelate... has... any authority ecclesiastical or spiritual within this realm.*[27]

The penalty for refusing the oath was loss of office.[28] All but one of the bishops refused and were deprived. House arrest and prison followed, as also for other key individuals associated with Pole; the last, Bishop Thomas Watson of the *[W]holesome and Catholic doctrine concerning the seven Sacraments*, died in Wisbech Castle in 1584. Intransigence was widespread elsewhere in the upper ranks of the church. The clerical proctors in the Canterbury Convocation voted solidly in defence of papal supremacy and the miracle of the altar. Figures for archdeacons and the staff of the cathedrals are incomplete, but the indication is that more than half opted out of Elizabeth's church. Resistance was particularly strong in the universities.[29] The head of all but one of the Oxford colleges resigned or was sacked, along with many of the college fellows. Cambridge was perhaps less affected, but even there, in three colleges alone, forty-eight new fellows were required in the two years 1560 and 1561. All this says a great deal for the success of Pole's efforts at renewal, but the consequence was that traditionalists in the parishes, both clergy and laity, were substantially left leaderless.

Roman Catholics did not have the option of do-it-yourself undercover meetings, which had sustained a number of Protestant dissidents under Mary. These had only needed access to a Bible. Catholic devotional life focused on the sacraments, but where could they find a priest to dispense sacramental grace once the *Book of Common Prayer* became mandatory? A handful of aristocrats and rich gentry were able to maintain a resident chaplain to celebrate mass in private, but for the great majority the future seemed to be the Church of England.

That prospect horrified a number of serving priests. Some abandoned their benefices and became "hedge-priests", offering the Catholic sacraments as and how they could, possibly in collaboration and in some cases supported and even organized by the few survivors of leading Marian clergy. How numerous they were we do not know. Deprivations nationally could have been as few as 300, but we know nothing about resignations.[30] The only reliable figures we have are for priests in the north who were summoned to take the oath of supremacy, and these suggest that only 10 per cent actually refused the oath, although perhaps a third were absent for reasons unknown.[31] Other priests became "liturgical hermaphrodites".[32] They retained their benefices and performed Prayer Book services but offered the mass in private, or else combined the new services with as much of the traditional ritual as they dared. Neither course was, however, easy or safe in towns or populous areas where it would be noticed, and at best the provision was sporadic and occasional.

The answer most convinced lay Catholics arrived at was the one Protestants had reached under Mary: Nicodemism, outward conformity. Robert Parsons, the most hated of Catholic exiles, wrote in 1580 that "at the beginning of the reign of the queen… for ten consecutive years practically all Catholics without distinction used to go to their [i.e. Protestant] churches".[33] "Practically all Catholics without distinction" was probably an exaggeration, but certainly it was true of the great majority. After all, why isolate yourself from your neighbours when on most Sundays all you would hear at morning prayer were psalms and Bible readings, and prayers which were rooted in the 1,000-year-old prayer traditions of Christianity? When there was anything offensive you could dissent mentally. The new communion service was admittedly a problem, but attendance was only compulsory at Easter and excuses could be found. Moreover, absence from church risked a one shilling fine, levied for the poor of the parish.[34] True, the services were in English, but that was an attraction. Catholics in exile abroad admitted in 1567 that "even under Catholic jurisdiction [i.e. Mary] people were bitterly unwilling to surrender" their English Bibles.[35] Even prominent conservatives endorsed Nicodemism. The Spanish bishop representing that pillar of orthodoxy, Philip II, advised enquirers that attending Protestant services was not of itself sinful.[36]

Outward conformity and a waning of zeal for the old ways were, of course, exactly what the crown wanted. When Elizabeth famously (but allegedly) said that she had no wish "to make windows into men's hearts", the implication was that she was only interested in conformity of body, but that was death to Catholic integrity. What it produced was the "church papist", who did attend the required services but as infrequently as possible and with as little participation and as much dumb insolence as he could get away with. Some brought their Latin primers with them to read, others told their beads, one played with a pet dog, some walked out in the sermon, others slept. Given the manpower problems of Elizabeth's bishops, church papists could have been a majority in many parishes. But powerful influences worked against the position in the long term. The royal supremacy had been dinned into English ears for twenty of the previous twenty-six years; anything else smacked of disloyalty. There were immediate pressures too – the pull of the parish community and the pull of the family, which commonly included both traditionalists and Protestants, sometimes even in the same marital bed. And particularly enticing to the younger generation, the future lay in accepting the system, not in maintaining the protests of their fathers.[37]

The Settlement Settled

By the end of Elizabeth's first ten years, the shape of that future had been set. On any Sunday in 1568 and after, the majority of England's parishioners would still be found wending their way to their local church just as they – or their parents – had done in 1530 and before. What they found, however, was very different. No holy water to cross themselves with, and everything plain and without colour. Whether that was so at All Saints North Street in the city of York we do not know. Queen Mary had presented Christopher Assheton to the living in June 1554 and he may have been one of that minority of priests who adhered as far as they could to the old ways.[38] The norm was for walls to be whitewashed and bare except, perhaps, for Bible texts. Where the high altar had had pride of place was a wooden table. Either side, where statues of the Virgin and the patronal saint had stood, were boards inscribed with the Ten Commandments. No side altars. The statues had gone from side chapels too, and possibly some or all of the windows which had held stained-glass likenesses of the saints. More revolutionary than anything else, the church was no longer dominated by life-sized figures of the crucified Christ with his mother and St John. Instead, there was the royal shield of arms. The parish was no longer part of Western Christendom answerable to the pope. It was a unit in a Church of England answerable to its supreme governor.

The Sunday Service

In conforming parishes (the majority), services were as radically different as the surroundings. There was no parish mass. The only ecclesiastical vestment the priest wore was the surplice.[39] Morning prayer was the main service, said in English as the liturgy was everywhere, except at the universities. However, unlike the Latin equivalent – matins – congregational participation was integral (the same was true at evensong). As well as being required to say "Amen" to the prayers, congregants had to recite the Lord's Prayer, the *Benedictus*, and the Apostles' Creed, all pieces previously said or sung in the mass in Latin by the priest or singing men.[40] In the absence of prayer books (and people who could read), the congregation must have repeated the phrases after the priest or parish clerk, until the changes had been memorized, a practice known as "lining out".[41] That must have been the case too with other elements in the service, such as the General Confession, the *Venite* [Psalm 95], the *Te Deum*, and the Responses.[42] Increasingly, the psalms for the day were sung in English metrical settings which had already circulated under Edward VI; *Sternhold and Hopkins*, the most famous psalter, was published in 1562. However, since not everyone in a village could read, "lining out" was often adopted to enable all to sing. The service included two Scripture readings, one from the Old and another from the New Testament. Also there were collects and prayers, including a prayer for the queen, and morning prayer concluded with the benediction. Evensong was similar, but the congregation recitations were the *Magnificat* ["My soul doth magnify the Lord"] and the *Nunc Dimittis* ["Lord, now let thy servant depart in peace"], again in English. As for the communion, as well as saying or singing the *Gloria* in English, the congregation now gave responses to the reading of the Ten Commandments and said the Nicene Creed. The peak of lay involvement is that a communicant could offer the confession:

> *Then shall this general confession be made, in the name of all those that are minded to receive the Holy Communion, either by one of them, or else by one of the Ministers or by the Priest himself.*[43]

Congregations no longer learned by looking. "God was to be heard, not seen."[44]

Consequences

The enduring consequences of the Elizabethan settlement were both destructive and constructive. On the negative, it put an end finally to ecclesiastically tolerated popular superstition which Mary had wanted to see revived.[45] The church would no longer offer holy bread, holy water, and other apotropaic remedies and protections. There were no statues to reverence and no saints to aid the prayers of supplicants. The collect for the feast of St Michael the Archangel [Michaelmas] simply asks God that the angels "by thy appointment may succour and defend us on earth", while that for All Saints' Day is merely a prayer "to follow thy blessed saints in all virtuous and godly living".[46] The church ceased to endorse charms and incantations; masses could no longer be commissioned for specific purposes. All that was now sanctioned was belief in evil and the devil as revealed in Scripture, while the accidents of life were rationalized as within God's providence.

The positive legacy of the Elizabethan settlement was the Prayer Book itself. Hearing and reciting the liturgy Sunday by Sunday could not fail to have an effect – Christopher Haigh has called it "osmosis".[47] By the end of the 1560s, the Prayer Book services – matins, evensong, and holy communion – had become the norm for most people. Indeed, in the twenty years since 1549, the continuity of Prayer Book worship had only been interrupted by six years of Mary's restored Catholicism. In contrast to the laissez-faire approach of some reformist ministers early in the reign, by the 1570s evidence begins of parishioners complaining when their priest departed from the set liturgy; some even brought their own Prayer Books to church in order to check. Politics too had an impact. We have seen how political loyalty was a factor in securing acceptance of religious change. This, as we shall see, was hugely reinforced by the perception of an increasing Roman Catholic threat, especially after a short-lived rebellion by traditionalist earls in the north in 1569, a papal bull deposing Elizabeth, the arrival of missionary priests, and Catholic plots against the queen's life.[48] Events on the Continent reinforced the fear. In the Low Countries a new Spanish governor, the duke of Alva, had arrived in 1567 with a large army and set about enforcing obedience to Philip II and the Church of Rome by violence and executions. In August 1572, the Massacre of St Bartholomew would see several thousand French Protestants butchered in Paris and the provinces, and led to a number taking refuge in England. Dislike of Spain – then Europe's dominant power – was also fed by friction over English incursions in the Caribbean, which Spaniards saw as their private lake. The climax came in 1588 with Philip II's attempt to invade England. His primary grievance was England's support for his rebellious Dutch subjects, but the Armada was equally a religious crusade intended to bring the country back to papal obedience. All this taken together made Protestantism the identifying mark of national identity. Confessionalization had come to England.

28

REVIVAL DIVIDED

'History is little more than the register of the crimes, follies and misfortunes of mankind' – so Edward Gibbon famously wrote in *The Decline and Fall of the Roman Empire*.[1] It is a conclusion which the story of the Reformation in the first three-quarters of the sixteenth century can seem to demonstrate. What had begun in longings for a deeper Christian spirituality appears to have ended in self-interest, political interference, division, religion as a confessional label, and all too many deaths. Yet that is not the whole story; the longed for religious revival was not aborted. Fragmented and incomplete – and could it have been otherwise? – it is nevertheless both detectable and vibrant within each branch of the now divided Christianities of Western Europe and England.

A Roman Catholic Future for England?

From the standpoint of Elizabeth and her ministers, church papists were a minor problem. Time and the spread of a Protestant ministry would deal with them; they had no future. But from a Roman Catholic position the reverse was true. They presented a huge opportunity and the faithful were not without resource. For the first time, leading Catholics chose to go into exile, and in some numbers. There had been occasional refugees under Henry and Edward, notably the remnants of Sir Thomas More's family and circle, but from Elizabeth's reign, exile became an enduring dimension of the English Catholic community. Initially the émigrés were drawn precisely from the social and academic elite that had experienced Pole's renewal and were desperate to continue the religious life they had recovered. Sir Francis

Englefield, Mary's privy counsellor, went abroad in May 1559, never to return. Jane Dormer, her favourite maid of honour, left England in July 1559 following her marriage to de Feria, the Spanish ambassador, but some thirty priests and gentlemen seized the chance to go with her. Their expectation, as of those who left subsequently, was to return to England when Roman Catholicism had triumphed – it was their turn now to "wait for a day". A number of the restored monks and nuns went with a more immediate object – to continue their vocation in a foreign house. Others, helped by de Feria, tried to stick together. The nuns of Syon were eventually able to settle in Portugal, and carried on getting recruits from England until the community returned in 1861, where it continues.

The exiles were out of the reach of England, but the reverse was not the case. Ties of family, friendship, and property persisted and the Channel was a most ill-guarded moat. With reasonable caution Roman Catholics were as able to communicate and even travel to and fro as readily as Protestant exiles had done in earlier years. Thus despite being abroad, the exiles remained part of the Elizabethan religious scene. This was particularly true of the significant number of academics who had abandoned Oxbridge – eventually over 100. They saw it as their mission to sabotage the intellectual respectability of the Elizabethan settlement. The principal initial base for the campaign was Louvain, nine miles west of Brussels, where the More family had sheltered. Over the next ten years, they produced some sixty books in English, the great majority of them apologetic, plus others in Latin. These were smuggled across the Channel, much as Tyndale's New Testament and other reformist literature had been in the reign of Henry VIII, with the authorities once more frustrated in their attempts to stem the flow. As John Jewel, the Elizabethan bishop of Salisbury, complained to Heinrich Bullinger in 1565, "the popish exiles are disturbing us and giving us all the trouble in their power".[2] They were so impressive academically and so productive that Protestant leaders in England were forced to respond in kind. In what has been called "The Great Controversy" (to distinguish it from several other debates), fifty-two titles were produced on both sides in eight years from 1562, with Jewel leading for England and Thomas Harding for Rome.[3] In effect, Catholic exiles compelled the Elizabethan settlement to define and justify itself, which Jewel did in his authoritative *Apology of the Church of England* (1562) and subsequent follow-up.

The intellectual assault from Louvain troubled the Church of England bishops but is unlikely to have reached the constituency of church papists. That required boots on the ground, and two men stand out as leaders in that role: Lawrence Vaux and William Allen. Vaux had been warden of the prestigious collegiate church of Manchester, and had from the start campaigned against the settlement and the temptation of Nicodemism, until England became too hot for him.[4] Allen was one of the academics who had left Oxford, but when ill health forced him back to his native Lancashire he too was horrified by what he found.[5] Rome was equally concerned, but it was not until 1566 that Vaux was able to bring to England a formal papal ruling which forbade conformism. Armed with this, the surviving loyal priests had the authority to instruct Roman Catholics to refuse to attend the established church – an offence technically known as "recusancy" and it becomes possible to talk of an emerging "recusant" community. In practice, however, the pastoral advice which the priests gave in private seems to have been less absolute than the theory. They accepted that circumstances would compel many would-be Catholics to continue toying with occasional conformity in order to protect themselves and their families. In consequence, recusancy had an intransigent core, but fuzzy edges. Historians continue to argue how long this penumbra of church papists remained important, but it is possible that part of the growing support for Prayer Book religion came from some who decided that its increasingly outdated liturgy was enough to satisfy their wish for tradition and ceremony.[6]

Allen, however, recognized that recusancy and occasional conformity would not guarantee the future of a Tridentine Catholicism. The reasons conservatives gave when charged with failing to attend the parish church were uniformly negative – a dislike of change, objection to what was lacking in the new non-Roman liturgies – no priest, no altar, no sacrifice – and a rejection of what they saw as lax moral discipline. Only positive input would correct that deficit in morale. A conformist device which was proving useful was for the father of a family to attend Protestant services alone. That was reckoned to cover his household, and so freed the wife to educate the children as Catholics. Yet if the community was to flourish, the Protestant monopoly of further education had also to be challenged. Allen returned to the Low Countries, was ordained, and in 1568 an English Catholic college was opened at Douai [south of Lille]. "Our aim", Allen wrote later, "is and always has been to train Catholics to be plainly and openly Catholics."[7] A decade later, Douai had eighty students. Also integral to the project was Allen's belief that "it would be an excellent thing to have men of learning always ready outside the realm to restore religion when the proper moment should arrive, although it seemed hopeless to attempt anything while the heretics were masters there".[8] Yet the clergy in England loyal to Rome were ageing, and having replacements "ready outside the realm" was not enough. For recusancy to survive, new priests had to be sent to keep open the channels of sacramental grace. Douai turned to producing missionaries. The first arrived in 1574 and over the remaining twenty-nine years of Elizabeth's reign, 438 came.

A Continuing Catholic Community

The missionary priests arrived to find a drastically changed situation. In April 1570 the pope had issued the bull excommunicating Elizabeth, depriving her of "her pretended title to the throne", absolving all oaths sworn to her and ordering the faithful to disobey her orders and laws.[9] The original intention had been to help the rebel northern earls, but the bull came too late.[10] To make matters worse, the following year Pius V and Spain joined in a plot to depose Elizabeth, which marginally involved Mary Queen of Scots and the duke of Norfolk (who was executed). Elizabeth still clung to the hope that a church of conformists would emerge over time and blocked legislation aimed at putting further pressure on the indigenous Catholic community, but she did accept measures against the pope. Expressing support for the papal bull or saying that the queen was a schismatic or a heretic was declared high treason. So too was bringing papal material into the country or attempting to convert anyone to Rome; importing Catholic artefacts such as rosaries was made a lesser offence. As for the exiles, any who did not return within six months were to lose their property. The hostile reaction in England to the pope's action meant that although the missionary priests arrived claiming that their purpose was exclusively spiritual, the crown, understandably and justifiably, saw them as traitors determined to set up a fifth column. Increasingly severe penal laws were passed against them and against laity who gave them assistance and soon against the whole recusant community. In 1577 the first missionary priest was executed. The situation became even worse in 1580 when Jesuits arrived, the counter-reformation *corps d'elite* swearing absolute and direct obedience to the pope.[11] In all some 124 Catholic clerics were put to death by Elizabeth, plus perhaps 59 lay folk.[12] It is understandable that Roman Catholics today regard these individuals as martyrs, but given the papal bull, the Elizabethan state could very reasonably conclude that they were political subversives.[13]

There has been considerable academic debate about the impact of the émigré priests on Roman Catholic fortunes in the last decades of the sixteenth century and beyond. These are outside the concerns of this book, but two general conclusions seem justified. First, the hardships and sacrifices of the priests and their supporters may have encouraged something like a surge in Catholics "coming out", and certainly did contribute significantly to ensuring that Roman Catholicism would remain a permanent element in English Christianity. It is hard to imagine that result otherwise. Second, their efforts did not in the end sound the "alarm spiritual against foul vice and proud ignorance" promised by Edmund Campion.[14] Indeed some historians suggest that the objective of Campion, Allen, and their fellow Jesuits to reconvert England was not shared by the other missionaries. There was no agreement on evangelizing the country, no coherent mission strategy, and little exploitation of the opportunity presented by the continued existence of church papists. In particular, there was a failure to prioritize the needs of the 40 per cent of the country's recusants who lived in the north and the many more in the region who were sympathetic to tradition. Reportedly, only one missionary in five ever penetrated this potentially rich field where the resources of the Church of England were stretched beyond the limit. The result was that although Catholicism remained strong in Lancashire and the North Riding of Yorkshire, it was the traditional Catholicism of parish and folk religion and festivals, effectively the broad popular culture of the pre-Reformation years.[15]

That, however, is a verdict heavily influenced by hindsight. At the time, the concentration of Tridentine missionary priests on the south and east must have seemed the sensible policy. The bulk of the population was there. Most priests arrived through a port on the Channel coast and in order to survive they had to be sheltered within the area network of sympathetic aristocrats or gentlemen. They also needed finance. It could be argued too – and with some justice – that leaders of Elizabethan society offered the most promising constituency for missionary work, given the influence they could exert over their tenants and neighbours. An individual peasant would count for little, but a Catholic gentleman had clout, and even more so if occasional conformity allowed him to remain a magistrate.[16] But there was a downside. Priests easily "went native". Their hosts did not want them to move, they had no sympathy with any campaign to reconvert England – let alone for the pope's instructions to disobey Elizabeth – and no intention at all of risking martyrdom; the less attention they and their families attracted, the better. The result was what is called "landlord [seigneurial] Catholicism", where priests (often disguised as tutors or gentlemen stewards) were effectively reduced to serving as domestic chaplains to propertied Catholic families and, at most, the families' immediate tenants and contacts.

Yet, by an irony, it was because of this retreat that the spiritual renewal longed for in the pre-Reformation years became possible. Much Catholic devotion is nurtured by actions rather than study – meditating on Christ's presence in the consecrated host, following the daily office, regularity at confession, observing the calendar with its fasting and festivals, appropriate rites of passage, especially at death. In isolation, a Catholic had no future.[17] In what could be a relatively segregated and protected gentry household, the whole rhythm and ethos of living could be Catholic, and intense Christocentric spirituality became a possibility. With a priest frequently in residence, a spiritual director would be on hand. When that was not the case and hence the sacraments were not available, devotional life could focus on the use of the (illegal) rosary, both privately and communally. In those houses where such a focus of devotion did develop, the principal ladies in the family were generally the driving force. Male members had to compromise in order to function in the wider society; women faced few public demands and were able to create the domestic godliness they sought. In such communities the longed for religious revival did find a Roman Catholic expression.

The Protestant Future?

Elizabeth's bishops, as we have seen, had a major problem in finding clergy which were both sympathetic and educated.[18] Thanks to the Catholic takeover of the universities under Mary, there was no possibility of an immediate supply of the educated personnel needed if Protestantism was to become the English religion. Suitable scholars were quickly appointed to the many academic vacancies, but time was needed to achieve a flow of educated clergy into the church. Not until 1571 were the bishops able to require ordinands not to have worked in "base and handicraft labour", to have some competence in Latin and the Scriptures, and to have been educated "either in the university or some other inferior school".[19] Bishops and archdeacons individually did what they could. One such was Richard Cox, bishop of Ely, whom we last saw at Frankfurt, tussling with John Knox. He resided as much as possible in his diocese and conducted visitations in person, focusing on the clergy. An early step was to tighten up on the quality of ordinands. His object was an active preaching ministry and four sermons a year in every parish, and with Cambridge in his see Cox was better placed than his colleagues to provide them. He also insisted on the young being taught the catechism. Absenteeism and pluralism were tackled as much as possible, although the poor salaries in many parishes were always a problem. Some urban centres too did what they could to provide reformist preaching. Early in the reign, Leicester, Colchester, Coventry, and Ipswich set up civic lectureships, well paid enough to attract the best preachers and not restricted by parish boundaries. Other towns followed suit. Another device to promote both clerical standards and Protestant ideas was the "prophesying". This was a training conference encouraged by the bishop to improve the standards of his clergy where sermons ["prophecies"] were delivered and Bible passages discussed in the presence of senior clergy and laity.[20] Elizabeth thought them dangerous and ordered them stopped – opposing her cost Parker's successor at Canterbury the leadership of the church.[21] However, stripped of the name, they re-emerged as "combination lectures".

Staff numbers and staff quality were not the only obstacles in the way of Protestant progress. Another was continued unhappiness over the 1559 settlement. Elizabeth's refusal to budge led to divisions among the reformers, with those keenest on change – "the hottest sort of Protestants" – learning the nickname "puritan". They were a spectrum of opinion rather than a party, but the more radical among them did begin to feel that the time for moderate persuasion was past. A new parliamentary campaign was begun to destroy the settlement and replace it with the presbyterian system: "either must we have right ministry of God and right government of his church according to the scriptures... (both of which we lack) or else there can be no right religion".[22] That campaign failed, but sympathy for presbyterianism grew as the existence of bishops was increasingly seen as part of the problem. Signs of organization appeared. Petitions were presented to parliament and bills introduced into the House of Commons.

Nothing came from this open political pressure, so in the last quarter of the century, a section of puritan ministers turned to undercover direct action. In various parts of the country they set up a secret structure of presbyterian "classes" [groups linking individual churches] – in essence subverting the established church from within. However, in the 1580s, the behaviour of hot-heads brought the whole weight of the establishment down on the puritans. The underground "classical" network was discovered and broken up, and this discredited further attempts to change Elizabeth's settlement while the queen was alive. Except, that is, among a tiny handful of puritans. Those who wanted presbyterianism had never intended to challenge the rightness of an established church, but this minority – they became known as "separatists" – accepted the logic that only a congregation exclusively comprised of believers could guarantee a true church. We have seen this do-it-yourself tradition in the Lollards and how this reasserted itself in the underground conventicles of Mary's reign.[23] Similar groups were found in London in the 1560s but it would not be until the 1580s that enduring "gathered" churches would appear. These would be formed on the principle of committed believers covenanting together to function as a community, agreeing among themselves on church practice and the choice of a pastor. Elizabeth's government felt that it had to stamp hard on these critics. There were executions for sedition and laws to drive separatists abroad. Their day would come in the non-conformist denominations of the United Kingdom and North America, but only after much more persecution.

The Puritan Way

We do not know how many convinced puritans flirted with radical policies, but as pressure failed to bring change, a majority of puritan clergy reconciled themselves to the settlement. However, they were not always comfortable colleagues or pastors, and were frequently criticized for their rigorous attitudes. Indeed, the epithet "puritan" was code for "holier than thou". It is a reputation kept alive ever since as plays from the period have remained in the repertoire. Shakespeare's Malvolio and Ben Jonson's characters "Tribulation Wholesome" and "Zeal-of-the-Land Busy" are hypocrites.[24] The reason for the stereotype is the effort puritans put into regulating and promoting improvements in public behaviour. In this, they were at one with Zwingli, Bucer, Calvin, and other reformers in Switzerland and the Rhineland who, as we have seen, were deeply concerned to promote a godly society.[25] Indeed, one of the puritan criticisms of the Elizabethan church settlement was that it did nothing for public "discipline", and Roman Catholics felt that too.[26]

In a parish where the parson held such views, the church could be an instrument of social pressure. He might believe that many of his congregation were destined for damnation, but that was no reason to allow them to go soft on God's moral law: swearing, drunkenness, idleness, sexual misbehaviour, and casual religion had all to be fought for the sake of society. Puritanism, therefore, caused division, with people resenting being preached at and the implication that if religion did not determine every moment of their waking day, they were irreligious. Shakespeare has Sir Toby Belch say to the puritan Malvolio, "Dost thou think, because thou art virtuous, there shall be no more cakes and ale?"[27]

The reformation of manners, however, was not of concern only to puritans. Preachers and writers were part of a widespread campaign in the last decades of Elizabeth's reign and into the next century to improve the nation's behaviour. It was the civic authorities of London who disliked theatres because of the danger they represented to the physical and moral health of the city. Among reputable sections of society a need for public discipline was widely recognized, including many magistrates and MPs. Indeed, repression by the authorities could be extremely harsh. In Bury St Edmunds in the 1570s, sexual miscreants were tied to a post on Sunday and only released on Monday after a severe whipping. Attacks on misconduct from the pulpit reflected "responsible" opinion just as much as puritan values.

On the positive side, puritans were the heirs of the fifteenth-century religious hunger, just as much as devout recusants. They shared the ideal of a life dedicated to personal spiritual experience, but this time as Protestants.

What characterized ministers was an overriding commitment to preaching. As for lay puritans, the emphasis was on attending "the preaching of the word", wherever occasion presented itself. Indeed, "gadding" was their hallmark – journeying to hear preachers who were "edifying" – if possible carrying along a *Geneva Bible* to follow the texts cited by the preacher. Enthusiasm for preaching also extended to sermons in print. In Elizabeth's reign more than 500 sermon collections were published. Puritans also wrote – and by no means only in controversy. Some seventy of the sermon collections were devoted to Bible exposition. Some were blockbusters – translating Calvin's 200 sermons on the book of Deuteronomy required 1,248 pages. Others were more manageable, even intended "for the better help and instruction of the unlearned" or specifically on the Bible passages read in Prayer Book services.[28] There was, too, a puritan market for books about spiritual discipline, especially helping with daily devotions. Edward Dering was a most outspoken (or tactless) puritan – he told Elizabeth to her face that she was personally answerable for the deplorable state of the church – but his *Godly private prayers for householders to meditate upon and to say in their families* went through four imprints in fourteen years.[29] Catechisms were also in demand and Dering hit the domestic theme again with *A brief and necessary catechism very needful to be known of all householders, whereby they may the better teach and instruct their families in such points of Christian Religion as is most meet.*[30]

Many, perhaps, most individual puritans had experienced the struggle to achieve assurance of being among the elect. The continuing proof of that was holy conduct both privately and in society, and that called for a serious religious lifestyle, just as it had seventy years earlier. Now instead of saying "the office", the daily discipline was self-examination and regular exposure to the Scriptures.[31] More and more, Sunday was observed as the Sabbath and devoted solely to religious activities. Groups met then and in the week for Bible study and mutual endorsement. The bishops became increasingly critical of such initiatives, classing such gatherings as "conventicles" which threatened the authority of the establishment and even the royal supremacy. But that was unjustified. Separatists apart, puritans remained faithful to the parish church. Their determination was to add the depth that they felt was lacking there. What soon became a standard resource was the whole day fast. This was a sequence of sermons, psalm singing, and prayers which ended in a communal meal – an activity paralleled in many Christian groups today. A primary focus of Puritanism was on the household – hence Dering's titles. He suggested that his *Catechism* should be learned by heart. Parents were also expected to follow up on the catechizing of their children as a vital reinforcement for the word preached. Families (and servants) discussed the sermons they heard, and rehearsed their contents. Puritans, apart from the limited and short-lived subversive "classes", had no formal organization, but they did have a strong sense of community, linked socially by ties of friendship, marriage, travel, and letter writing. Group dynamics matters and it is easy to appreciate the individual endorsement that came from "belonging". Puritans formed a very visible semi-separate network with all the marks of shared identity – even a vocabulary. Others might insult them as "puritans"; they called themselves "the godly".

Assessments of the impact of Puritanism have differed widely. One verdict is that, like Roman Catholicism, it failed as a missionary religion. There were too few puritan preachers in the early years and Patrick Collinson suggested that "there is no reason to believe that an intellectually demanding and morally rigorous religion transmitted by the written and spoken word had a broad, natural appeal".[32] That could be a factor, though intellectual content was not always an obstacle. "Over half the Marian martyrs" whose status we know "were rural labourers", indicating that at least some in England's villages were at ease with the doctrinal niceties of the time.[33] On occasion audiences did, to modern minds, show an impressive ability to cope with heavy exposition. In one such case, the puritan Laurence Chaderton suggested after preaching for two hours "that he had tired his hearers' patience and would leave off; upon which the whole congregation cried out: 'For God's sake, sir, go on, we beg you, go on'". He did, for another hour, "to the great pleasure and delight of his hearers". Many of them, however, were probably Cambridge academics.[34] The fundamental reason for limited puritan missionary success is not the message but the level of expectation. The New Testament had told them to preach the gospel, but also that the elect would never amount to other than a handful: "narrow is the way which leads to life and few there be that find it".[35] Thus although preachers welcomed converts, they never anticipated a major harvest. Puritans took for granted that a gulf would exist between the godly elect and a lax and only nominally Christian majority. Yet medieval parishioners had not been uniformly devout either, so puritans were perhaps only being realistic.[36] Historians need to ask whether the majority in English society has ever had more than a nominal religious commitment. Possibly the contrast between the Christian belief supposedly embattled in the twenty-first century, and belief during the so-called "Ages of Faith" is less than is often thought.

To draw an anachronistic analogy, the puritans were the early Methodists of Elizabeth's church – still part of it but, in obvious ways, distinct and alien. In their vibrant spirituality, we see the Protestant expression of the sought-for Christocentric revival. The puritan community and the elite of the Catholic recusant community are mirror images of each other.

29

ESTABLISHED RELIGION

As Protestantism moved towards acceptance, the notion spread that the English were now a "nation elect of God".[1] Catholics, by contrast, lamented that "the Virgin's Dowry" had been lost to the true church.[2] Neither myth is credible. Puritans and recusant Catholics were, however, agreed on one thing: neither had much respect for "religion established by law".

The Uninvolved

The Elizabethan compromise has not enjoyed a good press since. It has been denigrated as a state-imposed religious routine which over the years became accepted as "the done thing". Yet was that new? As we have seen, some English men and women had always taken their religion lightly, except for the rites of passage, especially baptism and burial.[3] That was not a consequence of the break with Rome. Indeed, the fact that a number of people were only marginally committed to the church was possibly one reason why the break was so little challenged. How many of the English just didn't care? Subsequently a number may have been reached by the Protestant message or the Catholic revival, but many no doubt remained happy to do the minimum necessary to conform to the law and to protect their reputation. They earned the name "statute Protestant" or even "atheist" – not in the modern sense, but meaning people who were minimally concerned about God.[4]

A revealing exchange took place in Mary's reign when Bishop Bonner's chancellor tried to persuade the Protestant Juliana Living to conform. He said to the parish constable who was offering to stand bail: "you be constable and should give her good counsel". "So do I," came the reply, "for I bid her go to mass and to say as you say. For, by the mass, if you say the crow is white, I will say so too."[5] We have no Elizabethan equivalent to the constable's cynicism, but when in 1564 the bishops were asked to survey the key constituency of JPs, they reported that while 18 per cent opposed the settlement and 51 per cent supported it (though with what degree of enthusiasm is not stated), 31 per cent were indifferent. The only religious event which most Elizabethans seem to have been careful to attend was the Easter communion, although with the same lack of decorum which the Wife of Bath knew.[6] Preachers and Protestant writers certainly suggest that nominal conformism was rife and there is regular complaint about the degree of absenteeism from services. We have noted that evidence from sermons and books of exhortation has to be taken with caution – godly ministers always see the glass half empty – but little seems to have changed since the poor attendances of the 1450s.[7]

The bishops might be told to recruit tell-tales in each parish and *The Act of Uniformity* might threaten absentees with a shilling fine, but neither seems to have been effectively implemented.[8] Only a busybody would harass a neighbour. In any case, where the poor were concerned, compulsion was meaningless: many needed to work on Sundays. The alehouse, too, continued to be a powerful and less demanding alternative to the church. James Pilkington, the bishop of Durham, reported in 1560 that "come to a church on the Sabbath day, and ye shall see but few, [even] though there be a sermon, but the alehouse is ever full".[9] For the majority, Sunday was the one chance to lie in or to relax. Tudor Englishmen were not Victorian Sabbatarians. In many places communal festivities based on the church were in decline, but secular gatherings drew crowds. The minister of King's Langley (Hertfordshire) complained that

> truly the people will not stick to go 10 or 12 miles upon the Sabbath
> Day in the morning unto a Silver game [charity event] there to spend the
> time in vanities all day long: so that a man may find the churches empty,
> saving for the minister and 2 or 3 lame and old folk.[10]

A factor in this was undoubtedly an irrepressible preference for dancing and football among England's young population. Even among the literate and well-to-do there was the feeling that adolescence and apprenticeship was a brief stage before adult solemnity and responsibility arrived all too soon. "Now is the month of Maying when merry lads are playing."[11] Socio-economic trends may also have increased the numbers disengaged from religion. The growing gap between the well-to-do and the rest is evident in the fashion for pews in church and, in any case, the poor might have nothing respectable enough to wear. Moreover, the population was expanding and the growth in the number of mobile poor and their migration to towns and areas of rural prosperity broke any habit of attendance. In any case, if they had wanted to go to Sunday services, few churches in such growth areas could have accommodated them.

Established religion did not, moreover, have the field to itself. The church may have distanced itself from the apotropaic and magical, but such beliefs continued to flourish. It has, indeed, been suggested that when clerics ceased to be massing priests possessed of supernatural powers, those anxious about the threat of the spirit world, or fearful of accident, calamity, and life's uncertainties, simply moved to "cunning men" and "wise women" or had recourse to "holy wells" or other sites of supposed magical authority. The church's message that everything should be accepted as God's providence stretched the faith of many people too far. The urge to find help from supra-natural forces may also have increased as social and economic pressures and hardships drove people to seek somewhere, anywhere, explanations for misfortune, and protection against the risks of life. Witchcraft accusations peaked in the harsh decades of the 1580s and 1590s. Nor was this an exclusively lower-class obsession. At a high intellectual and social level, alchemy and astrology flourished, fed by Renaissance discoveries of occult classical texts. The date of Elizabeth's coronation was chosen after consultation with the astrologer–mathematician John Dee. In London in the 1590s, the astrological and medical practice of the notorious Simon Forman was providing more than 2,000 consultations a year. The church had powerful competitors.

All in all, it could be that despite the energy poured into the Reformation, English men and women were no more religiously committed afterwards than they had been half a century earlier or, perhaps, than they have ever been.[12] We have heard the Jesuit missionary Edmund Campion declare that "my charge is of free cost to preach the Gospel,... to cry alarm spiritual against foul vice and proud ignorance wherewith many my dear Countrymen are abused".[13] John Penry, an obscure Welsh evangelist and a puritan, wrote:

> I see you my dear and native country perish; it pities me. I come with the rope around my neck to save you. Howsoever it goes with me I labour that you may have the Gospel preached among you. Though it cost me my life, I think it well bestowed.[14]

Neither saw the vision achieved. Campion was executed in 1581, John Penry in 1593.

Prayer Book Christianity

It would, nevertheless, be wrong to conclude that, during Elizabeth's reign, the English nation comprised a majority not engaged with religion and minorities of enthusiasts, puritans on one side and recusants on the other. Prayer Book Protestantism itself had a distinctive religious impact, which, arguably, was of greater significance than either Roman Catholicism or Puritanism. Extremes always catch the eye, make most noise, and create most evidence, but it is hard to believe that Catholics and puritans were numerically dominant, even aggregated together. For many, perhaps most of the English people, religion meant parish church and Prayer Book.

Parish activity in Elizabeth's plain churches was or was becoming very different from what it had been. True, a good deal of the old workload did remain and buildings continued in heavy use. For example, in the London parish of St Botolph's Aldgate, there were events every day; in a single month, January 1581, there were fourteen weddings, seventeen christenings, nineteen mothers churched, and thirteen funerals.[15] Yet aside from the provision of such rites of passage, the rest of the activity at St Botolph's was fundamentally different. No more provision to support the departed – no dirges, no requiems, no obits, no chantry priests offering soul masses – no individuals commissioning a mass for this or that private intention, no bidding of the bedes, and no holy bread or holy water. Instead, the Prayer Book reigned. Morning and evening prayer was said every Sunday, in each case with a sermon – the parish employed its own additional preacher. Communions were held and every Thursday there was a lecture. Collections for the poor took place weekly and the contents of the parish chest were distributed regularly.

St Botolph's was a city church of a mildly puritan complexion and probably above average, but throughout the country the new was taking over. Perhaps the most widespread indication of this was a revolution in the character and position of the clergy in English life and society. The parish priest might continue performing some of the old duties, but he himself was different. Historians count heads and emphasize the delay in bringing in new trained personnel. Yet 1559 saw the profession start to mutate from "celibate (and tonsured) confessor presiding over the mysteries of the sacrament in Latin, to married, bearded minister of the Word in English", a change which has been described as "one of the most striking transformations of the 16th century".[16]

A factor in gaining Prayer Book religion more than mere acquiescence was that, to an extent, it preserved the community character of the pre-Reformation parish. It avoided both the divisiveness implicit in extreme puritanism and the mental, and increasingly physical, alienation implicit in adherence to Rome. The single item of new church furniture which the settlement had insisted on was the strong box "to the intent the parishioners should put into it their oblation and alms for their poor neighbours".[17] Willingness to accept the Prayer Book regime was also helped by an initial lack of rigour in strictly enforcing attendance. In the early years too it accommodated existing culture. The metrical psalms in the services, which we have already noted, called for a greater lay involvement than even making the Prayer Book responses.[18] "Popular demand for the metrical psalter exploded in a way matched by no other text during the reign of Elizabeth."[19] A particular attraction was that for the first time women were able to join in. There was also provision to sing a hymn "or suchlike song" at the start or end of matins and evensong "to the praise of Almighty God in the best sort of melody and music that may be conveniently devised".[20] Congregational singing – facilitated by "lining out" – effectively saw off polyphony and put an end to parish choirs which had been previously comprised of selected men and boys. There were also many "Scripture songs", sung on the streets to popular (secular) tunes. Outside service time, communal games and dances were accommodated. Civic religious drama was censored for anything papist, but continued to be performed until the 1570s. New drama was produced to teach the Protestant message. For example, *A New Merry and Witty Comedy of Jacob and Esau* (1568) tells a story:

> *Whereby God's adoption may plainly appear*
> *Jacob was chosen and Esau reprobate;*
> *Jacob I love (said God) and Esau I hate,*
> *For it is not (says Paul) in man's refusal or will*
> *But in God's mercy who chooses whom he will.*[21]

And in case anyone in the audience missed the message about predestination, the epilogue announces that "all must be referred to God's election".[22] This cultural accommodation would wither in the 1570s and after, but for a decade it eased acceptance of the settlement.

The religious content of Prayer Book Protestantism was inculcated by the liturgy, in particular the repetition of the Apostles' Creed twice on every Sunday plus the Nicene Creed when there was communion. This was backed up by what eventually were the pretty successful efforts at catechizing the young. No doubt some individuals fell through the net, but for the majority of adults there was no excuse for not knowing the groundwork of the faith. The conservative modifications Elizabeth had insisted on, such as using communion wafers instead of "fine white bread", were increasingly ignored.[23] Services were more varied than it might appear. Instead of homilies trotted out again and again, they might feature the English version of Erasmus's *Paraphrases* or Thomas Becon's *A New Postil containing most godly and learned sermons upon all the Sunday Gospels* or Thomas Cooper's *Brief exposition* of the weekly Old Testament lessons.[24] Topical additional prayers were included from time to time, such as thanksgiving for the successful defence of Malta against the Turks in 1565. Prayer Book religion was not necessarily mind-numbingly boring.

Yet did it go beyond gaining a growing acceptance? Was there anything to encourage the personal Christocentric renewal which is evident in the Catholic and puritan communities? Was there Prayer Book spirituality? Some scholars answer "no". A puritan vicar alleged in 1581 that the common attitude was: "I mean well: I hurt no man; nor I think no man any hurt: I love God above all and put my whole trust in him."[25] Enquiries by the clergy towards the end of the century read similarly, as though most respondents saw upright living as the passport to heaven. Was this anything more than salvation by works, the "Pelagianism" of pre-Reformation days now shorn of the earlier reliance on the church and its sacraments?[26] It was certainly neither the Catholicism of the missions nor salvation as experienced by the puritan "godly". Indeed, even though a well-taught parishioner would have vehemently rejected the Catholic mass and the authority of the pope, should he be called a "Protestant" at all?

The answer is that loving God and one's neighbour is precisely the expression of reformed Christianity which the liturgy of the *Book of Common Prayer* sought to inculcate. The catechism, which increasingly people knew by heart, said much the same. Not many people, other than the clergy and "the godly", would have gone beyond that to study the reformed doctrines of salvation expounded in *Homilies* and the *Thirty-Nine Articles*. Certainly few non-readers. To promote greater understanding, the reformers put their confidence and energies in preaching. That was the God-ordained method and the church made a huge effort to remedy the earlier dearth of qualified preachers.[27] By the end of the century sermons were being preached regularly in most towns and many country parishes. The diocese of Peterborough, which had 8 licensed preachers in 1560, had 144 in 1603, all but one with university degrees. Yet how effective was preaching? It is notorious that only 10 per cent of any address remains in the mind by the time the listener gets to the door. So what did reach the people? The answer is the Prayer Book itself. The twenty-first century decries rote learning, but the majority of Elizabeth's subjects were not bookish; they were listeners. They repeated the liturgy aloud and they repeated it *regularly*. Many of them sang it. And the words they heard and repeated – the same words Sunday after Sunday – taught them the faith and two things in particular: rely on God and live a moral life.

Grant that we may live hereafter a godly righteous and sober life/
[beseech God] that the rest of our life hereafter may be pure and holy;
so that at the last we may come to his eternal joy/grant that… we may
put our whole trust and confidence in thy mercy and evermore serve thee
in holiness and pureness of living/dispose the way of thy servants towards
the attainment of everlasting salvation/vouchsafe… to direct, sanctify

and govern both our hearts and bodies in the ways of thy laws and in the
works of thy commandments; that through thy most mighty protection,
both here and ever we may be preserved in body and soul.[28]

Prayer Book services avoided the puritan temptation to theological complexity. Very simply, they assured people that they could and should depend for salvation on God's grace alone and otherwise live responsibly. Christianity, according to the catechism, was duty:

My duty towards God is to believe in him, to fear him, to love him
with all my heart, with all my mind, with all my soul, and with all my
strength, to worship him, to give him thanks, to put my whole trust in
him, to call upon him, to honour his holy name and his word and to
serve him truly all the days of my life… My duty towards my neighbour
is to love him as myself, and to do to all men as I would they should do
unto me.[29]

This was Protestantism of a distinctly cool order but arguably as much a genuine product of the fifteenth-century Christian revival as recusancy or puritanism. It stripped religion of the accretions of myth, legend, and superstition. It was Christocentric – teaching that salvation depended on Christ alone, not on good works and not on the church. Hence the good reformist language of the collect for Christmas Day, praying "that we being regenerate [born again] and made thy children by adoption and grace may daily be renewed by thy Holy Spirit".[30] Above all, Prayer Book religion exploited the Reformation's greatest achievement: the vernacular Bible. The requirement on the clergy to read morning and evening prayer daily meant that in twelve months they covered the Old Testament once and the New Testament three times. Over a year, Sunday readings introduced the laity to virtually every book of the Bible. Together, Bible and Prayer Book came to shape the way the nation thought, spoke, and sang. Because it was less prescriptive than either Catholicism or Puritanism, Prayer Book Protestantism could comprehend diversity, and, indeed, could accommodate much of both opinions. It did not offer the fierce spiritual emotion experienced by people such as Bilney and some of the puritans – not many parishioners saw heaven open during morning prayer. Nor did it provide the passionate intimacy with Christ which many Catholics sought. For those attending as a matter of routine, it could indeed be routine. But we cannot assume that was the only response. The 1559 liturgy could and did enable a person to express individual faith in Christ and a commitment to Christian discipleship. Not everyone was troubled by spiritual angst and for those unattracted by enthusiasm, the words of the Prayer Book could express real meaning:

If a man say his Lord's Prayer, his Ten Commandments and his Belief [Creed] and keep them and say no body harm, nor do no body harm and do as he would be done to, have a good faith God-ward and be a man of God's belief, no doubt he shall be saved without all this running to sermons and prattling of Scripture.[31]

30

RETROSPECT AND PROSPECT

When the Chinese statesman Zhou Enlai was asked for his assessment of the 1789 French Revolution he supposedly replied that "it was too early to say".[1] Whether or not he was properly reported, it clearly is still too early to assess the final impact of the Reformation on today's world.[2] It is difficult even to form interim judgements, especially in the case of a book such as this, which takes the story merely to a point where foundations – but only foundations – have been laid for expressions of Christianity which would emerge and endure in England over the next centuries and be in large measure exported worldwide.[3] The huge task of structuring and ordering which that future would require has barely been glanced at. Some historians have given that the label "England's second reformation" and it generated a new crop of tensions, divisions, and innovations. On the Continent too everything remained up for grabs and confessionalization would ultimately feed the horrors of the Thirty Years War. England and Wales too, along with Scotland and Ireland, would experience the trauma of confessional violence in the "Civil Wars" of the seventeenth century.

By 1570, therefore, the Reformation in England had barely reached "half-time". But what can be said of the score at that point? The original impetus for religious revival had certainly contributed to a fundamental and permanent transformation in the nation's religious structure and order, a change summed up in a royal supremacy and a church order established by parliamentary statute. Each remains in place to this day. There had been destruction on a huge scale, most obviously the plunder and demolition of the monasteries and other age-old religious institutions, the scars are again with us today. Even more profound was the impact on the religious experience of ordinary men and women. There was the revolution in the physical circumstances of the worship they engaged in – Roman Catholics and puritans as well as the parish majority. Activities and artefacts which had meaningfully expressed the Christianity of previous generations, such as pilgrimages and statues, were no more, along with age-old sacred rituals. There were fundamental changes in doctrine and what people were progressively being taught to believe. The most striking casualty was the sense of coherence between the living and the dead which had been nurtured by belief in purgatory and the whole industry of intercession for the departed. Mary's reign had shown that in the 1550s a counter to all this change was not impossible, but the arrival of the missionary priests in 1574 showed that even Douai now accepted that the battle to decide the religious complexion of the country was being lost. England would henceforward be in the Protestant camp. As Eamon Duffy has said that "by the 1570s there is a perceptible sense of the changing of the guard, even in many traditionalist parishes".[4]

What above all brought religious change past the point of no return was the free accessibility of the Bible in English. Cardinal Pole's synod had recognized the need for a traditionalist translation of the New Testament and the Roman Catholic Douai version did belatedly appear in 1582.[5] However, its prime concern was to ensure that the text endorsed existing church teaching and so it was based on the Latin Vulgate and full of Latinisms – indeed, sometimes it is hardly readable. In contrast, William Tyndale's object in translating had been to make the Scriptures intelligible "to the boy who drives the plough".[6] In consequence, from the time the *Great Bible* was placed in every parish church for all to read, individuals made of it what they would – as Henry VIII complained.[7] When in 1571 MPs refused to accept some of the *Thirty-Nine Articles*, it was because they "had no time to examine them, how they agreed with the word of God".[8]

Personal confrontation with the Bible also contributed to the gradual growth in individualism which, for a variety of reasons, was taking place during the sixteenth and seventeenth centuries in certain sections of English society. The medieval church had emphasized the reality of hell, and the possibility of damnation, but offered the assistance of masses and prayers on earth and the intervention of the saints in heaven. It would take the soul time, perhaps a long time, but paradise was attainable. Access to the Bible revealed a different picture: "there is [not] any creature that is not manifest in [God's] sight; but all things are naked and opened unto the eyes of him with whom we have to do."[9] The individual was alone. This exposure became even more immediate with the publication of the *Geneva Bible* in 1559, which was small enough (quarto) for individuals and families to have a copy in the home. The copious reformist notes had a Calvinist tinge, but the text remained sacrosanct and included for the first time an Old Testament completely translated from Hebrew. With the novelty of numbered verses and accompanied by a battery of maps, woodcuts, and indexes, the Geneva version made personal Bible study a practicality.[10] The reality of "nakedness" before God became inescapable. The *mise en scène* of John Bunyan's *Pilgrim's Progress* is the Bible so distressing "the Man" that in desperation he abandoned his home and family, and ignoring their cries to return "put his fingers in his ears and ran on crying Life, Life, eternal life!".[11]

Individual accountability was, indeed, synonymous with the Reformation. It had been precipitated by the desire for more personal spirituality, but the extreme demonstration of personal responsibility was martyrdom, the deliberate decision to defy the ruling norm. This is not to say that only dissidents had personal convictions. We have seen that real spiritual quality existed within the English church in the years before the Reformation, but challenging the norm to the point of death clearly represented a different order of response. That remained the case even when the numbers embracing Protestantism made the choice less isolating and risky. There could still be a cost in lost local status and friendships, and splits within families. After the 1559 settlement, Roman Catholics were faced with the precisely parallel decision. Indeed, enforcement of even more oppressive legislation which would be enacted in 1581 would make recusancy an increasingly costly choice.

Further evidence of the link between the Reformation and individual decision is provided by the book trade. In the second half of the century there is the massive output of aids for the Protestant religion which we have already seen – sermons, commentaries, catechisms, and prayers.[12] By 1600, over a hundred editions of the Bible had appeared, plus thirty of the New

Testament. All this publishing indicates the level of public demand. Roman Catholics sought to supply it too, though under the obvious limitations of clandestine production and distribution. Ironically the Catholic bestsellers were printed legally in England having first been purged of "superstition". One of the victims was an edition of *The Imitation of Christ*, "leaving out the corruption of it".[13]

During the twentieth century leading historians argued that a hugely significant consequence of the Reformation was the "Protestant work ethic". They pointed in particular to the Calvinist emphasis on being "called", that is to "a certain kind of life, ordained and imposed on man by God for the common good".[14] It was thus a Christian duty to work in a serious and responsible manner, with no indulging in the luxuries and pleasures of the flesh. The result was a "favourable ethical disposition… for bourgeois capitalism".[15] This proposition was rapidly accepted as self-evident and the term "Protestant" or "puritan work ethic" is now in popular use to describe a 24/7 business culture. Subsequent research has, however, shown that the hypothesis – for that is what it was – does not correspond to the evidence. For example, Calvin was not responsible for overturning the medieval prohibition on usury. Medieval thinking (and practice) had already accommodated the economic and moral difference between lending money to the desperate and lending money for investment. All that Calvin did was to clarify the difference between morally obnoxious loans to the needy and finance for business. What is more, the pre-Reformation world was already well familiar with the idea of "calling" – why otherwise was sloth a mortal sin? The concept of "calling" has always extended to human activity which was worthy, but against strict Christian criteria. Pursuing wealth for its own sake remained, as of old, the sin of "avarice".

There were also less personal consequences of the Reformation. One of the most malign was state intolerance. Before the break with Rome, deviant religion had been a matter for the church authorities, but in the Six Articles and even more the Marian persecution, the English crown joined rulers in Europe in accepting that force was the appropriate response to religious dissidence. Elizabeth followed suit, although she was careful to have Catholics executed for treason and Protestant separatists for subversion. As the seventeenth century progressed, the death penalty was more rarely enforced, and separatists could now take refuge in North America, but state persecution only tailed off in the last years of the seventeenth century. Even then, social and political discrimination against non-Anglicans would continue for a further century and a half. Among these outsiders, the lot of Roman Catholics was particularly bad. They were popularly branded as "un-English", quislings whose religion disposed them to sympathize with the designs first of Spain and then France and which threatened a return to the horrors of the Marian persecution. Although eventually they did benefit from the general relaxation of Anglican dominance, anti-Catholicism remained embedded in British national politics for many generations and survives vestigially in parts of the United Kingdom even in the twenty-first century.

A possibly more benign consequence of religious division which is recognizably still with us is party politics. So long as England was part of the Western church, kings were concerned with the loyalty of their subjects, not with their personal beliefs.[16] Henry VIII's claim to be "the supreme head in earth of the Church of England" introduced for the first time the question of ideological conformity. Henceforward it was not enough to be faithful to the rightful king. To that age-old requirement was added conforming to the monarch's religious posture. Increasingly under Elizabeth, men otherwise eminently suited for office remained out in the cold because their Christian belief meant they were "not one of us". The Reformation made division over ideas a permanent feature of English life – Catholics and Protestants, high churchmen and Calvinists, Cavaliers and puritans, Tories and Whigs, right and left.

A number of historians have argued that a further consequence of the emergence of the Reformation was the growth of toleration and religious liberty. In the time span covered by this book, quite the opposite was the case, as we have seen. It was almost universally accepted that stability in a state required uniformity in religion. As William Paget, a hugely experienced royal councillor, wrote in 1549, "society in a realm consists and is maintained by means of religion and laws. And these two or one lacking, farewell all just society, farewell kings, government, justice [and] all other virtue."[17] Hence the Tudor monarchs felt politically compelled to cleanse ideologically and to establish uniform belief. On the other hand, it is the case that it was in the Protestant territories of England and the Low Countries that a significant degree of toleration and religious liberty did eventually emerge. In part, this was because the will exhibited by Mary I (and her Habsburg relatives in Central Europe) proved to be politically unsustainable in these Northern territories, and in part because of economics – entrepreneurial energy and thought control were ill bed-fellows. Nevertheless, it is hard not to feel that the growth of individualism rooted in the vernacular Bible also played a part. Some scholars even draw a link between this and the development of science. After all, "Newton wrote as much about the Book of Revelation as about the theory of gravity".[18]

All of this takes us a long way in both time and topic from the religious experience of ordinary English men and women as they approached the final quarter of the sixteenth century. In particular, it may seem far removed from the pre-Reformation longing for spiritual revival. What then of that had been achieved? The parishes had had imposed on them a fundamental shift from the religion of images and actions to the religion of words and ideas. No doubt many individuals were left behind by this, but the demand for religious literature suggests that the move was inevitable in the long run, if the church was to keep up with the increasing level of lay education. A corollary of this was purging the superstitious elements in earlier English religious practice, though as we have seen these did not disappear but migrated elsewhere.[19] And, of course, there was the ending of the late medieval preoccupation with the departed, an emphasis which the Roman Church also pruned significantly. On the positive side, the church of 1571 now held to justification by faith in place of sacramental grace, the Bible as the sole authority for "all things necessary to salvation", and a liturgy which was corporate and in the vernacular – all key Reformation priorities.[20] The sweeping away of the old and the turmoil of the new had not, of course, produced a national religious revival. What, however, the experience of a vernacular Bible and services "in a tongue understanded of the people" had done was to encourage an increased exposure to the element of personal response demanded by Christianity.[21] For example, the Prayer Book General Confession was said at least every Sunday, and its six brief opening sentences aim nine personal pronouns at the conscience of the individual reciting it. For the reflective who did respond and seek a deeper spirituality, the years of contention had opened up three very different but positive options: the spirituality of the Tridentine Roman Church, the puritan experience of vibrant saving faith, and the quiet Prayer

Book understanding of faith and duty conscientiously done to God and man. An irenic assessment of the sixteenth-century Reformation has to be that overall, despite divisions which no one had anticipated, least of all wanted, and despite unfinished business, Christianity had been made more immediate to the people of England.

NOTES

1 Locating the Reformation
1. Actual fighting occupied fifteen weeks in a period of twenty-eight to thirty years.

2 The English at Church 1500
1. The following is substantially dependent on Barnwell et al., 2005.
2. Favoured laymen might also carry lit candles or torches.
3. Other cycles had ten repetitions.
4. Swanson, 1993, pp. 151–57.
5. Brereton, 1976, p. 244.
6. See below, p. 27.
7. For fraternities, see Scarisbrick, 1984, pp. 19–39. There is some evidence that fraternities became less buoyant in the early sixteenth century.
8. Ives, 1983, pp. 425–31.
9. Lomas, 1906, p. 8.
10. Colvin, 1963–82, iii, pp. 187–222, also for almshouses in Westminster and his chapel in Westminster Abbey.
11. Barnwell et al., 2005, pp. 25, 64–65.

3 Popular Religion: Observance
1. Williams, 1967, p. 195. The identification is conjectural.
2. I owe this quotation to Robert Swanson, cf. Swanson, 2007, p. 237.
3. Van der Goude, 1532, sig.Iiii^v–ki^v.
4. Fisher, 1532, sig.C1^v–2.
5. The story is probably apocryphal.
6. Van der Goude, 1532, sig.kii. This and similar promises in primers were, in fact, completely unauthorized.

7. Duffy, 1992, p. 287; "conversion" presumably refers to making moral changes in this life.
8. See above, p. 26.
9. See above, p. 26.
10. See above p. 25.
11. Galpern, 1976, p. 20.

4 Popular Religion: Criticism
1. Matthew 6:24.
2. Except among heretics: see below, pp. 55–58.
3. See below, p. 39.
4. Heal, 2003, p. 60.
5. Archbishop Stephen Langton, 1213: Neill & Weber, 1963, p. 113.
6. Neale, 1953, p. 205.
7. Heywood, 1533, sig.Bi.
8. See above, pp. 14–15.
9. For the following, see Brigden, 1989.
10. Williams, 1967, p. 656.
11. Lehmberg, 1970, pp. 81–82.
12. See below, p. 139.

5 Popular Religion: Challenges
1. See above, p. 27.
2. Litzenberger, 1997, p. 71. The figures may be affected by the answers being required in English. Would they have been able to repeat in Latin?
3. See below, pp. 47–50.
4. Duffy, 1992, p. 158.
5. See below, p. 203.
6. Duffy, 1992, p. 98.
7. Duffy, 1992, p. 94.
8. Chaucer, 1912, p. 424.
9. See above, p. 26.
10. The brass could have been on a tomb slab with the request for prayers round the edge of the slab itself.
11. Mercer, 1962, plate 78.
12. Swanson, 1993, p. 83.

13. Van der Goude, 1532, sig.ki–ki^v.
14. See above, p. 12.
15. Duffy, 1992, p. 273.
16. Duffy, 1992, p. 274.
17. Duffy, 1992, p. 271.
18. Duffy, 1992, p. 286.
19. Heywood, 1544.
20. Duffy, 2006, p. 4.
21. Duffy, 1992, p. 272.
22. Duffy, 1992, p. 282.
23. Duffy, 1992, p. 243.
24. Duffy, 1992, p. 236.
25. Duffy, 1992, pp. 281–82.
26. Parker, 1873.
27. Medieval proverb.
28. See above, p. 17.
29. See below, p. 162.
30. Dickens, 1959, p. 207.
31. Swanson, 1993, p. 252.
32. Tanner, 2009, p. 75.
33. Pollard, 1964, p. 179.
34. Collinson & Craig, 1998, p. 26.

6 Pre-Reformation Spirituality

1. See above, pp. 8, 51.
2. McSheffrey & Tanner, 2003, p. 69.
3. McSheffrey & Tanner, 2003, p. 91.
4. Dickens, 1959, p. 36.
5. St Cyprian, (d. 258).
6. Tanner, 1977, p. 111.
7. Foxe, 1563, p. 627 [recte 631]; Foxe, 1570, p. 1410.
8. Elton, 1972, p. 88.
9. Duffy, 1992, p. 391.
10. McSheffrey & Tanner, 2003, p. 104.
11. McSheffrey & Tanner, 2003, p. 183.
12. Duffy, 1992, pp. 106–108.
13. Higgs, 1998, p. 110.
14. McSheffrey & Tanner, 2003, p. 212.
15. Van der Goude, 1532, sig. hi^v.
16. Wabuda, 2002, p. 153.
17. Rubin, 1991, p. 144.
18. Van der Goude, 1532, sig.oiv ^{v}.
19. Duffy, 1992, pp. 239, 243; Rubin, 1991, pp. 302–306.
20. Wabuda, 2002, p. 150.
21. Wabuda, 2002, p. 165; Duffy, 1992, p. 115.
22. Duffy, 1992, p. 236.
23. Tanner, 2008, pp. 102–104.
24. Tanner, 2008, p. 58.
25. McNair, 1977, p. 354.
26. Thomas à Kempis was trained at Deventer and then moved to its offshoot, the Canons Regular at Windlesheim.
27. Swanson, 1993, pp. 88–89.
28. Swanson, 1993, p. 138.
29. Van der Goude, 1532, sig. Ei^v–Eii.
30. Doran, 2009, p. 46.
31. James 2:13, quoted from Swanson, 1993, p. 48 and Tyndale, 1534, fo. cccl.
32. Foxe, 1563, p. 473; Foxe, 1570, p. 1146; cf. McSheffrey & Tanner, 2003, pp. 52–54, 295–96, 304, 310.
33. Duffy, 1992 p. 79.
34. Daniell, 1994, p. 98.
35. Love, 1506, sig. Aiiii^v–Bii^r.
36. Love, 1506, sig. Fv–Gi.
37. Love, 1506, sig. Kvi^v.
38. Love, 1506, sig. Oiii–Oiv.
39. Daniell, 1994, pp. 97–100, 398–99.

7 Printers and Scholars

1. Eisenstein, 1983, p. 16.
2. MacCulloch, 2003, p. 82.
3. Hughes, 1984, p. 56.
4. McGrath, 1987, p. 140.
5. Hughes, 1984, p. 155.
6. Hughes, 1984, p. 157.
7. Hughes, 1984, p. 160.

8. Farge, 1985, pp. 178–80.
9. See above, pp. 29–30.
10. See above, p. 30.
11. 1 John 5:7–8.
12. See above, p. 70.

8 European Anxieties

1. See pp. 9–10, 98.
2. *Exsurge Domine*, 15 June 1520.
3. McGrath, 1999, p. 75.
4. McGrath, 1999, p. 106.
5. Febvre, 1957, p. 66.
6. Erasmus, 2008, p. 164.
7. Erasmus, 1964, p. 37.
8. Daniell, 1994, p. 67.
9. Bainton, 1972, p. 175.
10. Nicolls, 1996, p. 196.
11. Cousturier, 1525, pp. 167–68.
12. Foxe, 1563, p. 468.
13. Hughes, 1984, p. 115.
14. Rummel, 2004, p. 31.
15. See above, p. 71.
16. Hughes, 1984, p. 75.
17. Hughes, 1984, p. 74.
18. Hughes, 1984, p. 75.
19. Hughes, 1984, p. 78.
20. Hughes, 1984, pp. 80, 93.
21. Hughes, 1984, p. 97.
22. Lefèvre, 1964, fos. cciv^v–ccxv, cf.
Hughes, 1984, p. 81.

9 The Challenge to Authority

1. Quoted MacCulloch, 2003, p. 73.
2. See above, p. 30.
3. Luther, 2007, i, pp. 53–54.
4. Luther, 2007, i, p. 58: thesis 75.
5. Luther, 2007, thesis 82 cf. other
references to the St Peter's project,
Luther, 2007, i, p. 56: theses 50–51.
6. Luther, 2007, i, p. 52: thesis 5.
7. Luther, 2007, i, p. 52: thesis 11.
The reference is to the parable of the
weeds in Matthew 13:25.

8. Luther, 2007, i, p. 52: thesis 6.
9. Luther, 2007, i, p. 53: thesis 26;
p. 54: thesis 28.
10. Luther, 2007, i, pp. 56–57: theses
56–68; see above, p. 30.
11. Cameron, 1991, p. 100.
12. McGrath, 1999, p. 108.
13. Luther, 2007, i, pp. 54–55: theses
36–37.
14. Romans 1:17. Opinion on the date
of the *Turmerlebnis* is divided between
1515 and 1517–18: McGrath, 1999,
pp. 110, 311; MacCulloch, 2003,
pp. 118–19, 126–27.
15. Ephesians 2:8.
16. McGrath, 1999, p. 113.
17. McGrath, 1999, p. 109.
18. See above, p. 55.
19. Hillerbrand, 1975, p.22.
20. MacCulloch, 2003, p. 127.
21. Hendriz, 2004, p. 50.
22. Hillerbrand, 1975, p. 24. The
commonly supposed ending "Here
I stand. I can do no other. God help
me" is probably apocryphal.

10 Magnificent Religious Anarchy

1. Luther, 2007, i, p. 329.
2. See above & below, pp. 28, 33, 94.
3. MacCulloch, 2003, p. 580.
4. Rupp, 1958, p. 111; see below,
pp. 113–14.
5. Hillerbrand, 1975, p. 54.
6. McGrath, 1999, p. 122.
7. Lefèvre, 1976, p. 2.
8. Hughes, 1984, p. 85.
9. Heller, 1972, p. 50.
10. Heller, 1972, p. 57; Lefèvre, 1964,
fo.11^v; Lefèvre, 1976, p. 14.
11. Zwingli, 1523, no. 13.
12. See above, pp. 85–86.
13. This made for confusion since

Rome adhered to Augustine's understanding of justification.

14. Hughes, 1984, p. 75.

15. Hughes, 1984, p. 77.

16. Hughes, 1984, p. 78.

17. Hughes, 1984, p. 86.

18. Lefèvre too played with ideas of double justification: Hughes, 1984, p. 77.

19. See above, p. 95.

20. In Latin *Justificatio*, in Greek *dikaiosis*.

21. "Forensic justification" became the accepted understanding among Lutheran Christians.

22. See below, p. 87.

23. Hughes, 1984, p. 87.

24. Hughes, 1984, p. 89.

25. Hughes, 1984, p. 87.

26. Hughes, 1984, p. 89; Lefèvre, 1964, fo.clxxi^v; Lefèvre, 1976, p. 227.

27. Haller, 1528, theses 4 & 5: drafted by Berchtold Haller of Berne and revised by Zwingli: Potter, 1984, pp. 252–63.

28. MacCulloch, 2003, p. 173.

29. Bainton, 1964, pp. 47–48.

30. Kusukawa, 2004, p. 65.

31. Kusukawa, 2004, p. 65; MacCulloch, 2003, p. 228.

32. Ephesians 1:4.

33. Martin Luther, *Commentary* on Genesis 29:9.

34. Cameron, 1970, pp. 140–41.

35. Cameron, 1991, p. 129.

36. McGrath, 1999, p. 133.

37. Bainton, 1977, p. 228.

38. Hazlitt, 2004, p. 109.

39. Calvin, 1559, iii.7 [Battles, 1960, ii.931].

40. Calvin, 1559, III xxi.1.

41. *Thirty-Nine Articles*, no. 17.

11 The Wider Context

1. See above, p. 99.

2. Friedrich Myconius to Simprecht Schenck, 29 November 1531.

3. MacCulloch, 2003, p. 144.

4. Cohn, 1979.

5. Luther, 2007, iii, pp. 310–12.

6. Luther, 2007, iii, pp. 319, 325.

7. Luther, 2007, iii, p. 353.

8. Luther, 2007, iii, p. 350. The figure for deaths is a contemporary estimate.

9. Martin Luther, *On the Jews and their Lies* (1543).

10. St Cyprian (d. 258).

11. Payne, 1958, ii, p. 129.

12. Payne, 1958, ii, p. 109.

13. Reid, 1974, p. 132.

12 Spain, Italy, and France

1. See above, p. 98.

2. MacCulloch, 2003, p. 225.

3. MacCulloch, 2003, p. 231.

4. It is arguable that the statement, effectively adopting the reformed understanding of justification and expressing good works as free assent and co-operation with the grace of God, was less strong than it might have been.

5. Hughes, 1984, pp. 134–36.

6. Lefèvre, 1964, fos. xxiii–xxiv, clxx^v, ccxxiv; Lefèvre, 1976, pp. 31–32, 227, 297.

7. Lefèvre, 1964, p. 16. There were links with reform in Italy, especially Réne, Francis I's sister-in-law: Belligni, 2007.

8. Cameron, 1970, p. 143.

9. Lefèvre, 1964, pp. 41–51.

10. See above, p. 79.

11. See above, p. 70.

12. Knecht, 1994, pp. 314–15.

13. See above, pp. 98, 113, 117.

14. Reid, 2007, pp. 105–24.

15. Pettegree, 1996, p. 92.
16. Ditchfield, 2007, pp. 145–60;
Martin, 2007, pp. 305–59.
17. Groutacrs, 1963, p. 306.
18. See below, p. 258.
19. Southern, 1950, p. 154.

13 England: Before the Storm
1. See above, p. 39.
2. Brigden, 1989, p. 70.
3. See above, p. 78.
4. Dowling, 1986, p. 20.
5. McConica, 2004.
6. See above, p. 121.
7. Bowker, 2004.
8. See above, pp. 118–19.
9. Trapp, 2004.
10. McSheffrey & Tanner, 2003,
pp. 102–279.
11. See above, pp. 24–25, 36–37.
12. Marius, 1985, p. 270.
13. Dowling, 1986, p. 38.
14. Linberg, 1972, p. 63, quoting
Martin Luther, *Ad dialogum Silvestri
Prieratis de potestate papae* (1518).
15. Gwyn, 1990, pp. 481–82.
16. Foxe, 1563, p. 535.
17. See above, pp. 113–14, 118.
18. *L.& P.*, iii.ccccxxxviii.
19. *L.& P.*, iii.1193.

14 England: The First Decade
1. Sewn but not bound. Daniell, 1994,
pp. 110–11.
2. Daniell, 1994, p. 175.
3. Daniell, 1994, p. 175.
4. Sturge, 1938, p. 133.
5. More, 1528, i.379.
6. Foxe, 1583, pp. 1051–52.
7. *L.&P.*, iv.6385.
8. See above, pp. 79–80.
9. See above, pp. 131–32; Foxe, 1563,
p. 490.

10. See above, p. 134.
11. Foxe, 1570, p. 1119.
12. Higgs, 1998, p. 101.
13. Guy, 2000, p. 120.
14. Marius, 1985, p. 406.

15 Henry VIII and the Reformation
1. 1536 *Act in restraint of appeals to
Rome.*
2. Elton, 1982, p. 353.
3. See below, pp. 142–44.
4. *King's Book*, 1932, p. 4.
5. Daniell, 1994, pp. 382–83.

16 Evangelical Influences
1. Edward IV was the other. Since the
Norman Conquest, one heir apparent,
the Black Prince, had married an
Englishwoman. John, Henry IV,
and Richard III did so when not in
expectation of the throne, while Henry
VII committed himself to marry if
he became king and before meeting
Elizabeth of York.
2. See above, p. 116.
3. See above, p. 115.
4. See above, pp. 116–17.
5. See above, pp. 130–31. It is possible
that Anne was supporting Forman's
vicar, Thomas Garrard.
6. Ellis, 1824–46, I ii.46.
7. Ecclesiaste, fos. 147–48.
8. See above, p. 139.
9. See below, pp. 153–54.
10. Bray, 1994, pp. 171–72.
11. Bray, 1994, pp. 173–74.
12. See below, pp. 161–62.
13. Williams, 1967, pp. 811–14.
14. See above, p. 117.
15. Kreider, 1979, pp. 132–37.
16. See above, pp. 108–109.
17. Hughes & Larkin, 1964, p. 274.

18. See above, p. 126.
19. Ryrie, 2003, p. 29.
20. Bray, 1994, p. 224.
21. Duffy, 1992, p. 431.
22. *King's Book*, 1932, p. 159.
23. *King's Book*, 1932, p. 164.
24. This was the first actual reversal of Cromwell's evangelical reforms.
25. Dickens, 1989, p. 214.
26. Nichols, 1859, p. 258.
27. Nichols, 1859, p. 252.
28. Ryr ie, 2003, p. 52; see below, p. 160.
29. Foxe, 1583, p. 1269.

17 Bare Ruined Choirs

1. See below, p. 173.
2. Youings, 1971, p. 15.
3. 27 Henry VIII, c.28, clause 13.
4. Dodds, 1971, i.92.
5. *L.& P.* xi.789(2).
6. Fletcher & MacCulloch, 1997, p. 47.
7. *King's Book*, 1932, p. 158.
8. 27 Henry VIII, c.28, preamble.

18 Change in the Parishes

1. See above, p. 43.
2. Hughes, 1950–54, i, p. 264; Strype, 1822, I(ii).145–49.
3. Strype, 1822, i.266.
4. Williams, 1967, pp. 805–806.
5. Bray, 1994, p. 177.
6. Williams, 1967, pp. 811–14.
7. Bray, 1994, p. 173; cf. Hughes & Larkin, 1964, i.274.
8. See above, p. 149.
9. See above, p. 151.
10. See above, p. 151.
11. Hughes & Larkin, 1964, i.350.
12. Duffy, 2001, pp. 100, 106.
13. Dickens, 1982, p. 295.

19 Conflicting Narratives

1. Duffy, 1992, p. 382.
2. See above, p. 51.
3. Hoyle, 2001, p. 464.
4. Elton, 1972, p. 19.
5. Elton, 1972, p. 26.
6. Elton, 1972, p. 25.
7. Duffy, 1992, p. 405.
8. Hughes & Larkin, 1964, i.274.
9. Duffy, 1992, p. 162.
10. Whiting, 1998, p. 13.
11. Shagan, 2003, p. 44.
12. See above, p. 133–36.
13. Ryrie, 2002, p. 109.
14. Whiting, 1998, p. 58.
15. Brigden, 1989, p. 399.
16. But there is the possibility of some cross-infection with Lollardy: Dickens, 1959, pp. 51–52.
17. Mayhew, 1987, p. 62.
18. Ryrie, 2003, p. 247.
19. Hall, 1809, p. 827.
20. B. Gregory, quoted in Marshall, 2002, p. 28.
21. See below, p. 258.
22. Marshall, 2002, p. 30.
23. Marshall, 2002, p. 20. This echoes 2 Corinthians 5:17.
24. MacCulloch, 2003, p. 110.
25. See above, pp. 79–80.
26. '*subito conversio*': Pettegree, 2005, p. 4.
27. See above, p. 16.
28. Plumpton, 1996, p. 205.
29. See above, p. 42.
30. Bray, 1994, p. 163.
31. Hall, 1809, pp. 865–66; Williams, 1967, pp. 604–605.
32. This was not Henry being even-handed: "*mumpsimus*" was an ignorant error; "*sumpsimus*" is correct Latin.
33. See above, p. 15.

34. Hence the significance of taking communion in the correct order.
35. Williams, 1967, p. 910. For Gostwick, see above, pp. 12–13.
36. See above, pp. 44–45.
37. See below, p. 185.
38. See below, pp. 275–76.
39. *King's Book*, 1932, p. 88.
40. See above, pp. 24–25.
41. Quoted from Henry VIII's will; see below, pp. 178–79.
42. John Fisher, see above, pp. 29–30; More, 1529, is a response to Simon Fish's call for money to be diverted from post-mortem prayers to social relief.
43. Whiting, 1989, p. 70.
44. Leach, 1906, pp. 58–61.
45. Ryrie, 2002, p. 105.
46. Dickens, 1982, p. 295.

20 Henry VIII: Legacy

1. Strong, 1967, p. 57, trans. C.R. & E.W. Ives. Henry claimed that the *King's Primer* was the latest of his reforms: "as we have bestowed right great labour & diligence about setting a perfect stay in the other parts of our religion, we have thought good to bestow our earnest labour in this part also". *Primer*, 1545, fo.Bij^v
2. Acts 13:22.
3. Marshall, 1535, sig.Li; *Primer*, 1545, sig. Qi^v, Qii.
4. National Archives E23/4/1; transcribed in *Foedera*, 1704, xv.110–17. Compare with Henry VII, below, n.5.
5. Henry VII, 1775, nb. pp. 2–3: "[Lord Jesus Christ] I cannot attain to the life everlasting, but only by the merits of thy blessed passion... NONETHELESS... I trust by the special grace and mercy of thy most Blessed Mother ever Virgin, our Lady Saint Mary (in whom after thee in this mortal life, hath ever been my most singular trust and confidence)... will now in my most extreme need, of her infinite pity take my soul into her hands, and it present unto her most dear Son: Whereof sweetest Lady of mercy, very Mother and Virgin, well of pity, and surest refuge of all needful, most humbly, most entirely and most heartily I beseech thee. And for my comfort in this behalf, I trust also to the singular mediation and prayers of the holy company of Heaven; that is to say, Angels [& 7 more specified categories], and specially I call and cry to mine accustomed avours [patrons]: [St Michael & 9 named saints]."
6. See above, p. 152.

21 Edward VI: Reform Unleashed

1. MacCulloch, 1999, p. 57.
2. MacCulloch, 1996, p. 365.
3. Bray, 1994, p. 261.
4. Tanner, 1951, p. 103 and see above, p. 32.
5. See above, p. 144.
6. Hugh Latimer, Sermon on the Plough, St Paul's, 18 January 1548.
7. Hales to Somerset, 24 July 1548: Tytler, 1839, i.115.
8. Strype, 1822, II(ii).351–55.
9. Cf. placards above pp. 116–17.
10. BCP, 1549.
11. BCP, 1549, cxxij.
12. BCP, 1549, cxxviij.
13. See above, p. 99.
14. BCP, 1549, cxxviij^v.
15. BCP, 1549, clxix-clxx^v.
16. BCP, 1549, cxxvij [recte cxxxvij] .

17. Ordinal, 1549, sig.Hiiij; the new wording was "to preach the word of God, and to minister the holy sacraments".
18. See above, pp. 24–25.
19. BCP, 1552.
20. BCP, 1552, sig. M6.
21. BCP, 1552, sig. N6ᵛ, N7.
22. According to the use of York, Barnwell et al., 2005, p. 164.
23. BCP, 1549, fo. cxxxᵛ.
24. BCP, 1552, sig. N7.
25. BCP, 1552, sig.Oi, Nvij.
26. Dickens, 1982, p. 305.
27. Tytler, 1839, ii.142.
28. Dawson, 2004.
29. BCP, 1552, between sig.Oi and Oii.
30. Tytler, 1839, ii.153.
31. i.e. the command to obey rulers: *Spanish State Papers*, 1862–1954, xi.33.
32. Bray, 1994, p. 285.

22 Edward VI: Reform on the Ground

1. See above, pp. 184–85.
2. Fincham & Tyacke, 2007, p. 16.
3. Wriothesley, 1875–57, ii.9.
4. See above, p. 172.
5. Craig, 2011, p. 229. His comment refers to the Elizabethan church but is apposite generally.
6. Duffy, 1992, p. 495.
7. Bray, 1994, p. 281.
8. Fletcher & MacCulloch, 1997, pp. 50–63.
9. Fletcher & MacCulloch, 1997, p. 140.
10. Fletcher & MacCulloch, 1997, pp. 64–80.
11. Shagan, 1999, p. 62.
12. See below, p. 208.
13. See below, p. 266.
14. Brigden, 1989, pp. 422–519.
15. See above, p. 181.
16. Craig, 2011, pp. 233–34.
17. Fincham & Tyacke, 2007, p. 26.
18. See above, p. 181.
19. See above, p. 106.
20. Brigden, 1989, p. 443.
21. See above, p. 188.
22. See above, pp. 186–87.
23. See above, pp. 186–87.
24. Tawney & Power, 1924, ii.312.
25. *Grey Friars*, 1852, p. 67.
26. Paget to Somerset, 7 July1549: Strype, 1822, II,ii.429–37.
27. *Noailles*, 1763, ii.79–80.
28. Heal & O'Day, 1977, p. 66.
29. Brigden, 1989, p. 529.

23 Anticipating the Council

1. Duffy, 2009, p. 1.
2. See above, p. 181.
3. Bray, 1994, pp. 315–17. About 2,000 priests lost their livings.
4. Frere & Kennedy, 1910, ii.328.
5. See above, p. 166.
6. See above, pp. 113–14.
7. Mackie, 1952, p. 512.
8. Duffy, 1992, p. 532.
9. But Mary's will requests prayers for her mother but not her father. See below p. 219.
10. Wooding, 2006, p. 249; see above, p. 48.
11. Wooding, 2006, p. 244.
12. Bishop Thomas Watson, 1558 in Wooding, 2006, p. 244.
13. Bishop Thomas Watson, 1558 in Wooding, 2006, p. 251.
14. Watson, 1554, sig. & vᵛ–vj [sic].
15. Wizeman, 2007, p. 179.
16. Duffy, 1992, p. 540.
17. *Primer*, 1555, fos. ccv, ccviʳ.
18. See above, p. 199.

19. See above, p. 65.
20. Duffy, 1992, p. 530.
21. Duffy, 2009, p. 55.
22. Duffy, 1992, p. 531.
23. Duffy, 1992, p. 531.
24. Frere & Kennedy, 1910, ii.361–62.
25. Knowles, 1959, iii.440–41.
26. See above, p. 122.
27. Marshall, 1994, p. 232.
28. Marshall, 1994, pp. 225–26.
29. Frere & Kennedy, 1910, ii.359–75.
30. Frere & Kennedy, 1910, ii.401–408.
31. See above, pp. 112–15.
32. Loades, 2006, p. 51.
33. Loades, 2006, p. xxiv; see below, pp. 258, 279.

24 Catholic Priorities

1. Wriothesley, 1875–77, p. 25.
2. Dickens, 1982, p. 309.
3. Wriothesley, 1875–77, pp. 101–102; see below, p. 243.
4. Haines, 1888, p. 118.
5. Scarisbrick, 1984, p. 38.
6. *Homelies*, 1555. Bonner himself only wrote the sermon on love.
7. Homelies, 1555, fo.18v.
8. Homelies, 1555, fo.18.
9. Homelies, 1555, fos.20ᵛ–21.
10. Duffy, 1992, p. 535.
11. The others dealt with the fall of man, the threat of hell, the crucifixion, and two on charity.
12. *Benefit*, 1855, p. 144; see above, p. 114.
13. Watson, 1558; see above, p. 204.
14. Watson, 1558, sermon 22.
15. Watson, 1558, sermon 27.
16. Frere & Kennedy, 1910, ii.365–68.
17. Frere & Kennedy, 1910, ii.370–71.
18. *Godlye instruction*, 1556, sig. Avᵛ–Aviij.
19. Frere & Kennedy, 1910, ii.405–406.
20. Frere & Kennedy, 1910, ii.424.
21. Spufford, 1979, pp. 244–45.
22. 20 November 1553: *Zurich Letters*, 1846–47, i.369.
23. Dickens, 1982, p. 309; Fletcher & MacCulloch, 1997, p. 140.
24. Spufford, 1979, p. 239.
25. See below, p. 225.
26. Sampson, 1554, sig. Aiij.
27. Sampson fled England in May 1554; the letter was printed in August.
28. Gibbs, 2006, p. 304, in addition to the regular parish processions.
29. Machyn, 1848, p. 51.
30. Machyn, 1848, p. 62. St Peter's Cornhill was the company church. By 1557, 3 processional crosses and 100 priests: Machyn, 1848, p. 138.
31. See above, p. 145.
32. See above, pp. 26, 46.
33. Loades, 1989, p. 371.
34. See above, p. 24.
35. Duffy, 1992, p. 563.
36. Dickens, 1989, p. 312.

25 Protestant Dissidents

1. See below, p. 254.
2. Duffy, 2009, p. 115.
3. *Venetian State Papers*, VI(i), 110–11.
4. The most authoritative calculation of numbers is in the appendix to Doran & Freeman, 2011, pp. 225–71, but with the caveat (p. 225) that "the exact number of martyrs must remain uncertain". Freeman's list indicates a minimum of 313 deaths (excluding the Guernsey baby): 284 burned (229

male, 55 female); 28 died in prison (25 male, 3 female); 1 male executed for treason.

5. Hughes, 1950–54, ii.273.

6. Pollard, 1964, p. 179.

7. Byford, 1998, p. 34.

8. *Story*, 1571, sig. Di[r]. This book is a hostile account but contains what is said to be Story's verbatim statement before he was executed.

9. See above, pp. 213–14 . The five deaths at Canterbury on 10 November 1558, even though it was known that Mary was dying, are down to Pole.

10. Foxe, 1583, p. 2027.

11. Foxe, 1583, pp. 1594–96.

12. And for other offences, including women convicted of high or petty treason.

13. Foxe, 1583, p. 1679.

14. The veracity of Foxe was challenged at the time and has been subsequently. The literature is extensive. His concern was to warn England of what a return to Roman Catholicism would mean and so his overall interpretation is heavily partisan – e.g. his vendetta against Bonner and Gardiner and his omission of martyrs whom he thought heretical. But if his work was to carry conviction, the facts had to stand up, and intense scholarly scrutiny has established that in the main they do. Over successive editions he added, corrected, and revised as better information became available. Where he could, he cited official documents (some of which survive and can be checked), and where sources exist which he did not use, they also support him.

15. See above, pp. 126, 147. Wriothesley, 1875–77, i.89.

16. Executions occurred irregularly: Ryrie, 2003, pp. 261–65.

17. See below, n.25.

18. In 1546.

19. See below, p. 227.

20. See below, p. 227.

21. See the table in Duffy, 2003, p. 454.

22. Between 1547 and 1551: Pettegree, 1996, p. 161.

23. Duffy, 2003, p. 454.

24. Franciscan, Alfonso de Castro.

25. Figures for burnings only. These differ from others published because persecutions began in February 1555, so making a full year, February to January, not January to December.

26. Duffy, 2009, p. 168; Freeman, 2011, p. 179.

27. 113, compared with 70 in 1556–57 and 50 in 1557–58.

28. 47 per cent of the total. The spasmodic recourse to burnings could mean long periods of local inactivity, e.g. of the 27 burnings in Sussex, 3 occurred in June 1555, 14 between June and September 1556, 10 in June 1557 and none in 1558.

29. See above, p. 210.

30. Freeman, 2011, p. 203.

31. *Story*, 1571, sig. Di[v].

32. i.e. Brentford, on Bonner's authority after consulting Pole. Duffy, 2009, p. 160.

33. Foxe, 1563, p. 1686; see below, pp. 265–66.

34. In December 1557 and March 1558, five members of the same London conventicle were executed.

35. Tertullian (AD 197): "the blood of Christians is seed". Commonly quoted as: "the blood of the martyrs is the seed of the church".
36. The Imperial ambassador: *Spanish State Papers*, xi.147.
37. Huggarde, 1556, 2nd ed. fo.43.
38. Jordan & Gleson, 1975, pp. 342–54.
39. MacCulloch, 1996, p. 604.
40. Duffy, 2009, p. 169; *Privy Council*, v.224.
41. Literally "it moveth many minds to see an heretic constant and to die": Byford, 1998, p. 32.
42. Huggarde, 1556, 1st ed. fo.41.
43. Byford, 1998, p. 30.
44. See above, pp. 52–53.
45. Pollard, 1964, pp. 179, 186.
46. See above, pp. 117–18.
47. Dickens, 1997, p. 91.
48. See above, p. 117.
49. See above, p. 225.
50. Foxe, 1570, p. 1755.
51. Crankshaw & Gillespie, 2004.

26 Change Once More

1. Psalm 118:23, BCP version.
2. When zealots removed them she had them replaced.
3. Aston, 1988, p. 303.
4. Haigh, 1993, pp. 238–39.
5. Some accounts say two votes.
6. 1 Timothy 2:12.
7. See above, p. 185.
8. Bray, 1994, p. 348; see below, pp. 246, 270.
9. BCP, 1552, sig. Ciiii^v.
10. BCP, 1566, sig. Avi^r.
11. BCP, 1566, sig.Avi^v.
12. They became *Thirty-Nine Articles* in 1571 by inclusion of the statement that unbelievers taking communion do not partake of Christ.
13. See above, p. 99.
14. The definitive edition of *The Institutes* appeared in Latin in 1559 and in English translation in 1561. The only element in Calvin's teaching prominent in early Elizabethan England was predestination. Its connection was principally with Zurich and the Rhineland.
15. See below, p. 244.
16. MacCulloch, 1999, p. 192.
17. Knox, 1558, sig.B1: "To promote a woman to beare rule… above any realme… is repugnant to Nature, contumelie to God, a thing most contrarious to his reveled will."

27 Parish Responses

1. Bray, 1994, pp. 335–48.
2. Bray, 1994, p. 344.
3. Bray, 1994, pp. 255, 341.
4. Whiting, 1997, p. 126.
5. Machyn, 1848, p. 208.
6. Hutton, 1987, p. 135.
7. See above, p. 236.
8. Wriothesley, 1875–57, ii.143.
9. Wriothesley, 1875–57, ii.145.
10. See above, p. 240.
11. Mary had re-ordained or weeded out clergy recruited under Edward.
12. Haigh, 1993, p. 249.
13. See below, p. 271.
14. In 1561 and 1560 respectively.
15. Dodds, 1971, i.136.
16. Whiting, 1998, p. 94.
17. Hutton, 1987, p. 135.
18. Wriothesley, 1875–57, p. 146.
19. This could still be conservatism, cf. the preservation of rood screens: Duffy, 1992, p. 577.
20. Whiting, 1998, p. 94.
21. Duffy, 1992, p. 584.

22. Duffy, 1992, p. 570.
23. See above, pp. 217–18.
24. Spufford, 1979, p. 240.
25. Dickens, 1982, pp. 165–66.
26. Dickens, 1982, p. 166.
27. *Act of Supremacy* 1 Eliz. I c.1 (1559), clause 9.
28. In an attempt to win the bishops over, the crown seems to have indicated that they themselves could be excused the oath provided they agreed to enforce the changes and require others to swear. Hughes, 1950–54, iii.36 n.3.
29. Cross, 2006, pp. 57–76.
30. MacCulloch, 1990, p. 113.
31. Hughes, 1950–54, iii.39–40. The oath administered went beyond the *Act of Supremacy* by requiring acceptance of the Prayer Book as "according to the true word of God and agreeable to the doctrine of the primate church": Hughes, 1950–54, iii.38.
32. Haigh, 1993, p. 253.
33. Hughes, 1950–54, iii.248 n.1.
34. Equivalent to two days' pay; see below, p. 266.
35. Hughes, 1950–54, iii.247 n.3.
36. Hughes, 1950–54, iii.250–51.
37. See below, p. 255.
38. See above, p. 248. He remained in place until he died in 1573: Shaw, 1908, p. 4. I am indebted to Fr Andrew Horsman for this information.
39. For clarification of a requirement often misunderstood, see Harrison, 1946, pp. 137–40.
40. Also minor responses, recitation/ chanting.
41. BCP, 1566, sig. O(vi)ᵛ specifies that the Lord's Prayer should be said in that way at communion.
42. In the medieval church, the *Te Deum* was sung on special occasions.
43. BCP, 1566, sig. O(iii), O(iii)ᵛ.
44. Aston, 1997, p. 186.
45. See above, p. 201.
46. BCP, 1566, sig. O(iii), P(ii).
47. Haigh, 1984b, pp. 179–80.
48. See below, p. 256.

28 Revival Divided

1. Gibbon, 1983, i.92.
2. Ellis, 1846–47, i.138.
3. Southern, 1950, pp. 60–76; see above, p. 222.
4. Vaux had belonged to the college pre-dissolution and was appointed warden when Mary refounded it.
5. Date: 1563–64.
6. See above, p. 252.
7. Hughes, 1950–54, iii.285.
8. Haigh, 1993, p. 254.
9. *Regnans in Excelsis* 27 April 1570.
10. See above, p. 252.
11. The initial consensus approach of the Jesuits did not last: see above, pp. 114, 119.
12. It is possible to argue about exact numbers.
13. The crown insisted that they were executed for sedition, not for religious belief or Catholic practice: Cecil, 1583.
14. See above, p. 119.
15. Haigh 1987, p. 207. In 1571 there were possibly fifty Catholic priests active in south Lancashire: Haigh, 1993, p. 256.
16. See below, p. 266.
17. In Yorkshire "in 1582–1590 there existed practically no considerable centres of recusancy where the active support of the local gentry was lacking", Dickens, 1982, p. 181.

However, traditional religion did survive in the North Riding: see above, p. 257.

18. See above, p. 244.

19. Haigh, 1987, p. 271.

20. "Prophesy" = proclaiming the message of God, not making predictions.

21. Edmund Grindal was suspended in 1577.

22. Fielde, 1572, quoted in McGrath, 1967, p. 133.

23. See above, p. 231.

24. Characters in Ben Jonson's *Alchemist* and *Bartholomew Fair*.

25. See above, pp. 92, 109.

26. See above, p. 255.

27. Shakespeare, *Twelfth Night*, Act 2 Scene 3.

28. Bennett, 1965, p. 146.

29. Dering, 1576.

30. Dering, 1575.

31. See above, p. 49.

32. Collinson, 1982, p. 201.

33. Spufford, 1979, p. 248.

34. Bennett, 1965, p. 149; the story may be wrongly attributed.

35. Matthew 7:14.

36. See above, pp. 52–53.

29 Established Religion

1. Collinson, 1988, pp. 1–27.

2. This description of England dates back to the fourteenth century.

3. See above, p. 247.

4. Collinson, 1982, p. 200.

5. Foxe, 1563, p. 1687; see above, pp. 265–67.

6. See above, p. 46.

7. See above, pp. 52–53.

8. See above p. 249. Cf. Nicholas Bacon in the 1563 parliament: "no man, no, no man – or very few – have seen it executed": Collinson, 1982, p. 203.

9. Collinson, 1982, p. 205.

10. Collinson, 1982, p. 203.

11. Thomas Morley, 1595.

12. See above, pp. 52–53.

13. See above, p. 119.

14. Penry, 1588, p. 63.

15. Craig, 2011, p. 234.

16. Kaufman, 2010, p. 239.

17. Injunctions of 1559 repeating those of 1547: Bray, 1994, pp. 255, 341.

18. See above, p. 250.

19. Craig, 2011, p. 233.

20. Fincham & Tyacke, 2007, p. 65.

21. *Jacob and Esau*, 1568, sig. Aiv.

22. *Jacob and Esau*, 1568, sig. Giv^v.

23. Fincham & Tyacke, 2007, p. 72.

24. Becon, 1566; Cooper, 1573.

25. Collinson, 1982, p. 202.

26. See above, p. 75.

27. See above, p. 259. The authority was Romans 10:14: "how shall they believe in him of whom they have not heard? And how shall they hear without a preacher?"

28. BCP, 1566, sig. A(ii) [General Confession]; A(ii)^v [Absolution]; Bvi [Litany]; Q vii^v, Q viii [communion].

29. BCP, 1566, sig. S(iii)^v, S(iiii). Twice as much space is given to "love your neighbour".

30. BCP, 1566, sig. C(iii)^v.

31. Dent, 1601, pp. 25–26. The puritan author sets up this opinion in order to attack it as suggesting that "a man may be saved without the Word which is a gross error". His imagined respondent repeats his assertion and adds, "although I am not learned, yet I hope it will serve the turn for my soul's health: for that God which made me, must save me. It

is not you that can save me for all your learning, and all your Scriptures", which is very much the Prayer Book emphasis. Cf. Haigh, 2007.

30 Retrospect and Prospect

1. It is probable that he understood the question to refer to unrest in Paris in 1968.

2. See above, pp. 6–7.

3. For a lengthy discussion, see McCulloch, 2003, pp. 668–708.

4. Duffy, 1992, p. 586.

5. See above, p. 204.

6. Foxe, 1563, p. 570.

7. See above, pp. 150, 171

8. See above, p. 37.

9. Hebrews 4:13.

10. It remained the preferred English Bible until at least the Civil Wars of the next century. Thereafter the Authorised Version becomes dominant. A non-religious consequence was the impact of the vernacular Bible on the English language.

11. Bunyan, 1678, p. 3.

12. See above, p. 262.

13. Bennett, 1965, p. 132.

14. Perkins, 1626, i.750.

15. Troeltsch, 1931, ii.812

16. The crown would not have countenanced individuals whom the church labelled as heretics.

17. William Paget to the Duke of Somerset, 7 July 1549: see "Letters of Lord Paget", no. 33 in Beer & Jack, 1974.

18. McCulloch, 2003, p. 683.

19. See above, p. 267.

20. *Thirty-Nine Articles*, no. 6.

21. *Thirty-Nine Articles*, no. 24.

REFERENCES

Aston, M. 1988. *England's Iconoclasts* (Oxford: Oxford University Press).
Aston, M. 1997. "Iconoclasm in England", in Marshall, 1997.

Bagchi, D. & Steinmetz, D.C. (eds) 2004. *The Cambridge Companion to Reformation Theology* (Cambridge: Cambridge University Press).
Bainton, R.H. 1964. *Studies in the Reformation* (London: Hodder & Stoughton).
Bainton, R.H. 1972. *Erasmus of Rotterdam* (London: Fontana).
Barnwell, P.S., Cross, Claire & Rycraft, Ann (eds) 2005. *Mass and Parish in late Medieval England: the Use of York* (Reading: Spire Books).
BCP, 1549: *The boke of the common praier, and administracion of the Sacramentes and other rites and ceremonies in the Churche: after the use of the Churche of Englande*, STC 16269.
BCP, 1552: *The boke of common praier, and ministracion of the sacraments and other rites and ceremonies in the Churche of Englande*, STC 16284.5.
BCP, 1566: *The boke of common praier, and administration of the sacraments*, STC 16297.5.
Becon, Thomas. 1566. *A New Postil conteinyng most godly and learned sermons vpon all the Sonday Gospelles*, STC 1736.
Beer, B.L. & Jack, S.M. (eds) 1974. *Camden Miscellany* xxv, Camden Society, 4th series, 13 (Cambridge: Cambridge University Press).
Belligni, Elenora. 2007. "Renata di Francia", in Benedict, 2007.
Benedict, Philip, Menchi, Seidel Silvana, & Tallan, Alain (eds) 2007. *La Réform en France et en Italie* (École Française de Rome).
Benefit. 1855. *The Benefit of Christ's Death*, trans. Edward Courtenay (1548), ed. C. Babington (London: Bell & Daldy).
Bennett, H.S. 1965. *English Books and Readers, 1558–1603* (Cambridge).
Bowker, M. 2004. "John Longland", in *ODNB*.
Bray, G. (ed.) 1994. *Documents of the English Reformation* (Cambridge: James Clarke).
Brereton, William. 1976. *Letters and Accounts of William Brereton of Malpas*, ed. E.W. Ives, Record Society of Lancashire and Cheshire, cxvi (Chester: Record Society of Lancashire and Cheshire).
Brigden, Susan. 1989. *London and the Reformation* (Oxford: Oxford University Press).
Bunyan, 1678. *The Pilgrim's Progress*, Wing B5557.
Byford, Mark. 1998. "The Birth of a Protestant Town", in Collinson & Craig, 1998.

Calvin, John. 1559. *The Institutes* [*Calvin's Institutes*, trans. F.L. Battles (Philadelphia: Westminster Press, 1960)].

Cameron, Euan. 1991. *The European Reformation* (Oxford: Oxford University Press).

Cameron, R.E. 1970. "The charges of Lutheranism brought against Jacques Lefèvre d'Étaples, 1520–1529", *Harvard Theological Review* 63(1), pp. 119–149.

Cecil, William. 1583. *The execution of iustice in England… against certeine stirrers of sedition*, STC 4902.

Chaucer, Geoffrey. 1912. *Complete Works*, ed. W.W. Skeat (Oxford: Oxford University Press).

Cohn, H. 1979. "Anticlericalism in the Peasants' War, 1525", *Past & Present* 83(1), pp. 3–31.

Collinson, P. 1982. *The Religion of Protestants* (Oxford: Oxford University Press).

Collinson, P. 1988. *The Birthpangs of Protestant England* (Basingstoke: Macmillan).

Collinson, P. & Craig, J. (eds) 1998. *The Reformation in English Towns, 1500–1640* (Basingstoke: Macmillan).

Colvin, H.M. et al. (eds) 1963–82. *History of the King's Works* (London: HMSO).

Cooper, Thomas. 1573. *A briefe exposition of such chapters of the Olde Testament as vsually are red in the church at common praier on the Sondayes*, STC 5684.2.

Cousturier, Peter. 1525. *De tralatione Bibliae* [*sic*], in Bainton, 1969.

Craig, John. 2010. "Parish Religion", in Doran & Jones, 2010.

Crankshaw, D.J. & Gillespie, A. 2004. "Matthew Parker", in *ODNB*.

Cross, Claire. 2006. "The English Universities, 1553–56", in Duffy & Loades, 2006.

Daniell, David. 1994. *William Tyndale* (London: Yale University Press).

Dawson, J.E.A. 2004. "John Knox", in *ODNB*.

Dent, Arthur. 1691. *The PLAINE MANS Path-way to Heauen* (1601), STC 6626.5.

Dering, Edward. 1575. *A briefe [and] necessarie catechisme or instruction*, STC 6679.5.

Dering, Edward. 1576. *Godlie priuate praiers, for househoulders to meditate vppon, and to saye in theyre families*, STC 6685. [There was a 1574 edition with a briefer title: STC 6684.5.]

Dickens, A.G. 1959. *Lollards and Protestants in the Diocese of York* (Oxford: Oxford University Press).

Dickens, A.G. 1982. *Reformation Studies* (London: Hambledon).

Dickens, A.G. 1989. *The English Reformation*, 2nd edition (London: Batsford).

Dickens, A.G. 1997. "The Early Expansion of Protestantism in England, 1520–1588", in Marshall, 1997.

Ditchfield, Simon. 2007. "Innovation and its Limits: The Case of Italy (*c*.1512–*c*.1572)", in Benedict et al., 2007.

Dodds, M.H. & R. 1971. *The Pilgrimage of Grace* (London: Frank Cass).

Doran, Susan (ed.) 2009. *Henry VIII, Man and Monarch* (London: British Library).

Doran, S. & Freeman, T.S. (eds) 2011. *Mary Tudor, Old and New Perspectives* (Basingstoke: Palgrave Macmillan).

Doran, S. & Jones, N. (eds) 2010. *The Elizabethan World* (London: Routledge).

Dowling, Maria. 1986. *Humanism in the Age of Henry VIII* (Beckenham: Croom Helm).

Duffy, Eamon. 1992. *The Stripping of the Altars: Traditional Religion in England, c.1400–c.1580* (London: Yale University Press).

Duffy, Eamon. 2001. *The Voices of Morebath* (London: Yale University Press).

Duffy, Eamon. 2003. "The Repression of Heresy in England", in *L'Inquisizioni: Atti del Simposio Internazionale*, ed. A. Borromeo (Vatican City), pp. 445–68.

Duffy, Eamon. 2006. *Marking the Hours* (London: Yale University Press).

Duffy, Eamon. 2009. *Fires of Faith* (London: Yale University Press).

Duffy, Eamon & Loades, David. 2006: *The Church of Mary* (Aldershot: Ashgate).

Ecclesiate. "The Ecclesiaste", Alnwick Castle, Percy MS 465.

Eisenstein, E.L. 1983. *The Printing Revolution in Early Modern Europe* (Cambridge: Cambridge University Press).

Ellis, H. 1824–46. *Original Letters Illustrative of British History* (London).

Elton, G.R. (ed.) 1958. *New Cambridge Modern History*, ii (Cambridge: Cambridge University Press).

Elton, G.R. 1972. *Policy and Police* (Cambridge: Cambridge University Press).

Elton, G.R. (ed.) 1982. *The Tudor Constitution* (Cambridge: Cambridge University Press).

Erasmus. 1964. *Enchiridion Militis Christiani* (1503), in *The Essential Erasmus*, ed. J.P. Dolan (New York: New American Library).

Erasmus. 2008. *Praise of Folly* (Richmond: One World Classics).

Farge, J.K. 1985. *Orthodoxy and Reform in Early-Modern: the Faculty of Theology of Paris, 1500–1543* (Leiden: Brill).

Febvre, L. 1957. *Au Coeur Religieux du XVIe siècle* (Paris: École pratique des hautes etudes).

Fielde, John. 1572. *An Admonition to the Parliament*, STC 10847.

Fincham, K. & Tyacke, N. 2007. *Altars Restored, 1547–c.1700* (Oxford: Oxford University Press).

Fisher, John. 1532. *Hereafter ensueth two fruytfull Sermons*, STC 10909.

Fletcher, A. & MacCulloch, D. 1997. *Tudor Rebellions*, 4th edition (London: Longman).

Foedera. 1704. *Foedera*, ed. T. Rymer (London, 1704–35).

Foxe, John. 1563, 1570, 1576, 1583. *Actes and Monuments of these latter and perillous dayes touching matters of the Church* [known as *The Book of Martyrs*] (London).

Freeman, Thomas. 2011. "Burning Zeal", in Doran & Freeman, 2011.

Freeman, T.S. & Mayer, T.F. (eds) 2007. *Martyrs and Martyrdom* (Woodbridge: Boydell).

Frere, W.H. & Kennedy, W.M. (eds) 1910. *Visitation Articles and Injunctions*, Alcuin Club, xv (London: Longman Green).

Galpern, A.N. 1976. *Religions of the People* (Boston, MA: Harvard University Press).

Gibbon, Edward. 1983. *History of the Decline and Fall of the Roman Empire*, ed. B. Radice (London: Folio Society).

Gibbs, G.G. 2006. "Henry Machyn's Manuscript", in Duffy & Loades, 2006.

Godlye instruction, 1556: *An honest godlye instruction for the... bringinge vp of children*, STC 3281.

Grey Friars. 1852. *Grey Friars Chronicle*, ed. J. G. Nichols, Camden Society, 53 (London).

Groutacrs, J. 1963. "The Roman Catholic Church", in Neill & Weber, 1963.

Guy, J.A. 2000. *Thomas More* (London: Arnold).

Gwyn, P. 1990. *The King's Cardinal* (London: Barrie & Jenkins).

Haigh, C. (ed.) 1984a. *The Reign of Elizabeth I* (Basingstoke: Macmillan).

Haigh, C. 1984b. "The Church and the New Religion' in Haigh, 1984a.

Haigh, C. 1987. *The English Reformation Revised* (Cambridge: Cambridge University Press).

Haigh, C. 1993. *English Reformations* (Oxford: Oxford University Press).

Haigh, C. 2007. *The Plain Man's Pathways to Heaven* (Oxford: Oxford University Press).

Haines, W. (ed.) 1888. "Accounts of Stanford 1552–1602", *The Antiquary* xvii.

Hall, Edward. 1809. *Chronicle*, ed. H. Ellis (London: J. Johnson etc.).

Haller, Berchtold. 1528. *The Theses of Berne* (Berne).

Harrison, D.E. 1946. *The Book of Common Prayer* (London: Canterbury Press).

Hazlitt, Ian. 2004. "Bucer", in Bagchi & Steinmetz, 2004.

Heal, Felicity. 2003. *Reformation in Britain and Ireland* (Oxford: Oxford University Press).

Heal, Felicity & O'Day, Rosemary (eds) 1977. *Church and Society in England, Henry VIII to James I* (Basingstoke: Macmillan).

Heller, H. 1972. "The Evangelism of Lefèvre d'Étaples", *Studies in the Renaissance*, 19, pp. 42–77.

Hendriz, Scott. 2004. "Luther", in Bagchi & Steinmetz, 2004.

Henry VII. 1775. *The Will of Henry VII*, ed. Thomas Astle (London).

Heywood, John. 1533. *A mery play between Iohan Iohan the husbande, Tyb his wife [and]syr Iha[n]n the preest* (London), STC 13298.

Heywood, John. 1544. *The playe called the foure PP. A newe and a very mery enterlude of A palmer. A pardoner. A potycary [apothecary]. A peddler*, STC 13300.

Higgs, L.M. 1998. *Godliness and Governance in Tudor Colchester* (Ann Arbor: University of Michigan Press).
Hillerbrand, H.J. 1975. *The World of the Reformation* (London: J.M. Dent).
Homelies, 1555: *Homelies Sette Forth by... Edmunde Byshop of London*, STC 3285–1.
Hoyle, R.W. 2001. *The Pilgrimage of Grace* (Oxford: Oxford University Press).
Huggarde, Miles. 1556. *The displaying of the Protestantes and [sundry] their practises, with a description of diuers their abuses* (1st ed.1556) STC 13557; 2nd ed. (1556) STC 13558.
Hughes, P. 1950–54. *The Reformation in England* (London: Hollis & Carter).
Hughes, P.E. 1984. *Lefèvre* (Grand Rapids, MI: Wm.B. Eerdmans).
Hughes, P.L. & Larkin, J.F. (eds) 1964. *Tudor Proclamations*, i (London: Yale University Press).
Hutton, R. 1987. "Popular Reactions to the Reformation... 1530–79", in Haigh, 1987.

Ives, E.W. 1983. *The Common Lawyers of Pre-Reformation England* (Cambridge: Cambridge University Press).

Jacob and Esau. 1568. *A newe mery and wittie Comedie... of Jacob and Esau*, STC 14327.
Jordan, W.K. & Gleson, M.R. 1975. "The saying of... Northumberland upon the scaffold", *Harvard Library Bulletin*, 23, pp. 139–79, 324–55.

Kaufman, P.I. 2010. "The Godly, Godlier and Godliest", in Doran & Jones, 2010.
King's Book. 1932. *The King's Book*, ed. T.A. Lacey (London: SPCK).
Knecht, R.J. 1994. *Renaissance Warrior and Patron* (Cambridge: Cambridge University Press).
Knowles, D. 1959. *The Religious Orders in England* iii (Cambridge: Cambridge University Press).
Knox, John. 1558. *The First Blast of the Trumpet Against the Monstrous Regiment of Women* (Geneva), STC 15070.
Kreider, A. 1979. *English Chantries: The Road to Dissolution* (Cambridge, MA: Harvard University Press).
Kusukawa, Sachiko. 2004. "Melanchthon", in Bagchi & Steinmetz, 2004.
L.&P. 1862–1932. *Letters and Papers, Foreign & Domestic, Henry VIII* (London: HMSO).
Leach, A.F. 1906. *History of Warwick School* (Archibald Constable).
Lefèvre d'Étaples, Jacques. 1964. *Épistres et Évangiles pour les cinquante et deux dimanches de l'an*, facsimile of the Lyons printing (Etienne Dolet, 1542), ed. M.A. Screech (Geneva: Librairie Droz).
Lefèvre d'Étaples, Jacques. 1976: *Jacques Lefèvre d'Etaples et ses Disciples*, ed. G. Bedouelle & Franco Giacone (Leiden: E.J. Brill).

Lehmberg, S.E. 1970. *The Reformation Parliament, 1529–1536* (Cambridge: Cambridge University Press).

Linberg, Carter. 1972. "Prierias and His Significance for Luther's Development", *Sixteenth-Century Journal*, 3(2), pp. 45–64.

Litzenberger, Caroline. 1997. *The English Reformation and the Laity* (Cambridge: Cambridge University Press).

Loades, D. 1989. *Mary Tudor* (Oxford: Oxford University Press).

Loades, D. 2006. "The Marian Episcopate", in Duffy & Loades, 2006.

Lomas, S.C. (ed.) 1906. *The Edwardian Inventories for Huntingdonshire*, Alcuin Club, vii (London: Longman Green).

Love, Nicholas. 1506. *Incipit Speculum vite xpi*, STC 3263.

Luther, Martin. 2007. *Select Writings of Martin Luther*, ed. T.G. Tappert (Minneapolis: Fortress Press).

MacCulloch, Diarmaid. 1990. *The Later Reformation in England, 1547–1603* (Basingstoke: Macmillan).

MacCulloch, Diarmaid. 1996. *Thomas Cranmer* (London: Yale University Press).

MacCulloch, Diarmaid. 1999. *Tudor Church Militant* (London: Allen Lane, Penguin Press).

MacCulloch, Diarmaid. 2003. *The Reformation* (London: Allen Lane, Penguin Press).

Machyn, Henry. 1848. *Diary*, ed. J.G. Nichols, Camden Society, 42 (London).

Mackie, J.D. 1952. *The Earlier Tudors* (Oxford: Oxford University Press).

Marius, R. 1985. *Thomas More* (London: J.M. Dent).

Marshall, Peter. 1994. *The Catholic Priesthood and the English Reformation* (Oxford: Oxford University Press).

Marshall, Peter (ed.) 1997 *The Impact of the English Reformation* (London: Arnold).

Marshall, Peter. 2002. "Evangelical conversion", in Marshall & Ryrie, 2002.

Marshall, P. & Ryrie, A. (eds) 2002. *The Beginnings of English Protestantism* (Cambridge: Cambridge University Press).

Marshall, William. 1535. *A goodly prymer in englysshe*, STC1 5988.

Marshall, William. 1545. *The primer set foorth by the Kynges maiestie and his clergie*, STC 16034.

Martin, J.J. 2007. "Elites and Reform in Northern Italy", in Benedict et al., 2007.

Mayhew, G. 1987. *Tudor Rye* (Falmer: Centre for Continuing Education, University of Sussex).

McConica, J.K. 2004. "Erasmus' in *ODNB*.

McGrath, Alister. 1987. *The Intellectual Origins of the European Reformation* (Oxford: Blackwell)

McGrath, Alister. 1999. *Reformation Thought*, 3rd edition (Oxford: Blackwell).

McGrath, Patrick. 1967. *Papists and Puritans under Elizabeth I* (London: Blandford).

McNair, Philip. 1977. "Seeds of Renewal" in *The Lion Handbook to the History of Christianity* (Tring: Lion Hudson).

McSheffrey, S. & Tanner, N.P. (eds) 2003. *Lollards of Coventry, 1486–1522*, Camden Society, 5th series, 23 (Cambridge: Cambridge University Press).

Mercer, Eric. 1962. *English Art 1553–1625* (Oxford: Oxford University Press).

More, Thomas. 1529. *The Supplycacyon of Soulys; against the Supplycacyon of beggars*, STC 18092.

More, Thomas. 1981. *Dialogue Concerning Heresies*, ed. T.M.C. Lawler et al., Collected Works, vi (New Haven: Yale University Press).

Neale, J.E. 1953. *Elizabeth and her Parliaments, 1559–81* (London: Cape).

Neill, S. & Weber, H.R. (eds) 1963. *The Layman in Christian History* (London: SCM Press).

Nichols, J.G. (ed.) 1859. *Narratives of the Reformation*, Camden Society, 77 (London).

Nicolls, David. 1996. "Heresy and Protestantism, 1520–1542: Questions of perception and communication", in *French History*, 10(2), pp. 182–205.

Noailles. 1763. *Ambassades de Messieurs de Noailles en Angleterre*, ed. R.A. Vertot & C. Villaret (Leyden).

ODNB. Oxford Dictionary of National Biography (Oxford: Oxford University Press, 2004)

Ordinal. 1549. *The forme and maner of making and consecrating*, STC 16462.

Parker, W. 1873. *The History of Long Melford* (London).

Payne, E.A. 1958. "The Anabaptists", in Elton, 1958.

Penry, John. 1588. *An Exhortation unto the gouernours and people of… Wales*, STC 19605.

Perkins, William. 1626. *Works* (London: John Legatt).

Pettegree, Andrew. 1996. *Marian Protestantism* (Aldershot: Scolar Press).

Pettegree, Andrew. 2005. *Reformation and the Culture of Persuasion* (Cambridge: Cambridge University Press).

Plumpton. 1996. *Plumpton Letters and Papers*, ed. J. Kirby, Camden Society, 5th series, 8 (Cambridge: Cambridge University Press).

Pollard, A.F. (ed.) 1964. *Tudor Tracts, 1532–1588* (New York: Cooper Square).

Potter, G.R. 1984. *Zwingli* (Cambridge: Cambridge University Press).

Primer. 1545. *The primer in Englishe and Latyn, set foorth by the Kynges maiestie*, STC 16040.

Primer. 1555. *The Primer in English and Latin*, STC 16063.

Privy Council. 1890–1907. *Acts of the Privy Council* (London: HMSO).

Reid, J.A. 2007. "French Evangelical Networks before 1555", in Benedict et al., 2007.

Reid, W.S. 1974. *Trumpeter of God* (New York: Scribner).

Rubin, Miri. 1991. *Corpus Christi: the Eucharist in Later Medieval Culture* (Cambridge: Cambridge University Press).

Rummel, Erica. 2004. "The theology of Erasmus", in Bagchi & Steinmetz, 2004.

Rupp, E.G. 1958. "The Reformation in Zürich, Strasbourg & Geneva", in Elton, 1958.

Ryrie, Alec. 2002. "The Problem of Allegiance", in Marshall & Ryrie, 2002.

Ryrie, Alec. 2003. *The Gospel and Henry VIII* (Cambridge: Cambridge University Press).

Sampson, Thomas. 1554. *A letter to the trew professors of Christes Gospell* (Strasbourg), STC 21683.

Scarisbrick, J.J. 1984. *The Reformation and the English People* (Oxford: Oxford University Press).

Shagan, Ethan. 1999. "Protector Somerset and the 1549 rebellions", *English Historical Review*, 114, pp. 34–63.

Shagan, Ethan. 2003. *Popular Politics and the English Reformation* (Cambridge: Cambridge University Press).

Shaw, P.J. (ed.) 1908. *An Old York Church: All Hallows in North Street* (York: Mabel Leaf).

Southern, A.C. 1950. *Elizabethan Recusant Prose* (London: Sands).

Spanish State Papers. 1862–1954. *Calendar of Letters… between England and Spain* (London: HMSO).

Spufford, M. 1979. *Contrasting Communities* (Cambridge: Cambridge University Press).

Story. 1571. *A Declaration of the Lyfe and Death of Iohn Story*, STC 23297.

Strong, Roy. 1967. *Holbein and Henry VIII* (London: Paul Mellon Foundation).

Strype, John. 1822. *Ecclesiastical Memorials* (Oxford: Clarendon Press).

Sturge, C. 1938. *Cuthbert Tunstall* (New York).

Swanson, Robert. 1989. *Church and Society in Late Medieval England* (Oxford: Blackwell).

Swanson, Robert (ed.) 1993. *Catholic England: Faith, Religion, and Observance before the Reformation* (Manchester: Manchester University Press).

Swanson, Robert. 2007. *Indulgences in Late Medieval England* (Cambridge: Cambridge University Press).

Tanner, J.R. 1951. *Tudor Constitutional Documents* (Cambridge: Cambridge University Press).

Tanner, Norman P. (ed.) 1977. *Heresy Trials in the Diocese of Norwich, 1428–31*, Camden Society, 4th series, 20 (Cambridge: Cambridge University Press).

Tanner, Norman. 2008. *The Church in the Later Middle Ages* (London: I.B. Tauris).

Tanner, Norman. 2009. *The Ages of Faith* (London: I.B. Tauris).

Tawney, R.H. & Power, E. 1924. *Tudor Economic Documents* (London: Longman).

Trapp, J.B. 2004. "John Colet", in *ODNB*.
Troeltsch, Ernst. 1931. *The Social Teaching of the Christian Churches* (London: George Allen & Unwin).
Tyndale, William. 1534. *New Testament*, trans. William Tyndale, STC 2826.
Tytler, P.F. 1839. *England under the reigns of Edward VI & Mary* (London: R. Bentley).

Van der Goude, Gherit. 1532. *The Interpretacyon and Sygnyfycacyon of the Masse* (London: Robert Wyer), STC 11549.
Venetian State Papers. 1864–1940. *Calendar of State Papers Venetian* (London: HMSO).

Wabuda, S. 2002. *Preaching during the English Reformation* (Cambridge: Cambridge University Press).
Watson, Thomas. 1554. *Twoo Notable Sermons*, STC 25115.
Watson, Thomas. 1558. *Holsome and Catholique doctrine concerninge the seven Sacramentes*, STC 25114.
Whiting, R. 1989. *The Blind Devotion of the People* (Cambridge: Cambridge University Press).
Whiting, R. 1998. *Local Responses to the English Reformation* (Basingstoke: Macmillan).
Williams, C.H. 1967. *English Historical Documents, V, 1485–1558* (London: Eyre & Spottiswoode).
Wizeman, W. 2007. "Martyrs and Anti-martyrs", in Freeman & Mayer, 2007.
Wooding, L. 2006. "The Marian Restoration and the Mass", in Duffy & Loades, 2006.
Wriothesley, Charles. 1875–7. *Chronicle*, ed. W.D. Hamilton, Camden Society, ns.11, 20 (London).

Youings, J. 1971. *The Dissolution of the Monasteries* (London: Allen & Unwin).

Zurich Letters. 1846–7. *Original Letters relevant to the English Reformation*, ed. H. Robinson, Parker Society, 26 (London).
Zwingli, Huldrych. 1523. *Sixty-Seven Articles* (Zürich).

INDEX